W9-CEA-426

HOTEL *and* LODGING MANAGEMENT

HOTEL *and* LODGING MANAGEMENT

An Introduction

Allan T. Stutts

Conrad N. Hilton College of Hotel and Restaurant Management
University of Houston

Contributing Author

James F. Wortman

Conrad N. Hilton College of Hotel and Restaurant Management
University of Houston

JOHN WILEY & SONS, INC.

New York Chichester Weinheim Brisbane Singapore Toronto

This book is printed on acid-free paper. ♾

Published simultaneously in Canada.

Library of Congress Cataloging-in-Publication Data:

Stutts, Alan T.

Hotel and lodging management : an introduction / by Alan T. Stutts.

p. cm.

Includes bibliographical references and index.

ISBN 0-471–35483–X (cloth : alk. Paper)

1. Hospitality industry—Management. I. Title.

TX911.3.M27 S78 2001

647.94′068—dc21 00-043351

Printed in the United States of America.

10 9 8 7 6 5 4 3 2 1

Contents

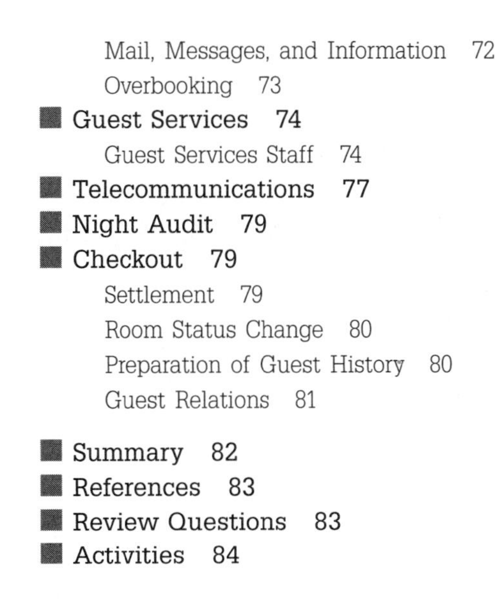

Foreword

Historically, people have always traveled for reasons of business, government, education, and religion. However, before the twentieth century, widespread travel for pleasure was another matter altogether. Today, holiday travel is increasingly justified by the need to find relief from the stress of work, to recuperate or improve one's personal health, or simply to escape from routine and the familiar.

Even with the advent of technology that is designed to reduce the need for business travel, face-to-face discussion and presentation still remains a standard means of developing and conducting business in the global marketplace. Thus, the development and successful management of hotels has become an increasingly important component of the economy of the United States and other countries.

I have spent most of my working life in the hotel business. I have found that the core principle of a successful hotel business must be the creation of an environment that will promote and enhance a feeling of well-being and enjoyment among guests. In the following pages, the author has provided the essential steps necessary for you, the student of hotel and lodging management, to understand the principles behind the development of a great hotel. The author then leads you through the key factors that are essential to the management of a great hotel.

The author is to be complimented on his thorough approach to the subjects included and to the new ideas that he has created for those who want to develop and manage a great hotel.

I know that each of you who choose a career in hotel and lodging management will find a bright future—one that is filled with challenges and excitement. Listen to your professors, read and reread this book, gain as much hands-on experience as you can while you are learning about hotel management, and above all, thoroughly enjoy what you are doing. I wish you the best of success.

Barron Hilton

Preface

Hotel and lodging management is a young discipline. The well-known lodging organizations of today are less than a century old, and the skills required to successfully manage a hotel or lodging establishment have evolved along with the companies themselves. Today, hotel and lodging management has its own skills, its own tools, and its own techniques. Yet, it will be clear to you from the first day that you are promoted to a management position in a hotel or lodging organization that there is still a great deal that remains to be learned about the business. What is clear is that managing these complex organizations requires more than just common sense. And while it is impossible to present all there is to know about hotel and lodging management in one book, this text seeks to equip the manager with the understanding, knowledge, and skills needed for tomorrow's job opportunities.

Hotel and lodging management is comprised of a variety of tasks. However, tasks alone are objective and impersonal, and while it is management that decides what tasks are needed and what is to be achieved, it is the employees and supervisors who perform them. Thus, the successful completion of those tasks almost always requires successful management of people. A manager's own vision, dedication, and integrity play a large role in determining whether there will be good management or mismanagement in a hotel.

This book recognizes that a hotel manager is a person and, therefore, seeks to create a framework of facts and concepts from which the manager can understand what people in a hotel or lodging business need to do, while also demonstrating how people and tasks can be integrated to achieve positive results.

This book addresses the critical topics and information that every hotel manager needs to know, but in a form that is understandable and reader friendly to students who aspire to become hotel and lodging managers but who have not yet worked as managers or even as employees. The book looks at the entire operation of a lodging facility, giving equal coverage to rooms management, front office operations, other supporting departments, and the responsibilities of the general manager. Special chapters on new hotel development, types of lodging environments, franchise companies, and management organizations broaden the scope of this text and introduce students to the key movements and challenges facing the industry.

The approach used in this text comes from my experiences, acquired over 30 years of operating hotel and lodging businesses and of teaching hotel and lodging management to many different kinds of students in colleges, universities, and executive programs and seminars. The subject matter has been developed largely from analyzing and evaluating firsthand those practices and procedures that have worked successfully in many different types of hotel business, large and small.

Students enrolled in the author's hotel management program tested preliminary versions of this manuscript and found it to be meaningful to them, as well as easily accessible. In addition, special recognition should go to those who have reviewed the manuscript and whose comments and ideas have helped enhance its content and relevance. They include the following:

Percival Darby, Florida International University

Sheryl Kline, Widener University

Thomas Jones, University of Nevada—Las Vegas

Robert Mill, Denver University

Ezat Moradi, Houston Community College

James Zielinski, College of DuPage

An Instructor's Manual (ISBN: 0-471-35739-1) is available to qualified adopters of this textbook. Please contact your Wiley sales representative for details.

Alan T. Stutts
University of Houston

HOTEL *and* LODGING MANAGEMENT

Introduction

If you are reading this book, most likely you are seriously considering a career in hotel management and may have asked yourself already the following important questions: What do I know about the hotel and lodging industry? What do I need to know to get ahead? Where will specific entry level positions lead? What do successful hotel and lodging executives do on a daily basis to make their businesses successful?

Alternatively, you may be one of thousands of managers who already are employed in the hotel industry and have found that additional training is necessary for advancement. What does a move into management mean? You know your job, but what do you know about the new position you have been offered? Have you seen others perform in similar positions? Are they really doing it the right way?

This book will not answer all of your questions—no book can. However, it will give you an overview of the hotel and lodging industry, as well as some important insights into hotel and lodging management and the job of the general manager. Most of the other books on the market concentrate on a single aspect of hotel and lodging management and leave the reader with a very narrow view of the hotel and lodging industry. This book will give you a general introduction to the hotel and lodging industry and then focus in on a number of departments, including the front office and housekeeping. After you finish reading the chapters in this book, you will understand the duties of the general manager of a full-service hotel as well as what an entry-level sales or food and beverage manager must do to be successful and be promoted.

Each chapter in this book includes a boxed feature, a biographical profile of some of the movers and shakers in the hospitality industry. Some, like Curtis Carlson, started out as newspaper boys; others, like Barron Hilton, were born into the industry. Each one has a unique story to tell about his or her career in the hotel and lodging industry.

Chapter 1 provides background on the growth and development of the hotel and lodging industry. This chapter does not take you through a long and ponderous discussion of the history of hotel and lodging in the United States but instead shows how the ebb and flow of supply and demand has led to the development of the various segments of the hotel and lodging industry. In addition, Chapter 1 introduces you to lodging industry classifications, that is, the wide range of facilities that are defined as "lodging," from the limited service facility to the full-service resort hotel. Lodging can be classified by quality of facilities and service, target market, or type of service. Appendix 1-1 provides one sample classification scheme. The classifications were developed by the American Automobile Association (AAA) and are accepted throughout the industry.

Chapter 2 takes you through the various operating departments of a lodging business and then discusses a number of ways of running the organization, including patterns of authority, span of control, and the pros and cons of functional organization design. The chapter concludes with discussions of the hotel staffing system and career paths and opportunities.

In Chapters 3 through 5, you will get an inside look at the key operating departments of a typical lodging business from the manager's perspective. What does each department do? How do the departments interface with each other? In Chapter 3, you will learn about the organization and staffing of the front office, as well as its reservations, registration, guest services, telecommunications, accounting, night audit, and checkout functions. Appendix 3-1 provides a list of some of the decision-making tools (stabilized occupancy rates, competitive index, REVPAR) that are used to evaluate the competitive position of a hotel or a lodging business.

In Chapter 4, we will describe the organization and staffing of a housekeeping department and then consider key procedures to guest room cleaning, public area cleaning, inventory control, and employee safety. Appendix 4-1 provides a listing of sample housekeeping routines.

This book directs considerable attention toward the front office and housekeeping departments, the heart of every hotel and lodging business. In fact, a lodging business cannot operate without them. If this is your first look at these two important departments, after reading Chapters 3 and 4, you will know how efficient operation of these departments maximizes both guest satisfaction and departmental productivity. For those of you who are already "in the business," these chapters will help you determine how the operation of your business measures up and will provide information on issues that may enhance the success of your business.

Chapter 5 examines the organization of the security department. Loss prevention involves preventing losses of persons as well as property and includes a discussion of safety issues to minimize the chances that an employee or guest will suffer an accident while staying at the hotel. Appendix 5-1 provides a hotel security audit that can and should be used to evaluate the security of a hotel or lodging business.

In Chapter 6, you will be given the opportunity to examine the other key operating departments of a lodging business and their relationship to the front office and housekeeping departments. These include the marketing and sales, food and beverage, engineering, and human resources departments. This chapter is intended as an overview. Each of these departments could fill an entire course or textbook, and some do! Those who are already in the lodging business will find solutions to some problems that undoubtedly they have already encountered, including how to establish a successful and integrated working relationship between the housekeeping and food and beverage departments to avoid confrontations over who cleans up after a major convention event.

One of the critical components of a lodging business is control. In Chapter 7, you will be introduced to the various mechanisms of control at the disposal of management. Guidelines for the type of control system mechanism that should be employed in different situations are given. Special attention is given to forecasting, business planning, and developing a monthly control or inventory cycle.

In Chapter 8, you will learn the elements that are essential to the development and preopening of a lodging business. These include the development of a product concept, the economic market study and appraisal, sources and types of financing, the development process, and preopening planning. Figure 8-1 provides a checklist of elements that lead to a successful opening day.

Readers who are preparing for a management career in the hotel and lodging industry have seen and heard the names Hilton, Marriott, Hyatt, Westin, Holiday, Motel 6, and so on. How and under what circumstances does a lodging corporation place its name on a specific hotel? In Chapter 9, you will explore the world of management contracts and franchise agreements. This chapter will explain the advantages and disadvantages of these two arrangements, outline the fees associated with a franchise and the financial expectations of a management contract, discuss the elements of a franchise agreement and a management contract, and explain the differences between franchise companies and management contractors. If you are an entrepreneur who is deciding between signing a management contract and purchasing a franchise, Chapter 9 will enable you to understand the key variables of the selection process. If you would like to become the manager of a franchise or work for a management contractor, after reading this chapter, you will better understand the working relationship that must be maintained between the franchisee and the franchiser or between the owner and a management company in order to realize the maximum return on your investment. Appendix 9-1 provides a draft franchise agreement, which will show you just how involved this arrangement can be.

The resort is one of the earliest types of hotel or lodging businesses in the United States. The names of such grand hotels as Cloister, Greenbrier, Broadmoor, Boulders, La Costa, and Pinehurst have graced the American lodging scene for more than a century. What are the special features of a resort? Does resort management differ from management of other types of lodging? What exactly is riverboat gaming? All of these questions and more will be explored in Chapter 10.

The time-share, or vacation ownership, is perhaps the fastest growing hotel and lodging business in the world. After reading Chapter 11, you will gain an understanding of the organizational structure of the business, key management responsibilities, the relationship between time-share hotels and marketers, and the role and function of companies that are in the business of time-share exchange. After reading this chapter, you will be able to determine whether this is a career path you wish to follow and, for those who are already in the business, to evaluate whether time-share or vacation ownership presents a viable business opportunity for your hotel or lodging business.

We conclude in Chapter 12 with a discussion of the role of the general manager of a hotel or a lodging business. Those of you who are just beginning your career in the hotel and lodging industry will have to wait some time for an opportunity to fill this position; it takes an average of 12 years of experience in the industry to become the general manager of a full-service hotel. In addition to learning the key components of the general manager's job, you will need to learn about the importance of total quality management and communication, and how to develop a performance culture among your employees. Appendix 12-1 provides a diary of a typical day in the life of a hotel general manager.

After reading *Hotel and Lodging Management: An Introduction*, you will be ready to move into the entry-level management ranks. More important, you will have the tools to select a hotel or lodging business that has carefully considered the structuring of these departments to maximize guest satisfaction and organizational productivity. Most important, you will have mastered the elements of managing a hotel or lodging business that will enable you to advance and facilitate your professional growth and development. As the comic strip character Pogo warns, "we have met the enemy and he is us!" For me, the hotel and lodging industry has been the most rewarding—and at times the most frustrating—life's work I could have chosen. If you are prepared to deal with the ups and downs of a career in which customer service rules, you are ready for the hospitality industry. The best of luck to you!

Chapter 1

Growth and Development of the Lodging Industry

CHAPTER OUTLINE

TRAVEL AND TOURISM

The travel and tourism industry includes many components: hotels and motels, transportation (airlines, buses, trains, rental car companies), cruise lines, entertainment and tourist attractions (theme parks, museums, zoos, and theaters), restaurants, travel and tour companies, travel industry associations, and public and private tourism promotion and marketing offices.

It is the top services export, one of the largest employers, and one of the top three industries in the United States. Over 47 million international travelers visit the United States annually. In addition, residents of the United States take in excess of 1 billion person-trips annually, including some 862.4 million for pleasure and another 275.5 million for business. These domestic and international travelers spend approximately $486.9 billion each year. In 1998, the industry employed 7 million workers and paid $128 billion in wages and salaries. That same year, an additional 2.2 million jobs were generated indirectly. The travel and tourism industry is estimated to produce more than $71 billion in federal, state, and local tax revenues.(1)

The Travel Industry Association, a consortium of corporations whose core business is the provision of travel services and products, which have joined together to influence policy that might positively or negatively impact upon their business, reported that all types of travel trips grew by 3.2% from 1991 to 1998. During those years, business trips grew by 1.1% and pleasure trips grew by 3.8%. For obvious reasons, the lodging industry is an essential component of the tourism industry in the United States and throughout the world—all those travelers need a place to sleep! Almost half of all trips involve a hotel stay, and the average stay per trip is 3.5 nights. In the United States alone, there are more than 3.7 million rooms available in lodging establishments. In 1998, the lodging industry generated nearly $95.6 billion in revenue and $18.9 billion in profits. By 2001, the industry should show an increase to 4 million rooms, $113.9 billion in revenues, and $25.1 billion in profits. (2)

The demand for lodging in the United States depends on three factors: airline ticket prices, oil prices, and population demographics. Logically enough, as air travel costs increase, lodging demand decreases; as air travel costs decrease, lodging demand increases. Changes in lodging demand seem to lag behind changes in the cost of airline travel by one year.

The price of oil has a less direct effect on lodging demand. Oil prices directly affect the prices of aircraft fuel and gasoline. This increase in the price of air and highway travel ultimately affects lodging demand. A 1 percent increase in the price of crude oil causes a 0.06–0.09 percent decline in lodging demand. Changes in the price of oil cause changes in lodging demand, with a two-year lag.

Almost half of all tourism trips involve a hotel stay. (Courtesy of the Hospitality Industry Archives and Library, Conrad N. Hilton College of Hotel and Restaurant Management, University of Houston, Texas.)

The third factor in lodging demand is population demographics—who is reserving these rooms? Survey data of business and pleasure travel suggest that people above 45 years of age tend to be the more intensive consumers of lodging. In the United States, this age group, commonly referred to as the "baby boomers," is becoming an increasingly significant segment of the traveling population.

The History of Lodging

The modern U.S. hotel industry emerged following World War II. The booming postwar economy enabled Americans to purchase automobiles and travel for leisure purposes. Motor hotels and motels blossomed along the roadsides in order to attract this new type of traveler. The operators of these businesses were small business owners who offered the traveler a bedroom, limited services, and parking right in front of the bedroom door. The quality of accommodations varied so widely that it was not uncommon for the traveler to ask to inspect the room before agreeing to spend the night.

Growth and Development

Kemmons Wilson reacted to what he described as the most miserable vacation trip of his life (presumably in some of the more substandard accommodations), by entering the lodging industry himself. Wilson opened his first Holiday Inn on August 1, 1952 in Memphis, Tennessee (see Box 1–1).

Holiday Inn was followed by Ramada, Howard Johnson, Marriott, Hyatt, and Radisson beginning in the late 1950s and early 1960s. The success of these chains and other brands that were established earlier, such as Hilton and Sheraton, aggressively franchised their brand of lodging, dramatically changing the accommodations of U.S. travelers.

Although it is best known for the birth of disco, the early 1970s was also a boom time for hotel expansion. The completion of the U.S. interstate highway system, along with aggressive sales activity by the major brands, opened new markets in many previously inaccessible cities and towns. In response to this surge in hotel development, companies developed multiple brands aimed at different segments of the traveling public. Segmentation was heaviest in the lower-priced portions of the industry, as budget and economy chains attempted to distinguish themselves from their competitors.

In the mid-1970s, the Arab oil embargo and the subsequent U.S. energy crisis, with its gas shortages, gas rationing, and higher oil and gas prices, crippled the travel industry. Inflation also had a dramatic impact on the lodging industry during this period. As the cost of borrowing funds for new hotel development soared, development all but ceased.

Because of this decline in development in the 1970s, in the early 1980s, demand for rooms exceeded supply. In 1981, changes in the U.S. tax law created a very positive climate for investment in hotel development. Accelerated depreciation schedules prompted hotel developers and operators to create paper losses, providing substantial tax shelters against other sources of income. Unfortunately, many hotels were built during this period to create paper losses rather than to attract guests and generate profit. Developers jumped in with great enthusiasm, giving rise to the construction boom of the "go-go eighties."

In 1986, the role of the hotel industry as a tax shelter backfired. In that year, the Tax Reform Act of 1986 increased the depreciation schedule from 18 years to 31.5 years, the investment tax credit was repealed, and earned income could no longer be sheltered by investment loss. This resulted in serious economic problems for many of the hotel development and operating deals that had been created in the early 1980s. Although catastrophic, the resulting impact was not felt immediately. To add to the challenges faced by the industry, demand began to lag behind the large number of new

BOX 1–1
Kemmons Wilson's Holiday Inn

Kemmons Wilson. (Courtesy of the Hospitality Industry Archives and Library, University of Houston, Texas.)

Kemmons Wilson (1913–) revolutionized the hotel industry by allowing children to stay for free and by providing swimming pools, air conditioning, free cribs, telephones, television, ice, and free parking, which provided comfortable accommodations to the middle class at prices they could afford.

Eleven Holiday Inns opened by the end of 1954. The 100th Holiday Inn opened in Tallahassee–Apalachee, Florida, on September 16, 1959. The following year, the Holiday Innkeeping School, predecessor of the Holiday Inn University, was created to teach new innkeepers the "Holiday Inn Way." The Holiday Inn company expanded outside the United States in 1960 with the opening of Holiday Inn–Chateaubrian in Montreal, Canada. In October of 1967, the Institutional Mart of America (IMA) opened in Holiday City, providing the company with its first year-round hotel supplies and equipment showplace.

The year 1968 was a busy one for Kemmons Wilson. The first European Holiday Inn opened on March 25 in Leiden, Holland, and the 1,000th Holiday Inn opened on August 1 in San Antonio, Texas. With the expansion of the Holiday Inn hotels abroad, in 1969, the corporate name was changed from Holiday Inns of America, Inc., to Holiday Inns, Inc. Similarly, the familiar slogan, "The Nation's Innkeeper," was revised to "The World's Innkeeper." Wilson, truly the "World's Innkeeper," believes that success means never having to settle for anything less than excellence and that you can always dare to do better.

By 1971, Holiday Inn became the first food and lodging chain in history to have facilities in operation in all 50 states. Most important, the company reached the 200,000 room mark in December 1971. Whereas it had taken 15 years to reach the 100,000 room mark, doubling that number took less than 5 years! In 1972, the grand opening of the world's largest Holiday Inn (719 rooms) occurred in Toronto, Canada, 20 years after the first opening of the first Holiday Inn property. In August 1989, Holiday Inn Corporation was acquired by Bass PLC, a corporation based in the United Kingdom. Today there are more than 1,900 Holiday Inn hotels throughout the world.

Source: "Kemmons Wilson," Cathleen Baird, Hospitality Industry Hall of Honor Archives, Conrad N. Hilton College, University of Houston, Texas, 1996.

projects being developed, and hoteliers began to lower rates in order to attract business.

The economic recession of the early 1990s and the limitations on travel caused by the Persian Gulf War caused demand for hotel rooms to falter once again. The rate cuts of the 1980s were followed by additional cuts in the 1990s. By 1991, an increasing percentage of each dollar earned was going to pay hotel debt service, and the "creative" financing of the 1980s was coming due. Hotel owners and operators were left with very few options to survive, resulting in massive loan defaults. Lenders virtually shut off funding to the entire industry.

In 1993, the hotel industry turned its first profit since 1985. As the economy recovered from recession, demand picked up again. With no new supply of hotel rooms, all demand in growth went straight to increased occupancy, improving the **average daily rate (ADR)**. The increase in ADR did not surpass inflation until 1994. New room construction began in earnest in 1995 and continued into 1997. The recovery did not last long. In 1998, the lodging industry again began experiencing problems. The supply of new rooms showed no signs of slowing. The **revenue per available room (REVPAR)**, the multiplication of average daily rate times **occupancy** percentage (i.e., ratio of the proportion of rooms sold to rooms available during a designated time period) also began to decrease. The combination of these two factors began to slow the availability of new capital. It has been suggested that the lodging industry will not rebound again until 2002, when supply and demand are expected to equalize.

Innovations in Lodging Management

One of the early pioneers in hotel management, Ellsworth Statler, opened his Statler Hotels in the early 1900s. In these early hotels, Statler made a number of important guest room innovations: (1) back-to-back rooms with common shafts for plumbing; (2) the first circulating ice water; (3) full closets with lights; (4) bedside reading lamps; (5) towel hooks in the bathrooms; (6) a modified door with enough room for newspapers to be passed underneath; (7) posted room rates; (8) radios; and (9) a generous supply of towels and stationery. Statler believed that, to be successful, a hotel company had to give its guests more and better service. Statler employees were required to learn and carry with them a set of rules called the Statler Service Code.

Until the 1950s, travelers called long distance to the hotel or motel of their choice to reserve a room. Once the telephone technology became available, such leaders in the motor hotel business as Kemmons Wilson automated the reservation system (he called his the Holidex) and made the telephone call available at no cost to the traveler. Other companies quickly followed suit.

Conrad Hilton, perhaps the best known hotel owner in the world, also made many innovations, which made his Hilton hotels stand out from the competition. Among these, Hilton introduced forecasting and control methods not previously used in the hotel business, which quickly became widely imitated. He used a forecasting committee to predict the number of rooms that would be sold a month in advance, a week in advance, and three days in advance, and scheduled employees to fit the anticipated volume of business.

Hilton also developed a concept called "digging for gold." "Gold" referred to unused space. Creating revenue centers out of space that was not otherwise being used became a Hilton signature.

In recent years, the automation and integration of all hotel services through a property management system that permits an instantaneous examination of financial data and daily status of all property operations, from the front desk to the engineering department, has revolutionized the way in which decisions are made in hotels. As hotel guests demand instant communication with others throughout the world, the Internet presents the next innovation in the lodging industry.

Lodging Industry Classification

Classifying lodging establishments into categories is not easy. The industry is diverse and there is no single, well-defined category. Lodging and accommodations can be classified in several ways: quality of facilities and services; target market; comparative statistics; and type of services provided to the guest. We will discuss each of these classifications in the following sections.

Quality of Facilities and Services

There are two systems of classification by quality of facilities and service in use in the United States. The Mobil Travel Guide, a division of the Mobil Oil Corporation, uses a star rating system, illustrated in Figure 1–1. The most widely recognized system is the diamond ratings issued by the American Automobile Association (AAA) beginning in 1907. A lodging establishment applies for evaluation voluntarily and can receive one to five diamonds, depending on the quality of the services and facilities it provides. Globally there are as many rating systems as there are countries. In most countries, the government ministry or department that is responsible for promoting tourism has an established rating system. While such systems are often patterned after the AAA or Mobil rating systems utilized in the United States, often there is considerable inconsistency between countries and often within countries. Often brand hotel companies operating internationally rely heavily on uniform standards that they have developed so as to ensure that their guests have a comfortable experience.

Appendix 1–1 provides AAA's lodging classifications, listing requirements, and diamond ratings. AAA classifications include apartments; bed-

★	***One-star*** lodging establishments must be clean and comfortable but not luxurious. However, they offer a minimum of services. There might not be a 24-hour front desk, phone, or housekeeping services, and there may or may not be a restaurant. If the facility is below the average in price charged for the area, a checkmark beside the star ✔ may indicate good value.
★★	***Two-star*** lodging establishments are slightly above a one-star establishment and may include better quality furniture, larger rooms, a restaurant, television in each guest room, direct dial phones, room service, and recreational facilities such as a swimming pool. Luxury is lacking, but cleanliness and comfort are essential.
★★★	***Three-star*** lodging offers all of the services of a one- and two-star establishment and has expanded upon these services so that one or more are truly outstanding.
★★★★	***Four-star*** establishments have rooms that are larger than average; furniture is of high quality; personnel are well trained, courteous, and eager to provide customers with everything they need. Guest complaints are minimal. Lodging in a four-star establishment should be a memorable experience.
★★★★★	***Five-star*** facilities are typically described as the best in the United States. A superior restaurant is required. Twice daily housekeeping services is standard; lobbies are comfortable and aesthetically attractive. The exterior is attractive and well maintained. A key factor is that the guest is made to feel like a very important person at all times by every employee of the establishment.

Figure 1–1 The Mobil Travel Guide lodging rating system

and-breakfasts; condominiums; cottages; country inns; hotels; lodges; motels; motor inns; ranches; and resorts. In order to be listed in the AAA system, a property must meet a minimum of 34 basic operating criteria that include management, public areas, guest room security, fire protection, housekeeping and maintenance, room decor and ambiance, and bathrooms.

First, an AAA inspector typically stays one or more times anonymously at the property to evaluate the total guest experience. Then, the inspector meets with the owner and/or general manager to collect factual data about the property and to conduct a physical examination of the entire property, including the grounds, landscaping, building, and other exterior elements. In addition, a random cross section of guest units is evaluated for quality and condition of the furnishings and decor. At the four- and five-diamond level, the inspector focuses his attention more intently on the services that are being provided to the guest.

At the conclusion of the evaluation, the inspector provides the owner, general manager, or other contact a written summary of the inspection and the rating decision.

Once a property is approved and included in the AAA system, it is reevaluated at least once a year. AAA pays close attention to comments on listed establishments that are submitted by its members. Any complaints are compiled by AAA and forwarded to the listed property. Of the more than 45,000 listings in AAA publications, the average ratio of member complaints is less than one per property.

Target Market

The number of markets targeted by the lodging business is as diverse as its customers. Under this classification system, lodging can be classified as commercial, airport, suite, residential, resort, bed-and-breakfast, time-share, casino, and conference center. Classification by target market is among the most traditional systems, but you may find this structure less useful because of the overlap among the categories.

Commercial lodging caters primarily to business guests. However, depending upon the location of the lodging establishment, many tour groups, individual pleasure travelers, and small conference groups may lodge at a "commercial" hotel. The commercial hotel must provide comfortable work spaces in the guest room that typically include a hand pullout return for a laptop computer, desk lamp, ergonomically designed desk chair, multiple electrical outlets conveniently located, a business center (i.e., fax machines, conference rooms, secretarial support), and food and beverage facilities that can serve the business traveler quickly and efficiently on a 24-hour basis.

You may have guessed that airport hotels are located near major travel centers. Although they target the business traveler, they are also heavily utilized by leisure travelers. However, they are rarely the final destination of the leisure traveler. The airport hotel must provide the business traveler with facilities and services that are similar to a commercial hotel and the leisure traveler with a comfortable accommodation that minimizes noise and the stress of a busy airport with prompt and efficient front office services (i.e., wake-up calls, check-in, and checkout) and quick and efficient restaurant and room services.

The guest rooms of suite hotels include a separate bedroom and a living room. Suite hotels appeal to multiple market segments. They can be the temporary living quarters of business travelers who are relocating or of leisure travelers who are not interested in standard lodging accommodations. In the early 1900s, residential lodging was one of the most common types of accommodations. Guests contracted to stay from a few weeks to a few months. The accommodations and type of guest were similar to the present-day suite hotel. In the suite hotel, every attention is given to providing or making available any product or service that guests may require or use if they were in their own home.

A resort is the planned destination of its guests. Typically, the resort has been used for pleasure or leisure travel. However, the resort also has become the destination for corporate meetings and conventions or group meetings. Resort hotels typically feature a special facility or environment, such as water sports, golf, tennis, skiing, history, or culture. Thus, the success of resort hotels depends heavily on its providing products and services to its guests that increase the pleasure they will derive from participation in and/or observation of the special environment that the resort features.

Bed-and-breakfast inns range from houses with a few rooms to larger facilities with as many as 20 to 30 guest rooms. There are thousands of bed-and-breakfasts operating in the United States today. A bed-and-breakfast guest is typically a leisure traveler who is looking for simple accommodations with an intimate atmosphere and personal service. Bed-and-breakfast inns are often located in proximity to a significant cultural, historical, or natural attraction and thus are successful when they provide the guest not only with comfortable accommodations but also with details and access to programs that expand the guests' knowledge of the cultural, historical, or natural attraction.

Time-share or vacation ownership lodging, which is discussed in more detail at the end of this chapter and in Chapter 11, typically provides the guest with a self-contained unit consisting of bedroom(s), living room, dining area, and kitchen. Guests purchase a specified period of time in the facility (one week, two weeks, one month) for their lifetime, unless they choose to sell it, and even for their children's lifetime, which can be used during certain seasons of the year. Particularly popular with the leisure traveler, time-share facilities are generally located in resort areas.

During the early development of casinos, lodging was often an afterthought. Early casino executives typically considered their facilities as casinos with rooms. However, since the late 1980s, lodging has become a more important source of revenue for casinos and has thus received increased attention. Since it can be considered a type of resort, a more detailed discussion of casinos and their lodging appears in Chapter 10. Casinos attract guests to their facilities by promoting gaming and other types of entertainment. While the majority of the casino lodging guests are leisure travelers, increasing numbers of conferences and business groups are selecting casinos as their destinations.

Conference centers, designed to handle large group meetings or conventions, cater to the business guest. Typically, the full-service conference center offers overnight accommodations; large areas for exhibits; and smaller, fully equipped meeting rooms. In recent years, increasing numbers of commercial hotels and resort properties have added conference centers, forcing the traditional conference center to add features to make them more competitive, further clouding the distinctions between categories in this classification system.

Comparative Statistics Comparing your hotel to others, in terms of number of rooms, rates, or geographic location, is often the best gauge of its success. PKF Consulting, one of several businesses that develops statistics and information for the lodging industry, provides a tool for comparison in its annual report, which includes operating statistics for the lodging business, such as average daily rate, occupancy percentage, revenues, and departmental costs. The report also breaks down expenses by number of rooms, rate group, and geographic location. PKF categorizes facilities by numbers of rooms (under 125 rooms; 125 to 200 rooms; and over 200 rooms), rate group (under $50; $50–$75; and over $75), and by geographic location (New England, Mid-Atlantic, North Central, South Atlantic, South Central, Mountain, and Pacific).

Types of Services Provided Another classification system categorizes lodging according to the level of services provided to its guests. This system of classification is perhaps the easiest to understand and includes the principal characteristics of the classifications by quality of facilities and services and by target market. The three levels of service are limited service, extended stay, and full service. In future years, these categories may expand to include time-share lodging, which is not currently covered by this system (see Figure 1–2). Service level should not vary, regardless of the size of a particular lodging establishment.

Limited-Service Lodging. Limited-service lodging establishments traditionally have been referred to as motels or motor hotels. However, since the early 1990s, limited-service lodging establishments have further segmented into midscale establishments without food and beverage economy, and budget establishments, with midscale being the highest priced of the three and budget, the lowest. The guest of the limited-service lodging establishment is the price-sensitive business or leisure traveler. Examples of limited-service lodging establishments include La Quinta, Hampton, Holiday Inn Express, Super 8, and Motel 6. The average length of stay at a limited-service facility is typically one or two nights.

As its name implies, limited-service lodging provides a limited number of services to its guests. If available, food and beverage service is limited to complimentary breakfast or a happy hour (there may be no restaurant on the premises). Meeting rooms, banquet facilities, bell service, and valet parking may be limited or absent. Limited-service lodging has been hit hard by

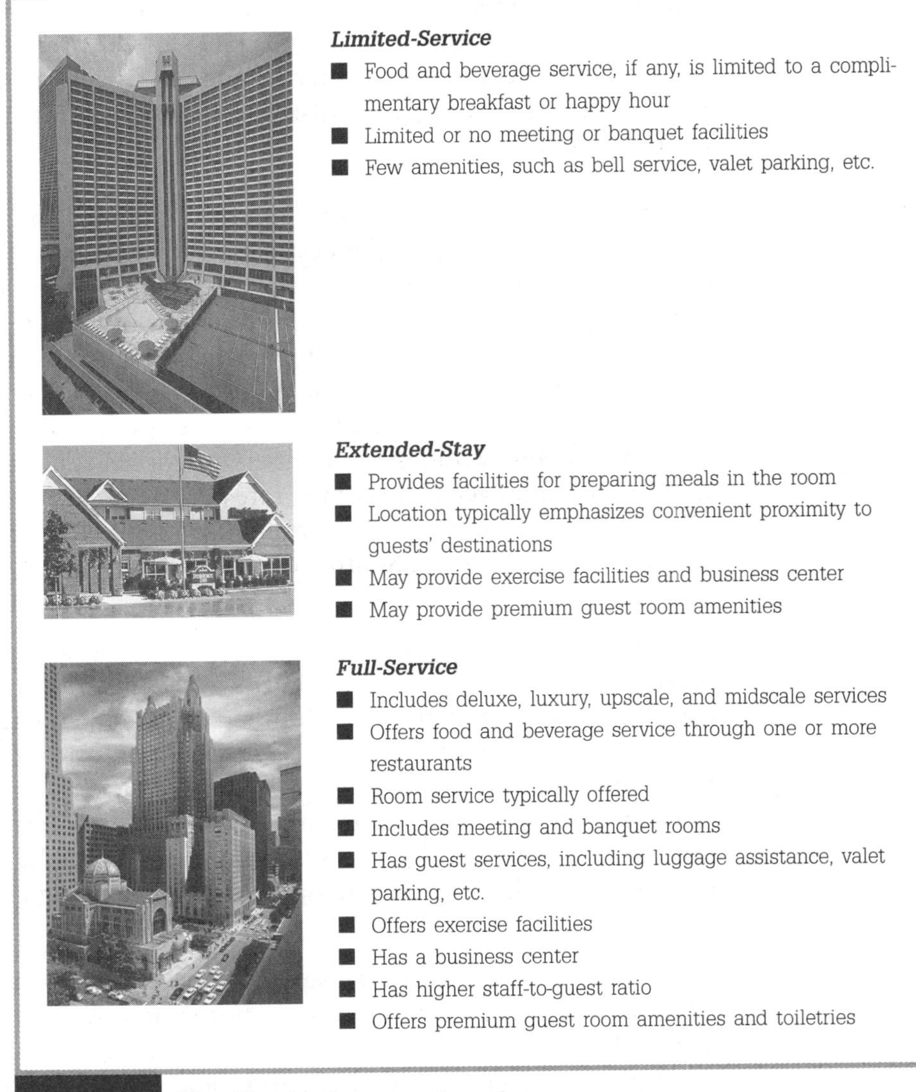

Figure 1–2 **Classification by type of service**

factors that affect their customers' price sensitivity, such as increases in gasoline prices or airline fares. However, lower departmental expenses and higher margins allow the limited-service lodging operator to remain profitable at lower levels of occupancy. Table 1–1 shows the number of properties and available rooms of the leaders in the limited-service segment of the lodging industry.

Table 1-1 Limited-Service Lodging

Company	Number of Properties	Total Number of Rooms
Midscale Without Food and Beverage		
Comfort Inn	1213	100,271
Hampton Inn	619	67,390
Holiday Inn Express	504	41,741
La Quinta	242	31,289
Economy		
Days Inn	1,659	151,741
Travelodge	393	31,227
Fairfield Inn	281	26,813
Ramada Limited	186	14,524
Budget		
Motel 6	987	111,761
Super 8	1,454	88,863
Econo Lodge	687	45,723

Source: Hotels, Vol. 33, No. 7 (July 1999): 45–68.

The limited service, midscale lodging establishment without food and beverage facilities is among the fastest growing segment of the industry. The reason for its lengthy, rather awkward name is that, as you will see shortly, the lowest tier of the full-service category is designated "midscale with food and beverage." (If you come up with a better name for these categories, the hotel industry will thank you!) In 1987, this segment represented only 5 percent of all rooms, while in the current market, it represents over 12 percent. In recent years, this subsegment has posted an ADR of from $53 to over $60. Comfort Inn, Hampton Inn, and Holiday Inn Express have been leaders in the midscale segment.

The economy subsegment of limited service lodging includes 307,983 rooms total. The average size property has approximately 89 rooms. Days Inn, with over 1,659 properties, is the leader in the economy subsegment. The ADR for economy facilities has hovered at around $50 in recent years.

The budget subsegment of limited service lodging, with over 37 companies, accounts for the largest number of companies in the business. Super 8 has been the dominant company in this subsegment with over 1,454 properties. The ADR for the budget subsegment is typically around $38.

Extended-Stay Lodging. Extended-stay lodging emerged in late 1995 as an alternative to more traditional lodging for those business and/or leisure travelers who anticipate visiting an area for more than an overnight visit. The guest of an extended-stay facility is provided all of the amenities of furnished apartment-style living, with only some of the services of a full-service hotel. There may or may not be exercise facilities, a business center, or premium guest room amenities. Extended-stay facilities provide the guest with most of the comforts of their own home, but without all of the services of a full-service hotel. Whereas full-service hotels may provide conference and meeting facilities, valet parking, 24-hour restaurants or food services, special leisure facilities (i.e., spa, retail, etc.), the extended-stay lodging establishment does not. The supply of extended-stay lodging has grown at such a rapid rate that supply has exceeded demand since 1997. Leaders in extended-stay lodging include Residence Inn, Extended Stay America, Homestead, and Villager Lodge (see Table 1–2).

Extended Stay America has the greatest geographic distribution. The three brands in its portfolio include Extended Stay America, StudioPLUS, and Crossland. Residence Inn operates the most hotels in this segment and continues to lead the extended-stay segment in number of rooms.

As with limited-service lodging, facilities in the extended-stay segment fall into two categories based upon price point. The upper tier is dominated by Residence Inn. In 1998, the occupancy of the upper-tier segment was 77.9 percent, with an ADR of $97.51. The lower tier includes 61 percent of the guest rooms and over 70 percent of the brands in the extended-stay segment. In 1998, the occupancy of the lower-tier segment was 67 percent, with an ADR of $43.10.

Perhaps the earliest of the extended-stay hotels was the all-suite hotel, which was considered to be a luxury, full-service hotel. It was pioneered in the late 1960s by Marriott. The guest rooms are larger than those in the full-service hotel and have a living and dining area that is separated from the sleeping area. Continental breakfasts, cocktails, and newspapers are generally provided for guests. (3)

Full-Service Lodging. The segments of the full-service lodging industry include (from most expensive to least expensive) deluxe, luxury, upscale, and mid-scale with food and beverage. Typically, the range of food and beverage ser-

Table 1–2 Extended-Stay Hotel Companies

Company	Number of Properties	Total Number of Rooms
Residence Inn	290	34,382
Extended Stay America	179	20,656
Homestead	119	15,975
Villager Lodge	107	8,496

Source: *Hotels*, Vol. 33, No. 7 (July 1999): 45–68.

vice is wider and the quality is higher at a full-service facility than at limited-service and extended-stay facilities (this applies to the subsegments within this category as well). In addition, more guest services are available, such as assistance with luggage from curb to room, room service, and the provision of a fully equipped business center. Table 1–3 provides the names of the leaders in the deluxe and luxury segments of the full-service industry, along with the number of properties and total number of rooms for each.

Deluxe full-service lodging typically includes hotels rated with four or five stars according to the Mobil Travel Guide Lodging Rating System (see Figure 1–1). The guests of deluxe hotels are corporate, group, and leisure travelers who are not sensitive to price. Four Seasons, Ritz-Carlton, and Fairmont are examples of companies with multiple properties in this category. Hotels such as the Waldorf-Astoria and the Plaza in New York City, Mansion on Turtle Creek in Dallas, Texas, and the Palmer House in

Table 1–3 Full-Service Deluxe and Luxury Hotel Companies

Company	Number of Properties	Total Number of Rooms
Deluxe		
Preferred	62	15,152
Ritz-Carlton	20	7,161
Four Seasons	20	6,228
Fairmont	7	4,260
Deluxe Independent	100	25,386
Luxury		
Marriott	245	102,796
Sheraton Hotel	173	64,689
Hyatt	104	53,324
Hilton	49	36,326
Westin	54	26,921
Renaissance	33	14,852
Omni	38	14,100
Wyndham	33	13,422
Loews	11	4,552
Inter-Continental	8	4,344
Nikko	5	2,586
Helmsley Hotel	5	2,042
Hotel Sofitel	7	1,971
Meriden	4	1,920
Doral	6	1,521
Raphael Hotel	2	295

Source: U.S. Lodging Almanac 1999 Edition, Jason N. Ader, Robert A. LaFleur, and Joseph J. Yurman (New York: Bear Stearns & Co., Inc., 1999).

Chicago, Illinois, are examples of individual properties in this category. Boulders in Arizona, Broadmoor in Colorado, Breakers in Florida, Cloister in Georgia, and Greenbriar in West Virginia are examples of deluxe full-service hotels. In 1998, the occupancy of deluxe full-service facilities was 72 percent, with an ADR of $138.36. (4)

Luxury full-service lodging has slightly lower service levels, fewer amenities, and a lower ADR than deluxe lodging. Marriott is the largest operator in this segment, with 245 hotels and 102,796 rooms. Among the leaders in the luxury segment is Starwood Hotels & Resorts. Starwood controls a collection of very well-regarded lodging brands. Its Sheraton Hotels is among the most widely distributed and familiar names in the global travel market, and its Westin brand is consistently recognized as offering the highest service level among luxury hotel brands.

The upscale segment of full-service lodging includes all-suite brands such as Embassy Suites and Doubletree Guest Suites. Radisson, Hilton Inns, and Embassy Suites are the largest chains in the upscale segment. Table 1–4 lists the major upscale hotels along with the number of properties and total num-

Table 1–4 Full-Service Upscale and Midscale Hotel Companies

Company	Number of Properties	Total Number of Rooms
Upscale		
Radisson	219	52,219
Hilton Inn	163	42,388
Embassy Suites	142	34,374
Crowne Plaza	62	19,952
Clarion	110	17,905
Adam's Mark	21	11,601
Wyndham Garden	60	10,984
Midscale with Food and Beverage Facilities		
Holiday Inn	1,066	199,894
Best Western	2,104	188,234
Ramada	729	108,057
Courtyard	386	53,089
Quality Inn	425	49,896
Howard Johnson	299	35,909
Doubletree Club	103	31,028
Holiday Inn Select	64	17,043
Four Points	71	13,713

Source: U.S. Lodging Almanac 1999 Edition, Jason N. Ader, Robert A. LaFleur, and Joseph J. Yurman (New York: Bear Stearns & Co., Inc., 1999).

ber of rooms for each. In 1998, occupancy for this segment of the lodging industry was 69.4 percent, with an ADR of $95.60.

The biggest differences between upscale hotels and midscale hotels with food and beverage facilities are that the rates charged to their guests all lower, the amenities are of a lower quality, and there is a decreased availability of facilities in midscale hotels. In 1998, the occupancy rate of midscale hotels with food and beverage facilities was 60.8 percent, with an ADR of $67.07.

The resort is a special type of full-service hotel. Unlike other types of hotels, the resort is often the final destination of the pleasure traveler, with a superior location and/or facilities. Although the vacation market has long been the principal target for the resort, in recent years, an increasing number of resorts has begun to include conventions, corporate meetings, and incentive groups in their market mix. Resorts are typically in the deluxe or luxury categories; however, some resorts, such as hunting and fishing resorts, might be in the midscale category.

Another variation on the full-service hotel is the convention hotel, which provides facilities and services that are geared to meet the needs of large group and association meetings and trade shows. Typically, these hotels have in excess of 400 guest rooms, with substantial function and banquet space flexibly designed for use by large meeting groups. The convention hotel often works with other hotels and convention centers to provide facilities for citywide conventions and trade shows.

Time-share Lodging. Time-share lodging is a unique type of lodging arrangement. Also known as vacation ownership or holiday ownership, time-share lodging offers the purchaser the right to use lodging that is equipped with a variety of services and facilities for a set interval (one week, two weeks, etc.) each year. The purchaser pays a capital sum to acquire the time-share for a lifetime. It becomes his or her property. The time-share owner then pays an annual contribution, known as a maintenance or management fee.

In the United States, the states with the most active time-shares are Florida, Hawaii, California, and Nevada. Time-share units are typically studio, one bedroom, two bedroom, or three bedroom apartment-style accommodations.

Time-share facilities most frequently include swimming pools, whirlpools and spas, and tennis and exercise facilities. The most successful ones utilize the geography of the area, whether it be the availability of downhill skiing, direct ocean beach access, or location on a golf course.

Depending upon the location, time-share prices range from a low of $6,225 per week for a studio unit in the low season to $8,635 for the same studio unit in the high season. The cost of a week will be determined by location and amenities and may rise to as much as $35 per week. Average maintenance fees range from $290 per year for a studio to $425 per year for a three-bedroom unit.

Time-sharing has grown into a $6 billion dollar industry, with over 4 million owners and 4,800 resorts worldwide. Time-sharing is considered to be among the fastest growing components of the travel and tourism industry in the world.

Leaders in time-share development include Fairfield Communities, Signature Resorts, and Vacation Break. In addition, Disney Vacation Club, Marriott Ownership Resorts, and Hilton Grand Vacations Club have aggressively moved into this growing segment of the lodging industry.

In 1974, a company currently known as Resort Condominiums International (RCI) created the time-share exchange concept. The exchange allows time-share owners to swap the holiday intervals they own for different intervals of time in alternative properties around the world. In 1997, RCI processed over 1.8 million exchanges, covering about 3,200 resort affiliates in 90 countries.

SUMMARY

The travel and tourism industry is the top services export, one of the largest employers, and one of the top three industries in the United States. One of its many components, the lodging industry, includes 3.7 million rooms. In 1998, the lodging industry generated nearly $95.6 billion in revenue.

Lodging demand in the United States is driven by the cost of airline tickets, oil prices, and population demographics. The lodging industry emerged in the United States following World War II with a booming postwar economy. However, the quality of the facilities varied widely. In 1952, one of the pioneers of the lodging industry, Kemmons Wilson, opened his first Holiday Inn, and others quickly followed his lead, offering standardized, quality lodging at affordable prices. The boom time in U.S. hotel expansion of the early 1970s was due in large part to the completion of the interstate highway system. Demand for rooms exceeded supply to such an extent in the 1980s that the construction boom in this period was labeled the "go-go eighties." The U.S. recession of the early 1990s caused the demand for hotel rooms to decline. Recovery from the recession beginning in 1993 signaled another upturn in the cycle. Currently, the industry is in another downturn, from which it is expected to recover around 2002.

Lodging can be classified by quality of facilities and services (using the AAA and Mobil Travel Guide ratings), target market (commercial, airport, suite, residential, resort, bed-and-breakfast, time-share, casino, conference center), comparative statistics, and type of service (limited service, extended stay, full-service). Two variations on the full-service hotel are resorts and convention hotels, and time-shares, or vacation ownerships, are a unique type of lodging experience. These classifications are by nature artificial, and there is a great deal of overlap among the various categories. In the next chapter, you will learn about the organizational structure of an individual lodging business.

References

1. Dolores Minic, ed., *Tourism Works for America* (Washington, D.C.: Travel Industry Association of America, 1998).
2. Dolores Minic, ed., *Tourism Works for America* (Washington, D.C.: Travel Industry Association of America, 1998).
3. Chuck Y. Gee, *Resort Management*, 2nd ed. (East Lansing, MI: Educational Institute of the American Hotel and Motel Association, 1988).
4. *Trends In The Hotel Industry USA Edition*—1998 (San Francisco: PKF Consulting, 1998).

Review Questions

1. What three factors influence lodging demand?
2. At what time in history did the modern hotel industry emerge? What were the contributing factors to its emergence?
3. The Lost Island Inn features curb-to-room luggage service, lovely rooms furnished with top-quality antiques, a full-service restaurant, an exercise room and sauna, room service, and top-quality amenities at its remote island location. Would you classify this establishment as a limited-service, extended-stay, or full-service business? Would the Lost Island Inn appeal to the leisure traveler or to the business traveler? Why?

Activities

1. List the names of two businesses in each component of the travel industry that are found in your city.

2. Request from the Chamber of Commerce or the Convention and Visitor's Bureau in your city the number of jobs that each component of the travel industry contributed to the local economy.
3. List the number of rooms by lodging industry segment that are in operation in your city.
4. Visit a lodging establishment in your city that is listed by either Mobil or AAA. Then visit another lodging establishment in your city that is not listed by either rating system and compare the two.

Appendix 1-1

AAA Lodging Classifications

Apartment (limited service)—Establishments that primarily offer transient guest accommodations with one or more bedrooms, a living room, a full kitchen and an eating area. Studio-type apartments may combine the sleeping and living areas into one room.

Bed-and-Breakfast (limited service)—Usually smaller, owner-operated establishments emphasizing a more personal relationship between operators and guests, lending an "at-home" feeling. Guest units tend to be individually decorated. Rooms may not include modern amenities such as televisions and telephones, and may have a shared bathroom. A common room or parlor, separate from the innkeeper's living quarters, allows guests and operators to interact during evening and breakfast hours. Evening office closures are normal. A continental or full, hot breakfast is served and is included in the room rate.

Complex (service varies depending on type of lodging)—A combination of two or more types of lodging classifications.

Condominium (limited service)—Privately owned guest accommodations that can include apartment-style units or homes. A variety of room styles and decor treatments as well as limited housekeeping services is typical. May have off-site registration. The lodging provided by time-share and vacation ownership is reflected in this category.

Cottage (limited service)—Individual housing units with one or more separate sleeping rooms, a living room, and cooking facilities. They usually incorporate rustic decor treatments and are geared to vacationers. A limited-service lodging business would be typical of this category.

Country Inn (moderate service)—Although similar in definition to a bed-and-breakfast, country inns are usually larger in size, provide more spacious public areas, and offer a dining facility that serves breakfast, dinner, and sometimes lunch. It may be located in a rural setting or in a downtown area.

Hotel (full service)—Usually high-rise establishments, offering a full range of on-premise food and beverage service, cocktail lounge, entertainment, conference facilities, business services, shops, and recreational activities. A wide range of services are available 24 hours, provided by uniformed staff. Parking arrangements vary. As noted in the chapter, full-service lodging is placing a premium on exceptional service and products for their guests.

Lodge (moderate service)—Consist typically of two or more stories, with all facilities in one building, and have a rustic decor. They are located in vacation areas that provide skiing, fishing, and so on. They usually have food and beverage service. Again, a limited-service property as described in the chapter is reflective of this category.

Motel (limited service)—A low-rise or multistory establishment offering limited public and recreational facilities.

Motor Inn (moderate service)—A single or multistory establishment offering on-premise food and beverage service. Meeting and banquet facilities and some recreational activities are provided. Usually there is complimentary onsite parking.

Ranch (moderate service)—Often offers rustic decor and food and beverage facilities. Entertainment and recreational activities are geared to a Western-style adventure vacation. Some meeting facilities may be provided.

Resort (full service)—Geared to vacation travelers. It is a destination offering varied food and beverage outlets, specialty shops, meeting or conference facilities, entertainment and extensive recreational facilities for special interests such as golf, tennis, skiing, fishing, and water sports. Assorted social and recreational programs are typically offered in season, and a variety of package plans are usually available, including meal plans. Larger resorts may offer a variety of guest accommodations.

Subclassifications

The following subclassifications may appear, along with the classifications listed above, to provide a more specific description of the lodging:

Suite—Have one or more bedrooms and a living room/sitting area, which is closed off by a full wall.

Extended Stay—Properties catering to longer-term guest stays. Guest rooms have kitchens or are in the form of efficiencies, with a double-burner cooktop and a refrigerator. Guest rooms may have separate living room areas. Evening office closure and limited housekeeping services are common.

Historic—Accommodations in restored structures built prior to 1920, reflecting the historical ambiance of the surrounding area. Antique furnishings complement the overall decor of the property. Rooms may lack some modern amenities and may have shared bathrooms.

A sample of AAA Listing Requirements

Style of Operation

1. The facility must accommodate primarily transient guests.
2. The facility must be operated as a full-time, seven-day-a-week business (during periods of operation if seasonal).
3. Incoming phone calls must be available on a 24-hour basis, and a system must be in place to ensure that messages are delivered on a timely basis.
4. Guests must have 24-hour access to outgoing phone service.
5. Staff must be willing to assist in resolution of member complaints.
6. Staff must be willing to accommodate unannounced property inspections.
7. There must be a minimum of four rental units.
8. Management must be willing to provide and honor room rates.
9. There must be 24-hour access to a property management representative, in person or by telephone.
10. Properties must be clean, safe, and well maintained.
    - Management and staff must present a neat appearance and operate ethically and professionally.
    - Staff must provide attentive, conscientious attention to guest service.
11. There must be appropriate, visible signage.
12. All facilities associated with a property must meet listing requirements.

Guest Room Security

13. Each door leading to a common walkway must be equipped with a primary lock and a secondary dead bolt lock (see definitions). This may be a single lock with dual functions.
    - A *primary lock* is a device that permits a guest to enter a rental unit using some form of key and allows the door to be locked while the unit is occupied and when the guest leaves the unit. Passkeys assigned to appropriate staff members operate only these locks (not dead bolt locks).

- A *dead bolt lock* is a mortised, locking device with a throw that extends at least one inch from the edge of the door, providing an extra measure of security against any unwanted intrusions. Unlike the primary lock, dead bolt passkeys are not provided to guests or to staff. Any dead bolt passkeys are for restricted use by management staff only.

In certain instances, with the approval of the AAA ,the requirement for secondary locks may be modified. The most common modifications are noted below.

- Sliding glass doors—An assortment of acceptable secondary locking devices is available for these doors, but the most common is a metal bar that folds down and extends from the frame to the door. A chain lock is not acceptable.
- French doors—In addition to the dead bolt lock requirements, surface-mounted slide bolts must be provided at the top and bottom, extending into the upper door frame and the lower door frame or floor.
- Historic doors—If a door is considered integral to an establishment's historic registry and is too thin to accommodate a standard, mortised dead bolt lock, a surface-mounted dead bolt locking device will be considered and approved on a case-by-case basis.

14. Each door must have a viewport or window that is convenient to the door.
15. Each door to connecting guest units or maintenance corridors must be equipped with a dead bolt lock.
16. Each window overlooking a common walkway or in a ground-floor room must be equipped with a functional locking mechanism.
17. An operational, single-station smoke detector is required in each guest unit.
18. An operational, single-station smoke detector or an automatic sprinkler system is required in public areas that are connected to guest units.
19. From each guest unit exit, there must be two separate means of egress to emergency exits.

Housekeeping and Maintenance

20. At minimum, each guest unit must be thoroughly cleaned, with complete bed and bath linens changed between guest stays.
21. All areas of a property's operation must be in good repair and in good working order.

22. Within the room, there must be an adequate open area, allowing guest(s) to move freely about the unit.
23. Privacy coverings, such as shades, draperies, or blinds, must cover all windows or other guest unit areas.
24. There must be sufficient soundproofing to muffle outside noises, normal sounds in adjacent units, and sounds from public areas.

Furnishings

25. A comfortable bed with two sheets, one mattress pad, pillows and pillow cases, a suitable bedspread, and a blanket is required.
26. A nightstand or equivalent must be placed beside the bed.
27. There must be one or more chairs in each guest unit.
28. Clothes-hanging facilities with hangers for two people and drawers or clothes storage space are required.
29. A minimum of 75-watt illumination (or equivalent) is required at each bed, at the writing surface (if present), and at the sitting area.
30. There must be an active light switch at the main entry to each guest unit.
31. Each guest unit must have its own private bathroom, with no carpeting in the commode area.
    - Bed-and-breakfasts, country inns, and historic properties may have shared bathrooms.
    - If there is a shared bathroom, each guest unit must have adequate shelf space, a lighted mirror, and a convenient electrical outlet.
32. An electrical outlet convenient to the bathroom mirror is required. An electrical outlet must accommodate such items as shaver, hair dryer, curling iron, and so on.

Fixtures

33. Bathroom fixtures must include a commode, sink, shelf space, well-lighted mirror at sink, shower, tub, or combination tub/shower with nonslip surface.
    - Multiperson hot tubs and whirlpools do not need to be enclosed. They must have a nonslip surface.

Amenities

34. Required amenities include one cloth bath mat, toilet tissue, one wastepaper basket, drinking glasses, at least one large bath towel, one

hand towel and facecloth per guest, two individually wrapped bars of soap (or liquid soap, with at least one wrapped bar).

In addition to the above, at the four- and five-diamond levels, the following services should be be evaluated: reservations, arrival, check-in, bell services, evening housekeeping, wake-up calls, checkout, room service order taking, room service delivery, miscellaneous additional services, staff.

Diamond Ratings

A diamond rating is assigned to a property based on the conditions noted at the time of the inspection. All physical attributes and the quality of services are considered.

One Diamond ◆
Property meets all listing requirements. It is clean, safe, and well maintained.

Two Diamond ◆◆
Property exhibits all attributes offered at the one-diamond level, with noticeable enhancements in room decor and quality of furnishings.

Three Diamond ◆◆◆
Property shows a marked upgrade in physical attributes, services, and comfort from the two-diamond level. Additional amenities, services, and facilities may be offered.

Four Diamond ◆◆◆◆
Property reflects an exceptional degree of hospitality, service, and attention to detail, while offering upscale facilities and a variety of amenities.

Five Diamond ◆◆◆◆◆
Property facilities and operations exemplify an impeccable standard of excellence and exceed guest expectations in hospitality and service. These renowned properties are both striking and luxurious, offering many extra amenities.

Chapter 2

Organizational Structure

CHAPTER OUTLINE

- Overview of Organizational Design
- Job Specialization
- The Organization of a Lodging Establishment
  - Rooms Department
  - Food and Beverage Department
  - Marketing and Sales Department
  - Human Resources Department
  - Accounting Department
  - General Manager
  - Resident Manager
- Patterns of Authority
- Span of Control
- The Pros and Cons of Functional Organization Design
- Meetings and Committees
- The Hotel Staffing System
- Career Paths and Opportunities

Overview of Organizational Design

Organizing, the process of structuring human and physical resources in order to accomplish organizational objectives, involves dividing tasks into jobs, specifying the appropriate department for each job, determining the optimum number of jobs in each department, and delegating authority within and among departments. One of the most critical challenges facing lodging managers today is the development of a responsive organizational structure that is committed to quality. (1)

The framework of jobs and departments that make up any organization must be directed toward achieving the organization's objectives. In other words, the structure of a lodging business must be consistent with its strategy. (2)

Managers give structure to a hotel and lodging through job specialization, organization, and establishment of patterns of authority and span of control. (3)

Job Specialization

There are as many degrees of job specialization within the lodging industry as there are different types of organizations. And as you learned in Chapter 1, there are many different types of organizations. One extreme is the case of a hotel where the owner/operator is responsible for checking in the guests, servicing their needs, taking care of the housekeeping for the guest rooms, maintaining the building and grounds, and checking out the guests. There is, to be sure, much to recommend this method of work. It is rewarding to have total control over a project from beginning to end, and many people find it motivating to see the results of their efforts. However, as the demand for additional products or services increases (i.e. , if additional rooms are added or another hotel is purchased), it becomes more and more difficult for an individual to do his or her job well. One benefit of the increased workload is increased revenue, which would enable the individual hotel operator to add housekeeping staff, one or more front desk agents to check in and check out the additional guests, and engineering and maintenance personnel to care for the building and grounds.

As a general rule, specialization increases worker productivity and efficiency. On the other hand, delegating jobs increases the need for managerial control and coordination. Someone has to make sure that housekeeping staff come in *after* the painters have repainted a room (and that the paint is dry), not before! One of the crucial elements of hotel and lodging management is coordinating the many specialized functions within hotels so that the organization runs smoothly.

Specialization has its own set of problems; it can result in workers performing the same type of tasks over and over again. A point can be reached where the degree of specialization so narrows a job's scope that the worker finds little joy or satisfaction in it. Signs of overspecialization include workers' loss of interest, lowered morale, increasing error rate, and reduction in service and product quality.

One solution to this problem is to modify jobs so that teams can perform them. Instead of a single guest room attendant being assigned to a group of rooms, a **work team** in a hotel housekeeping department might clean all of the rooms on a particular floor. Some establishments use teams throughout the organization on a regular basis; others use teams more selectively. Teams can be directed by a manager or can be self-managed. The idea behind self-managed work teams is for workers to become their own managers, which increases their self-reliance as well as develops a talent pool.

A concept called the quality circle is based on the belief that the people who actually do the work, rather than their managers, are the ones who are best able to identify, analyze, and correct any problems they encounter. The idea originated in Japan in 1962. The **quality circle** is a group of employees, usually fewer than ten, who perform similar jobs and meet once per week to discuss their work, identify problems, and present possible solutions to those problems. For example, a quality circle might be formed among front desk agents. The group's findings and proposals are then forwarded to management for evaluation and action. Quality circles are most successful when they are included as part of an organization-wide improvement effort. American business picked up on the quality circle concept in the mid-1970s. (4)

THE ORGANIZATION OF A LODGING ESTABLISHMENT

As their facilities grow in size, lodging managers are faced with the need to group certain jobs together in order to ensure efficient coordination and control of activities. These job groupings are usually called departments. In general, departments might be grouped as **front of the house** or those departments in which employees have guest contact, such as front desk, and **back of the house**, where employees have little guest contact, such as accounting. However, separating departments by function is the most common method of organizing a hotel or a lodging business. Figure 2–1 outlines the departmental structures of a limited-service hotel, a full-service hotel with under 500 rooms, and a full-service hotel with over 500 rooms. There may be as few as 2 or as many as 50 employees in a particular department.

In a very small lodging business, such as a bed-and-breakfast, the owner can supervise each department. However, as the lodging business increases in size (i.e., above 20 rooms), it is most effective to create managerial positions within departments.

Rooms Department Typically, the **rooms department** (called the front desk department in a limited-service facility) includes reservations, the front office, housekeeping, and telephone or PBX. In smaller full-service hotels, security and engineering might also be included in the rooms department. Responsibilities of the rooms department include reservations, guest reception, room assignment, tracking the status of rooms (available or occupied), prompt forwarding of mail and phone messages, security, housekeeping of guest rooms and public spaces such as lobbies, and answering guests' questions. To perform these many duties effectively, the rooms department may be divided into a number of specialized subunits. To complicate matters, in many instances, these subunits are also referred to as departments. For example, the laundry department shown in Figure 2–1b is responsible for cleaning and pressing all the hotel's linens and employee uniforms as well as guest laundry. Because of its specialized function, little of the knowledge and skills required to manage a laundry operation are transferable to other areas of hotel operations.

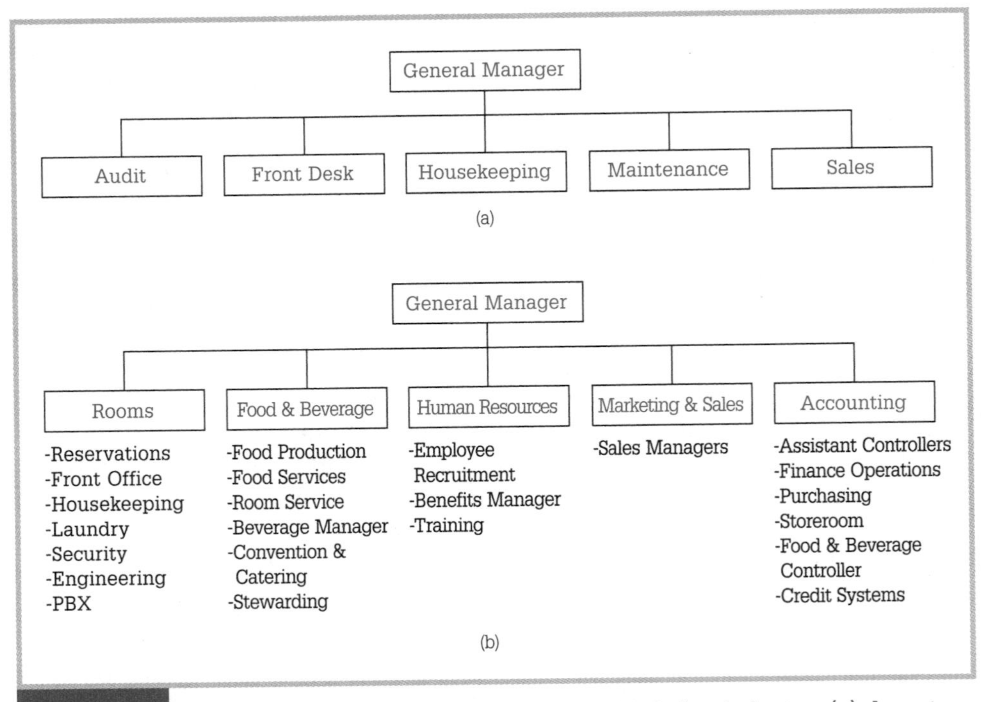

Figure 2–1 Departmental structure in the hotel and lodging industry: (*a*) departments of a Limited-Service Hotel; (*b*) departments of a full-service hotel (under 500 rooms)

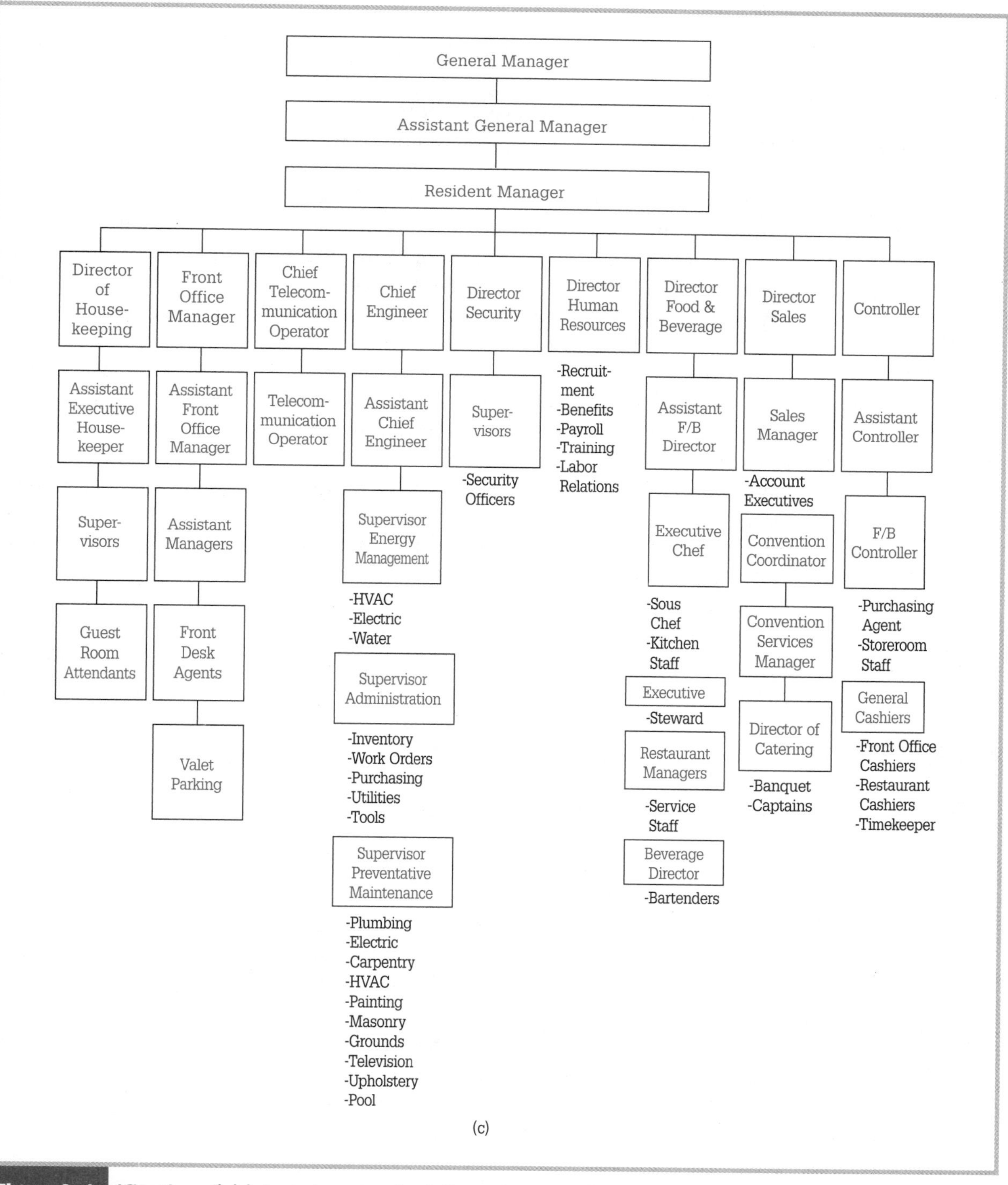

Figure 2–1 **(*Continued*) (*c*) departments of a full-service hotel (over 500 rooms)**

The front office is one of the most important departments in a hotel, as it often offers the only contact that may occur between guests and staff. A hotel's front office is where guests are greeted when they arrive, where they are registered and assigned to a room, and where they check out. Usually, the telephone operator, other guest communications functions, and the bell staff or those employees responsible for delivering luggage, messages, and attending to special requests that a guest might have also fall under the front office umbrella. The reservations department takes and keeps track of the hotel's future bookings. The housekeeping department is responsible for cleaning guest rooms and public spaces. Because of their specialized nature, the security and engineering departments will be discussed in separate sections.

A great deal of interdependence exists within the subunits of the rooms department. For example, reservations must inform the front office of the number of presold rooms each day to ensure that a current inventory of salable rooms is always available. On the other hand, the front office must let reservations know whenever walk-in guests (those who do not have reservations) are registered. A similar level of cooperation is required between the front office and housekeeping. When a guest checks out, the front office must inform housekeeping so that the rooms may be cleaned. Once a room is cleaned, housekeeping must inform the front office so that the room may be sold. Certain tasks within the rooms department must occur in a specific order. For example, housekeeping cannot properly provision a guest room if the laundry does not supply enough clean towels or bed sheets. Engineering cannot replace a defective light switch in a guest room if housekeeping does not report the problem. Effective management of this busy department calls for standardized plans, procedures, schedules, and deadlines, as well as frequent direct communication between executives that are managing the key operating units of the rooms department.

Security. The hotel and lodging business is vulnerable to security and safety problems. Problems can be created by guests, employees, or uninvited intruders. Security breaches can result in embezzlement, theft, arson, robbery, and even terrorism. Depending upon the size of a hotel or a lodging establishment, the security function may be handled by a fully staffed department on site, contracted out to an outside security company, or assigned to designated staff members or on-premise supervisory personnel in the rooms department. In a larger, full-service hotel, the director of security may report directly to the general manager. In smaller hotels, the security function might become a task of the rooms department (see Figure 2–1b).

Engineering. Typically, the engineering department's responsibilities include preventive maintenance; repair; replacement; improvement and modification to furniture, fixtures, and equipment (FFE); and ensuring uninterrupted provision of utilities (gas, electricity, water). (5) Preventive maintenance involves routine checks and inspection of the key components of all equipment. Maintenance of recreational facilities may be part of the engineering department's responsibilities. In particular, swimming pools require extensive maintenance to ensure proper filtration and to prevent the accumulation of algae and other conditions that are not suitable for swimming.

Prompt repair minimizes loss of productivity in other hotel operating departments and inconvenience to hotel guests. When a particular FFE has reached the end of its useful life and repair is no longer cost-effective, replacement is indicated. Improvement projects enhance the existing operation or reduce operating costs of the facility. Modification projects alter the existing operation to accommodate one or more new functions.

One hotel might have a large engineering staff that includes plumbers, carpenters, painters, electricians, and other technicians. Another might have maintenance personnel who have general knowledge and understanding of the hotel's operations but rely on outside contractors for specialized jobs. In larger, full-service hotels, engineering may be a separate department, with a director who reports directly to the resident manager (see Figure 2–1c).

Food and Beverage Department

The primary function of the *food and beverage department* is to provide food and drink to a hotel's guests. In earlier times, when an inn had a single dining room that could hold a limited number of guests, this was a much simpler task. Today, however, providing food and drink is much more complicated. A large hotel might well have a coffee shop, a gourmet restaurant, a poolside snack bar, room service, two banquet halls, and ten separate function rooms where food and beverages are served. It might also have a lounge, a nightclub, and a lobby bar. On a busy day (or night), it's quite likely that functions will be booked in many different outlets at the same time. In addition, some outlets may have multiple events scheduled for a single day. As you can see, there is great diversity in the types of activities performed by a food and beverage department, requiring a significant variety of skills on the part of its workers.

Because of the diversity of services provided, the food and beverage department is typically split into smaller subunits. The executive chef, a person of considerable importance and authority in any full-service hotel, runs the food production, or kitchen, department. A variety of culinary specialists who are responsible for different aspects of food preparation report to the executive chef.

In a large hotel, the actual serving of food in a hotel's restaurants is usually the responsibility of a separate department, headed by the assistant food and beverage director. The food service department is composed of the individual restaurant and outlet managers, maitre d's, waiters, waitresses, and bus help.

Because of their special duties and concerns, many large hotels have a separate subunit that is responsible only for room service. Because of the high value and profit margins associated with the sale of alcoholic beverages, some hotels have a separate department that assumes responsibility for all outlets where alcoholic beverages are sold. The person responsible for this department is the beverage manager.

Most full-service hotels also do a considerable convention and catering business. The typical convention uses small function rooms for separate meetings and larger rooms for general sessions, trade shows, exhibits, and banquets. As a hotel or lodging business increases the use of its facilities for conventions and meetings, it may form a separate convention services department. The convention services department and its personnel are introduced to the client, a meeting planner, or association executive by the marketing and sales department. The convention services department then handles all of the meeting and catering requirements. Individually catered events include parties, wedding receptions, business meetings, and other functions held by local groups. To provide for the unique needs of these particular types of customers, hotels often organize separate catering and convention departments.

Depending on the size of the hotel, the job of cleaning the food and beverage outlets themselves, as well as of washing all of the pots and pans, dishes, glasses, and utensils, is often delegated to a separate subunit known as the stewarding department.

It is only through continuous cooperation and coordination that a hotel's food service function can be carried out effectively. A guest who is dining in a hotel restaurant requires the joint efforts of the kitchen, food service, beverage, and stewarding departments. A convention banquet cannot be held without the efforts of the convention and catering department, along with the food production, beverage, and stewarding departments. The sequence of events and cooperation required among the food and beverage staff is even more important than in the rooms department, thus increasing the importance of communication between managers and employees alike. Another challenge faced by management is the diversity of the employees in the food and beverage department: the dishwasher in the stewarding department is at a dramatically different level than the sous chef.

Marketing and Sales Department

Coordination is not as important an issue in the **marketing and sales department**, which is generally a much smaller department. The primary responsibility of the sales managers who make up the marketing and sales department is **sales**, or the selling of the hotel facilities and services to individuals and groups. Sales managers sell rooms, food, and beverages to potential clients through advertising, attendance association and conference meetings, and direct contacts. The marketing and sales department is also removed from most of the day-to-day operational problems faced by other departments. The division of work among the sales managers is based on the type of customers a hotel is attempting to attract. Individual sales managers often specialize in corporate accounts, conventions, or tour and travel markets. Sales managers' accounts are sometimes subdivided along geographical lines into regional or national accounts. The sales staff of the largest, full-service hotels usually does not exceed a dozen or so. These sales managers work more or less independently in their particular market segments.

Human Resources Department

The **human resources department** serves no customers, books no business, and prepares no meals, yet it plays a vital role in a hotel's efficient operation. As shown in Figure 2–1b, the three functions of the human resources department are employee recruitment, benefits administration, and training. The director of human resources is also expected to be an expert on federal and state labor laws and to advise managers in other departments on these topics. The human resources department's major challenge is in its interactions with other hotel departments. Although the human resources department recruits, interviews, and screens prospective employees, the final hiring decision rests within the department in which the employee will be working. The same is true of promotion and disciplinary decisions; the human resources department's input is, in most cases, limited to advice and interpretation of legal questions. The human resources department's effectiveness depends on its manager's ability to form effective working relationships with managers of other departments.

Accounting Department

In many hotels, the **accounting department** combines staff functions and line functions or those functions directly responsible for servicing guests. The accounting department's traditional role is recording financial transactions, preparing and interpreting financial statements, and providing the managers of other departments with timely reports of operating results (line functions). Other responsibilities, carried out by the assistant controller for finance, include payroll preparation, accounts receivable, and accounts payable (staff functions).

Another dimension of the accounting department's responsibilities deals with various aspects of hotel operations, cost accounting, and cost control throughout the hotel. The two areas that are of central concern to the accounting department are rooms and food and beverage. The accounting department's front office cashier is responsible for keeping track of all charges to guest accounts. At the close of each business day, which varies by hotel but typically occurs at midnight or after the bulk of guests' transactions have been completed (i.e., check-in, restaurant charges, retail charges, etc.), the night auditor is responsible for reconciling all guest bills with the charges from the various hotel departments. Although the front office cashier and the night auditor physically work at the front desk and, in the case of the cashier, have direct contact with guests, they are members of the accounting department and report to the assistant controller of operations.

The food and beverage department may be responsible for food preparation and service, but the accounting department is responsible for collecting revenues. The food and beverage controller, and the food and beverage cashiers keep track of both the revenues and expenses of the food and beverage department. The food and beverage controller's job is to verify the accuracy and reasonableness of all food and beverage revenues.

In addition to keeping track of and preparing daily reports on the costs of the food and beverages used in the hotel, in many cases, the accounting department is also responsible for purchasing and storeroom operations. Finally, the director of systems is responsible for designing the accounting and control systems used throughout the hotel. As you can see, the accounting department is anything but a passive staff unit contending with routine record keeping. The accounting department is also responsible for collecting and reporting most of a hotel's operational and financial statistics, which provide important data for decision making and budget preparation purposes. The head of the accounting department may report not only to the hotel's general manager but also to the hotel chain's financial vice president or to the hotel's owner. The reason for this dual responsibility and reporting relationship is to afford the hotel corporation an independent verification of the financial and operating results of the hotel.

General Manager

In addition to being in charge of overseeing all of the departments that we have discussed, the hotel's **general manager (GM)** is responsible for defining and interpreting the policies established by top management. The general manager serves as a liaison to the hotel's owner or corporate parent, sets (or communicates) the overall strategic course of the hotel, sets hotel-wide goals, coordinates activities between departments, and arbitrates interdepartmental disputes. It is common practice in a large, full-service hotel for a director of public relations to report directly to the GM. Additional responsibilities of the GM include corporate-level responsibilities, participating on civic boards and committees, and engaging in industry-related activities, such as serving on the local tourism commission or hotel–motel association.

In addition to possessing a high level of technical skill (i.e., a thorough understanding of each operating department in the hotel), the general manager must also be decisive, analytical, and skilled with both computers and people. He or she must be able to see the big picture and how all of the various parts of a hotel fit into the overall organization.

Resident Manager

An executive may be promoted to relieve the general manager of some operational duties. This is often accomplished by elevating the duties and responsibilities of one particular department head, without relieving that person of his or her regular departmental duties. The title of this position is usually **resident manager**. It is quite common (and logical) for the general manager to select the manager of the rooms department to be resident manager. Responsibilities of the resident manager include serving as acting GM in the GM's absence, representing the GM on various hotel interdepartmental committees, and taking responsibility for important special projects such as major hotel renovations, VIP guests, or operating reports that require in-depth analysis for the regional or corporate offices.

PATTERNS OF AUTHORITY

The delegation of authority creates a chain of command, the formal channel that defines the lines of authority from the top to the bottom of an organization. As shown in Figure 2–2, the chain of command consists of a series of relationships from the highest position in the organization to the lowest. The chain of command specifies a clear reporting relationship for each person in the organization and should be followed in both downward and upward communication. Following the chain of command enables each new employee, no matter what his or her position is, to know exactly for whom and to whom he or she is responsible.

When designing an organizational structure, managers must also consider the distribution of authority. Defined simply, authority is the organizationally sanctioned right to make a decision. Authority can be distributed

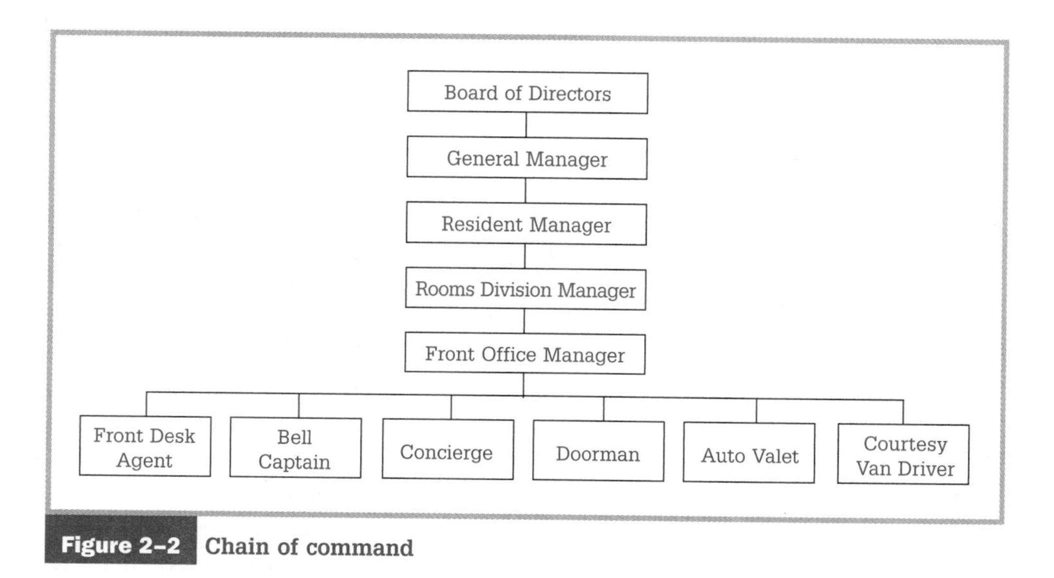

Figure 2–2 **Chain of command**

throughout an organization or held in the hands of a few select employees. **Decentralization** is the process of distributing authority throughout an organization. In a decentralized organization, an organization member has the right to make a decision without obtaining approval from a higher-level manager. **Centralization** is the retention of decision-making authority by a high-level manager.

Traditionally, hotel and lodging management has been very centralized, probably due to its roots in small, owner-operated lodging. In recent years, as the hotel and lodging industry has expanded, decentralization has become a more frequent style of operation.

Decentralization has several advantages. Managers are encouraged to develop decision-making skills, which help them advance in their careers. The autonomy afforded by this style of operation also increases job satisfaction and motivation. When employees are encouraged to perform well, the profitability of the organization increases.

Many hotel and lodging organizations have begun to empower employees and supervisors to make decisions that typically have been made by managers. One example that we have already discussed is the use of the quality circle. For example, if a front desk agent determines that a guest's bill is incorrect, in a decentralized organization, the agent has the power to make the correction immediately. If that same front desk agent determines that a guest's stay has been unsatisfactory, he or she has the power to reduce the guest's bill by an amount previously specified by management. Additional challenges, control of the process, and quality assessment become part of everyone's job, and each employee is given the authority to take positive actions that will lead to high quality and improved performance. (6)

SPAN OF CONTROL

Span of control refers to the number of people who report to one manager or supervisor. A wide span of control results in a *flat organization*, that is, a large number of employees reporting to one supervisor (see Figure 2–3a). A narrow span of control results in a *tall organization*, in which a small number of employees report to a supervisor, necessitating a larger number of supervisors (see Figure 2–3b). (Note that the organizations represented in Figures 2–3a and 2–3b have the same number of employees.) No formula exists for determining the ideal span of control. The following factors determine the most appropriate span of control: task similarity, training and professionalism, task certainty, frequency of interaction, task integration, and physical dispersion.

When a large number of employees perform similar tasks, the span of control can be increased. When the employees perform very different tasks,

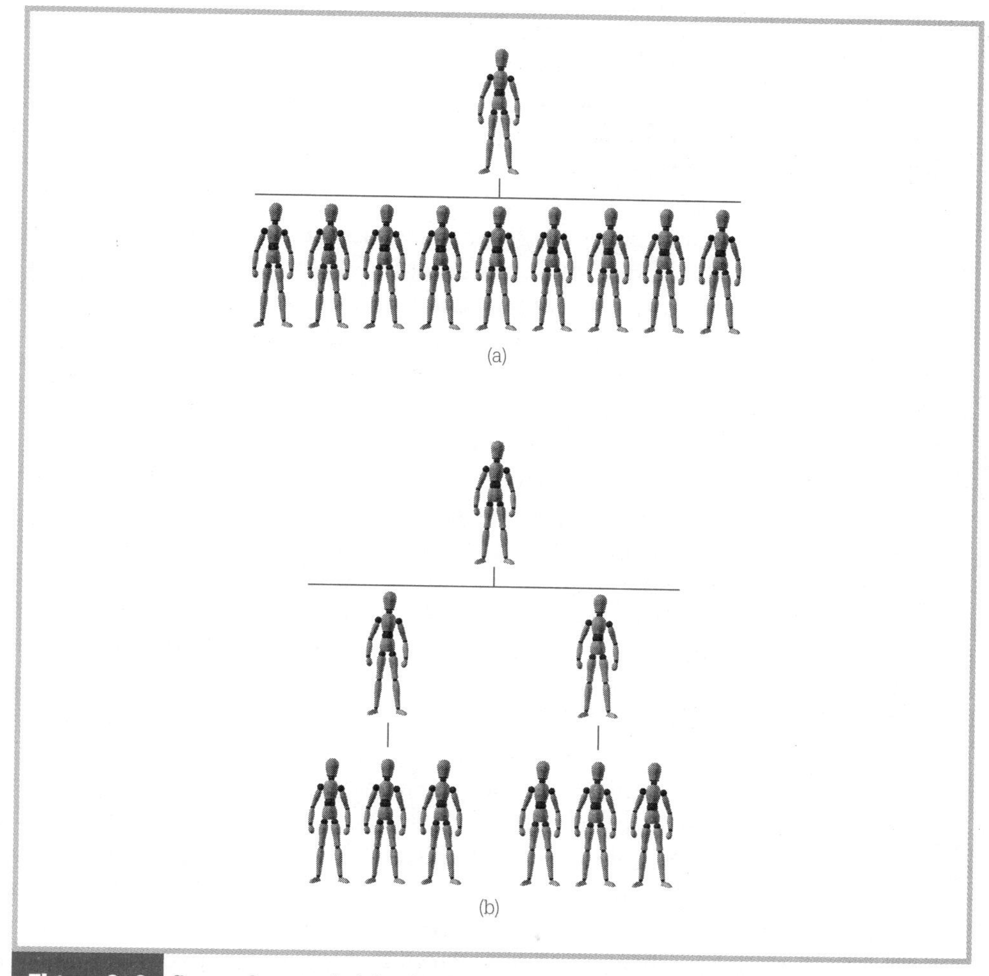

Figure 2–3 Span of control: (*a*) wide span of control (flat organization); (*b*) narrow span of control (tall organization)

the supervisor must give each subordinate more individual attention in order to keep in touch with the different types of tasks; this requires a narrower span of control. For example, the rooms department manager might easily manage the front desk agents and housekeepers until the brand standards for check-in or checkout of a guest increased in complexity and the standards for the various types of rooms and their cleaning procedure increased in detail. At this time, the rooms department manager's span of control would have to be narrowed.

The better trained and more skilled a subordinate is, the less supervision is required. For example, a front desk agent might require a higher level of training and skill than a room service waiter. Thus, a front desk supervisor can supervise more employees (wider span of control) than the room service supervisor (narrower span of control).

Task certainty refers to the predictability of a task. Routine tasks allow management to devise standard procedures for subordinates to follow, minimizing questions about the job and widening the span of control. On the other hand, closer supervision is called for when tasks are ambiguous and uncertainty is great. For example, the task of checking a guest in or out of the hotel can be documented and standard procedures can be created, so the front desk manager can have a relatively wide span of control over the front desk agents. However, because of the diversity of customers that the sales manager encounters, the tasks of a hotel sales manager are less certain. The director of sales is responsible for coaching the sales managers, observing sales calls, and ensuring deal closings; these tasks require a hands-on approach that limits the number of employees that the director of sales can handle, narrowing the span of control.

If the supervisor–subordinate relationship requires frequent interaction, the span of control must be narrow. If interaction is infrequent, the span of control can be wide. For example, the hotel controller must review on a regular basis the status of collections and payments with staff. On the other hand, the frequency of interaction between the chief engineer and his or her subordinates is directed by written work orders in most circumstances and thus requires less direct communication, enabling a wider span of control.

If the supervisor must integrate and coordinate the tasks of subordinates, the span of control narrows. For example, in the production of a meal for one table of four guests with different appetizers, salads, and entrées, the chef must have a narrow span of control to ensure that each component of the meal is assembled correctly and delivered to service personnel on a timely basis. The span of control of the executive housekeeper can be much wider, because the procedure for cleaning and preparing each guest room will be similar, if not exactly the same, for every room.

Physical dispersion refers to the distribution of employees within the lodging establishment. For example, if the executive housekeeper has guest room attendants on 20 floors in two different buildings, and the front desk manager has all front desk agents located in one place, the span of control would narrow for the executive housekeeper and widen for the front desk manager.

The ideal number of people that one person can supervise depends on a variety of factors. Consistent with some of the trends in organizational structure, such as teams, quality circles, and employee empowerment, many hotel and lodging organizations are widening their span of control. The objective behind these trends is to develop a flatter, more responsive organizational structure in which decisions can be made without going through several levels of management. (7)

The Pros and Cons of Functional Organization Design

The most important strength of a functional organizational design is efficiency. The performance of common tasks allows for work specialization, which increases overall productivity. Workers develop specialized skills and knowledge more rapidly. Training is easier because of the similarity of tasks and the resulting opportunities for inexperienced workers to learn from experienced workers. This helps new employees quickly learn the kinds of behavior that lead to success and promotion. Coordination of activities within functional departments is easier than in more broadly based organizations.

A functional organization fosters efficiency, teamwork, and coordination of activities within individual units. However, the functional organization's most important strength is also the source of its greatest shortcoming. The success of a hotel as a business is measured by its overall performance and not by the performance of any one department. A hotel with the most spotless rooms will not be successful if guests' front desk experiences are not up to par. Even if guests' dining experiences are superb, the hotel will fall flat on its face if its rooms are dismal. It is sometimes difficult for the various departments to fully appreciate their role in the overall success of the organization. It is vital that each department keep in mind the hotel-wide goals of customer service and profitability rather than focus narrowly on its own concerns. Some means must be found to coordinate the activities of individual functional departments and to set hotel-wide strategies and goals. A hotel's functional organization demands strong leadership.

New initiatives in hotels often require cooperation and coordination between functional departments. New ideas tend to be stillborn if department heads lack a hotel-wide perspective or have difficulty coordinating their activities. The tendency to concentrate on *doing things right* often overshadows the organization's ability to *do the right thing*. (8)

The GM, as the chief executive of the hotel, emerges as the single person who is capable of providing the overall organizational direction, decision making, coordination, and arbitration needed to make a hotel's functional departments work together effectively. A hotel simply cannot run itself from the departmental level. Thus, the GM must be a strong leader to be effective.

Meetings and Committees

An organizational chart, such as those depicted in Figure 2–1, is useful in identifying the formal reporting and authority relationships of a hotel or a lodging enterprise. However, it is not of much help in coordinating administrative units at the department and subdepartment level.

Consider this scenario. If the director of sales increases group bookings without consulting other hotel departments, a disaster is in the making. If the reservations department is not consulted, the sales department might guarantee more rooms to a group than are actually available at a price lower than the reservations department's quarterly goal. If the convention services manager is not consulted, necessary meeting rooms might not be available. If the food and beverage department is not consulted in the process, the group might be sold a banquet that exceeds the hotel's capabilities. If the accounting department is not consulted, credit terms might be extended that violate the credit manager's policies. If the front office is not included, the group might experience lengthy delays in check-in (groups are usually pre-assigned rooms and keys).

The *executive operating committee (EOC)* of a hotel, made up of the general manager and senior executives from each department, is designed to increase the level of coordination between departments. There is no standard membership for this committee, but it usually includes those executives who report directly to the general manager. The EOC is also responsible for a hotel's major budgetary units, such as the hotel's food and beverage and housekeeping units. EOC functions depend on how each hotel general manager chooses to use the group, the general manager's style, and the structure of other management meetings in the hotel. Typically, the EOC meets weekly, focusing on matters ranging from day-to-day operational issues (daily function schedules and labor and food cost control) to comparing budgets with actual operating results.

Many hotels increase communications through an elaborate structure of additional committees and meetings, including some or all of the following: operations, staff, sales forecast and marketing, departmental, subdepartmental, credit, safety, energy conservation, and employee meetings.

The operations committee is comprised of the general manager, department heads, front office manager, manager on duty, and representatives from housekeeping, security, engineering, and food and beverage. This committee might meet four or five times per week for 15 to 20 minutes to review upcoming activities and assess the results of previous activities.

The staff committee might include the general manager, department heads, and all subdepartment heads who report to the department heads. This committee, which might meet weekly for one or two hours, reviews the prior week's performance, the current week's activities, the next week's plans, and any special projects. The staff committee also presents performance awards to employees.

The concept of forecasting, pioneered by Conrad Hilton (see Box 2–1), was introduced in Chapter 1. The sales forecast and marketing committee might meet one to four times per month for several hours so that the general manager and the department heads can review room demand for the

BOX 2–1
Conrad N. Hilton

Conrad N. Hilton (Courtesy of the Hospitality Industry Archives and Library, University of Houston, Texas.)

Conrad N. Hilton (1897–1979), the son of a Norwegian immigrant father and a German-American mother, had a strong belief in the American Dream. He derived his strength from his faith in God, his belief in the brotherhood of man, his patriotic confidence in the United States of America, and his conviction that a natural law obliges all mankind to help relieve the suffering, the distressed, and the destitute.

Conrad Hilton was educated at St. Michael's College in Santa Fe, New Mexico and the New Mexico School of Mines. He entered the hotel business by buying the Mobley Hotel in Cisco, Texas, in 1919. The first hotel that he constructed, the Dallas Hilton, opened on August 2, 1925. While the Dallas Hilton was being constructed, he married Mary Barron. Conrad and Mary had three children: Conrad N., Jr.; William Barron; and Eric Michael. He later divorced Mary and had a fourth child, Francesca, with his second wife, actress Zsa Zsa Gabor.

Hilton maintained operations during the Great Depression of the 1930s by giving up many of his hotels and by learning to operate with economy—one of the keys to his future success. This enabled him to expand his empire by purchasing other hotels throughout the United States, including the Sir Francis Drake in San Francisco, the Plaza and the Waldorf-Astoria in New York City, and the Palmer and the Stevens in Chicago (the latter currently is known as the Chicago Hilton & Towers). He developed his business in the international arena by building hotels in such exotic locales as San Juan, Puerto Rico; Madrid, Spain; Istanbul, Turkey; Havana, Cuba; Berlin, Germany; and Cairo, Egypt.

The expansion of his business in the international arena cemented his belief in world peace and global economic stability. He vigorously opposed the spread of communism and used corporate advertising to promote world peace through international trade and travel. His concern for the public was heightened by the formation of the Conrad N. Hilton Foundation in 1944, which has continued to carry forward Conrad Hilton's vision by providing resources to organizations that focus on social issues, health issues, and education. The Conrad N. Hilton College at the University of Houston, Texas, was a designated recipient of resources from the foundation because of Conrad Hilton's belief that tourism and travel were a way to promote global understanding and world peace.

Conrad Hilton's vision for Hilton Hotels Corporation was carried on by two of his sons, William and Eric.

Source: "Conrad N. Hilton," Cathleen Baird, Hospitality Industry Hall of Honor Archives, Conrad N. Hilton College, University of Houston, Texas, 1996.

coming 90 days and devise strategies to increase room nights and thus bring in more revenue and to increase average daily rates by up-selling potential guests to a higher-rated room with perhaps more amenities or services.

The departmental committee meeting consists of the department head and his or her subdepartment heads, managers, and supervisors. Meeting once or twice per month for an hour or so, the group reviews departmental issues. Similarly, subdepartment committees meet monthly for about an hour so that the subdepartment head, managers, and supervisors can address issues unique to their subdepartment, such as the selection of a new type of floor cleaner by the housekeeping department or a more energy efficient lightbulb by the engineering department.

The credit committee meeting includes the general manager, the controller, sales, the front office, reservations, catering, and the credit manager. Meeting monthly for an hour, the committee reviews those guests and clients of the hotel who have been granted credit and have not settled their account.

Safety committees typically are comprised of members from human resources, food and beverage, housekeeping, and engineering. Meeting monthly for an hour or so, the committee reviews safety programs and safety records, addresses any problems, and discusses implementation of any new safety regulations.

In some full-service hotels, an energy conservation committee includes the chief engineer, resident manager, food and beverage staff, human resource representatives, rooms staff, and housekeeping representatives. The committee typically meets monthly for an hour to discuss strategies and programs for controlling energy costs.

Most full-service hotels convene a monthly meeting or at least an annual meeting of all hotel management and employees to review performance and to distribute awards. This event ranges from an hour-long meeting to a company-wide celebration lasting several hours.

The Hotel Staffing System

Staffing, which is one of a hotel's most important management functions, is an ongoing challenge because of the high rate of employee and management turnover. Full-service hotels can experience turnover rates in excess of 100 percent in certain employee classifications. Some managers consider an annual employee turnover rate of 33 percent as being low. (In other words, in a single year, one-third of a hotel's employees will need to be replaced.) At such a turnover rate, the entire hotel will have to be completely restaffed every three years. The higher the turnover rate is, the larger the number of employees who will need to be replaced. For example, if a hotel with 450 employees has a 75 percent annual turnover rate, a complete restaffing will occur every 16 months. Staffing is the responsibility of the human resources department, which will be considered in more detail in Chapter 5.

In an attempt to reduce employee turnover, hotel and lodging businesses are giving increasing attention to job design, seeking to enhance those job characteristics that give the employee the greatest satisfaction and motivation. Good job design must take into account the needs of employees as well as the demands of the job. Well-thought-out job design begins when management conducts a job analysis. A **job analysis** is a thorough evaluation of the specific tasks performed for a particular job and the time required to perform them. Job analysis is an ongoing process, as many jobs change with improvements in technology and pressure to improve product quality.

The job analysis is the basis for the job description and job specification. A **job description** includes the job title, pay, a brief statement of duties and procedures, working conditions, and hours. The **job specification** is an outline of the qualifications necessary for a particular job.

In response to the limits of specialization, organizations can redesign jobs to improve coordination, productivity, and product quality, while at the same time responding to an employee's needs for learning, challenge, variety, increased responsibility, and achievement. Such **job redesign** often involves *job rotation*, the systematic movement of employees from one job to another; *job enlargement*, an increase in the number of tasks an employee will do in the job; *job enrichment*, the attempt to give the employee more control over job-related activities; and *flextime*, a flexible work schedule that permits employee input in establishing work schedules. In *team-driven job redesign*, a concept similar to job rotation, employees can transfer back and forth among teams that are providing different services or products.

Hotels recruit employees from a variety of sources. Newspapers and employee referrals are used to recruit nonskilled hourly employees. Supervisory and management employees generally are recruited through colleges and universities, promotions from within, professional associations, and/or management recruiters. Those hotels that take more time in making their selections are more successful in retaining employees.

Discussions of employee training and development often concentrate on training techniques without giving a full explanation of what a hotel is trying to accomplish. As training and development impart job skills and develops employees, supervisors, and managers, they also improve current and future employee performance, which affects the bottom line. Effective training includes problem solving, problem analysis, quality measurement and feedback, and team building.

Performance evaluation, also called performance appraisal, is the systematic review of individual strengths and weaknesses of an employee's performance. The major difficulty in a performance appraisal is quantifying those strengths and weaknesses. The performance of some jobs is easy to quantify, while for others it is more difficult. An important part of the appraisal process is a well-established job description, so that the employee and the supervisor have similar expectations.

Compensation includes the monetary and nonmonetary rewards that managers, supervisors, and employees receive for performing their jobs. In order to set compensation levels, the human resources department must periodically conduct *job evaluations*, which determine the value of the job to the hotel. Knowledge of the value of the job to the organization and of wage rates for each job classification allows the hotel to establish a fair compensation policy.

Career Paths and Opportunities

If you complete your course of study and graduate with a Bachelor of Science degree in hotel management, most likely you will enter the business at some managerial level. Hopefully, along the way you will have learned that a successful manager provides clear direction; encourages open communication; coaches and supports people; provides objective recognition; establishes ongoing controls; follows up and gives subordinates feedback; selects the right people to staff the organization; understands the financial implications of decisions; encourages innovation and new ideas; gives subordinates clear-cut decisions when needed; and consistently demonstrates a high level of integrity. (9)

There are three levels of management careers in the hotel or lodging business: first-line, middle, and top. "First-line" refers to those who have day-to-day contact with a lodging business's guests and clients. The first-line manager oversees the work of the supervisors and line employees. In a hotel or lodging business, this might be the position of assistant manager of housekeeping, assistant front office manager, or assistant restaurant manager. First-line managers are responsible for a hotel's basic work, such as checking guests in and out, making up the guests' rooms, preparing and serving the meals. First-line managers are in daily or near-daily contact with line employees.

Middle management of most hotel or lodging businesses includes the department manager, general manager, and any position in between. Depending upon the size of the hotel, the regional manager (who supervises the general managers of the hotels in his or her region) can also fall into this category. Unlike first-line managers, those in middle management plan, organize, lead, and control other managers' activities, in addition to being responsible for the performance of their departments.

Top management is comprised of a small group of managers, such as the chief executive officer, president, or vice president. Top management is responsible for the performance of the entire hotel business, as well as for supervision of the middle managers. The top manager is accountable to the owners of the financial resources used by the organization, such as the stockholders or an executive board.

As you have already seen, there are numerous attractive careers in the hotel and lodging business. The following is one of the many paths your career might follow:

1. Assistant manager of the reservations department
2. Reservations department manager
3. Rooms department manager
4. Resident manager
5. General manager
6. Regional manager

In a full-service hotel or lodging business, the movement from entry-level position to general manager might encompass 15 years. Career advancement in a limited-service hotel or lodging business can occur more rapidly. A career in limited-service hotel or lodging establishment might commence at the assistant general manager level, with movement to general manager within three years and to district or regional manager within five to eight years. This accelerated pace is due in large part to the more restricted range of services that the manager must master before advancing to a higher level.

SUMMARY

The four basic components of organizational structure include job specialization, departmentalization, patterns of authority, and span of control. Job specialization includes increased worker productivity and efficiency, but it increases the need for managerial control and coordination. Work teams can be used to alleviate the routine caused by job specialization. A similar concept, the quality circle, can also enhance employee productivity.

The departments of a full-service hotel and lodging establishment include rooms, food and beverage, marketing and sales, human resources, and accounting. These departments report directly either to the general manager or to a resident manager who is responsible to the general manager. In smaller hotel or lodging businesses, the audit, front desk, housekeeping, maintenance, and sales departments all might report directly to the general manager.

While patterns of authority remain centralized in many hotel or lodging businesses, increasingly employees have become empowered to make decisions that typically have been made by managers. Decentralization is the distribution of authority throughout an organization. Centralization is the retention of decision-making authority by a high-level manager.

Span of control refers to the number of people who report to one manager or supervisor. In a narrow span of control, fewer subordinates report to each supervisor, resulting in a tall organization. In a wide span of control, a larger number of subordinates report to each supervisor, resulting in a flat organization.

The level of coordination and communication between departments can be increased by the activities of various committees. The executive operating committee includes the general manager and designated department heads. Other committees include operations, staff, sales forecasting and marketing, departmental, subdepartmental, credit, safety, and energy conservation. Larger organizations also will include an annual employee meeting for all employees of the organization, to discuss company performance and to distribute awards.

Staffing is an ongoing challenge because of the high percentage of employee turnover in the hotel and lodging industry. Successful staffing depends on providing adequate job descriptions, including job specifications, as well as realizing that the job description must be flexible. In some cases, it becomes necessary to redesign jobs, which can involve job rotation, job enlargement, job enrichment, and flextime. Employees also must be properly trained; effective training includes problem solving, problem analysis, quality measurement, feedback, and team building.

Successful managers enjoy certain common characteristics, including, but not limited to, providing clear direction, feedback, and recognition; encouraging open communication and innovation; and establishing ongoing controls. The management of a hotel or a lodging business falls into one of three categories: first-line, middle, and top.

References

1. John M. Ivancevich, Peter Lorenzi, and Steven J. Skinner, with Philip B. Crosby, *Management: Quality And Competitiveness* (Boston: Richard D. Irwin, 1996): 254.
2. Raymond J. Aldag and Timothy M. Stearns, *Management* (Cincinnati: Southwestern Publishing Co., 1987).

3. Frank Shippes and Charles C. Manz, "Employee Self-Management Without Formally Designated Teams: An Alternative Road to Empowerment," *Organizational Dynamics* (Winter 1992): 48–61.
4. Tom Peters, *Thriving on Chaos*, (New York: Knopf, 1988).
5. Frank D. Borsenik and Alan T. Stutts, *The Management of Maintenance and Engineering Systems in the Hospitality Industry*, 4th ed. (New York: John Wiley & Sons, Inc., 1997).
6. Robert D. Dewar and Donald P. Simet, "A Level-Specific Prediction of Spans of Control Examining the Effects of Size, Technology, and Specialization," *Academy of Management Journal* (March 1981): 5.
7. J. Barton Cunningham and Ted Eberle, "A Guide to Job Enrichment and Redesign," *Personnel* (February 1990): 56–61.
8. D. Dann and Timothy Hornsey, "Towards a Theory of Interdepartmental Conflict in Hotels," *International Journal of Hospitality Management*, no. 5 (1986): 23.
9. Brian Dumaine, "The New Non-Managers," *Fortune*, 22 February 1993, pp. 80–84; and "A Checklist of Qualities That Make a Good Boss," *Nation's Business*, November 1984, p. 100.

Review Questions

1. What is the difference between work teams and quality circles?
2. Compare centralization and decentralization.
3. Which span of control results in a tall organization? A flat organization?
4. Should a first-line manager delegate more or less responsibility than a top manager? Explain your answer.
5. List the principal functions of each major department of a full-service hotel.
6. A customer notifies the front desk that a table in her room has a broken leg and that when she set her room service tray on it, it tipped over and scattered the food on the floor. List the departments to which this information needs to be conveyed and the actions they must take.

Activities

1. Diagram the organizational structure of a local limited-service hotel and of a local full-service hotel. Compare them with one that has been illustrated in this chapter.

2. If you were able to reorganize the limited-service or full-service hotel that you diagrammed in question one, how would you do so?
3. Interview an assistant department manager, a department manager, and a general manager from a limited-service or a full-service hotel. Determine the functions of management in which he or she is actively involved.

Chapter 3

The Front Office

CHAPTER OUTLINE

ORGANIZATION

As you learned in Chapter 2, the **front office department** is a subdepartment of the rooms department. However, the importance of this vital service link cannot be overemphasized. The services provided by the front office, including processing guest reservations and room assignments, handling guest and house mail, and providing guest information, message service, and other related functions, are often the only contact the guest has with the hotel's staff. Each staff member must be competent, responsible, and courteous to assure efficient functioning of the front office as well as a pleasant guest stay.

As noted, the primary responsibility of the front office is to provide the most excellent service possible to the hotel's guests. However, the front office is also responsible for controlling costs, overseeing payroll and supplies, controlling reservations, and coordinating information on room availability.

The front office department of a full-service hotel includes a registration desk; key, mail, and information desk; service department; and telecommunications department. In hotels of less than 500 rooms, the reservation and security employees may report directly to the front office manager. This is due in large part to the strong working relationship that must be maintained between the front desk agents and the reservationists. The activity of all of these areas is directed by the front office manager, with the assistance of departmental supervisors such as the assistant front office manager, the reservations manager, the concierge, the night manager (senior assistant manager), and the chief security officer. The departmental supervisors are responsible for hiring, training, disciplining, and terminating employees who are working in their areas.

The key staff positions and the reporting relationships of the front office are shown in Figure 3–1.

In a larger, full-service hotel, the **front office manager** typically reports to the resident manager. Hotels with less than 500 rooms may not have a rooms department manager but, instead, may have a front office manager. As the hotel increases in complexity, typically, the separation of front desk and reservations occurs and a rooms department is established with a manager. The front office manager directs and/or coordinates the activities of the registration desk; reservations office; key, mail, and information desk; service department; front desk; and security department. He or she develops and maintains operating procedures for both individual and convention reservations; controls open and closed dates of rooms and reservations; and is responsible for room keys and the flow of house mail, guest mail, and messages.

An effective front office manager establishes efficient methods for the coordination of all departments, particularly cashiers, credit, sales, house-

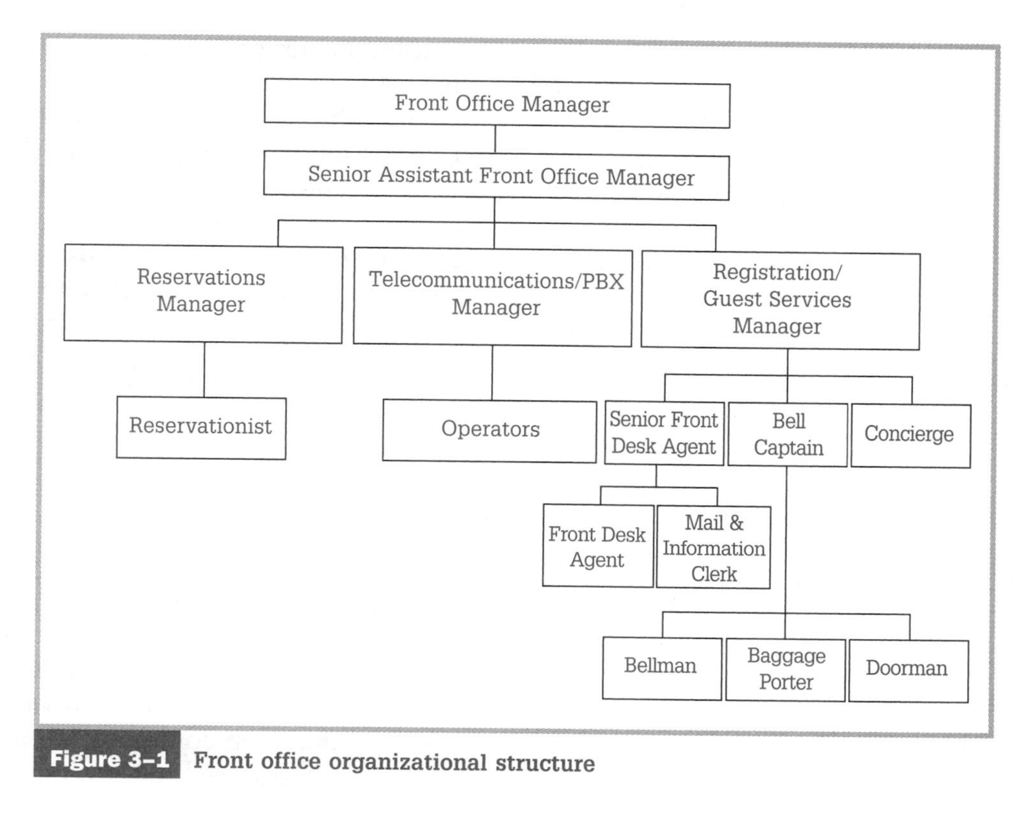

Figure 3–1 **Front office organizational structure**

keeping, engineering, telephone, and security, and is responsible for the efficient processing of information on guest room availability.

Additional responsibilities include working closely with the sales department to aid conventions and groups in planning housing requirements, room assignments, and rooming lists; preparing reports and forecasts on anticipated room occupancy, reservations, expected arrivals and departures, house count, estimated revenues, and other statistics; and obtaining the highest possible room revenues to achieve the desired departmental profit.

The *senior assistant front office manager* reports directly to the front office manager. Responsibilities of this position include assisting the front office manager in the direction and coordination of the various front office departments; supervising the daily functioning of the front office department and the reservation office in cooperation with the reservation manager; helping to develop and maintain operating procedures; and cooperating with related departments, such as accounting, sales, housekeeping, and engineering. The senior assistant front office manager also meets regularly with the front office manager, reservation manager, chief room clerks, and assistant managers to assure an efficient operation, and checks the daily forecasts and reports of the senior front desk agent.

The senior assistant front office manager assists the front office manager in hiring, training, and dismissing front office personnel; carrying out any necessary disciplinary actions; and implementing hotel-employee relations policies and programs, such as courtesy programs, work performance records, vacation schedules, and so on. The senior assistant front office manager also helps the reservation manager maintain the room availability board. Discussions of the other positions shown in Figure 3–1 will be included in discussion of their respective departments.

RESERVATIONS

The key duty of the reservations department is to sell every available room at the most profitable rate possible. In order to accomplish this task effectively, the reservations department must be able to anticipate future room availability, must be aware of existing reservations and their sources, must have effective procedures for handling telephone reservation requests, must coordinate with the sales department on convention or group reservations, must adhere strictly to policy on guaranteed reservations, must have an efficient reservation processing system that is flexible enough to handle reservation revisions, and must provide written confirmation of reservations.

Reservations Department Staff

The reservations department staff includes the reservations manager and a staff of reservationists. The **reservations manager** works under the direction of the front office manager and the senior assistant front office manager. All reservationists report to the reservations manager. The reservations manager is responsible for complete processing of reservations and reservations correspondence. This is accomplished by supervision of the reservations filing system so that front office personnel have quick access to accurate information on current and future reservations; maintenance of up-to-date information concerning room availability and appropriate records for statistical control of rooms and reservations; issuance of reports on reservations changes to all relevant departments; prompt changes and updates to the availability board (see below) as needed; and preparation and distribution of a document called the sell and report chart, which identifies the agents who have booked various room blocks and the status of remaining room blocks in various available periods.

Under the direction of the reservation manager, the **reservationist** maintains up-to-date, accurate reservation records, including a record of advance reservations, a daily reservation tally, and a daily departure tally; keeps con-

A reservationist taking reservations. (Courtesy of the Hospitality Industry Archives and Library, University of Houston, Texas.)

vention history records and suite and VIP accommodations lists; supervises daily preparation and distribution of the **special attention list (SPALT)**, which identifies persons who are VIPs and those guests who have special rooming requirements; and takes charge of the reservations office and all of its functions during the absence of the reservations manager. Additional responsibilities include maintaining all records for the statistical control of rooms and reservations; inputting and processing of reservations, confirmations, and reservation change requests; selling rooms by telephone in accordance with existing procedures; exchanging room availability information with front desk personnel; and assisting in maintaining the availability board.

Future Room Availability

To avoid **overbooking** (accepting more reservations than the hotel can fill), the reservations department keeps a document known as an **availability board**. While in some cases the availability board is in the form of a large, wall-size board, more typically it is automated and easily updated with each entry made by a reservationist. The reservations manager is responsible for maintaining the availability board. With the automation of the reservation function, the availability board is now a computer screen in the reservation system that, while monitored by the reservation manager, is automatically updated with new events, reservations that are booked, and circumstances that require the available number of rooms to change.

Typically, hotels process reservations through a reservation module included in the property management system. The reservation module can generate a forecast report that projects reservation data for the next day or the next year and can even break this down by room category. Appendix 3–1 provides a closer look at maximizing room and occupancy rates through reservations.

Whether manual or automated, the availability board is a convenient visual guide controlling overbookings. The board reflects a true picture of the room availability status for a six-month period. When space becomes critical for a particular day, the reservations manager restricts the sale of all or certain types of rooms for that day.

Five basic symbols are used on the availability board to describe room availability. These symbols are the same whether the board is manual or automated. Each symbol has a definite meaning (see Table 3–1).

Reservation Sources

Generally, reservations are received through four different sources: by mail, by telephone, through a central reservation system, and in-house. Reservation requests received through the mail are generally handled and processed exclusively by the reservations department.

Table 3-1 Availability Board Symbols

Symbol	Meaning	Procedure
No symbol	Open date	Reservations or walk-ins may be accepted for all open dates.
Black X	Closed date	Reservations or walk-ins cannot be accepted for closed dates. Arrivals prior to a closed date may stay through the closed date.
Red square	Boxed date	Reservations or walk-ins for a boxed date cannot be accepted under any circumstances. When negotiating a reservation request, if the guest wants to stay through a boxed date, the guest must be informed that it is not possible due to capacity booking.
Green circle	Restricted date	(1) A certain type of accommodation is no longer available for a particular day; (2) there is a rate restriction for that day; or (3) except for a group block, the hotel is booked to capacity.
Blue X	Housing bureau (convention reservations that are being made through the Convention and Visitors Bureau)	Rooms blocks that have been assigned to a Housing Bureau to accommodate city-wide events.

By far the most common type of reservation is the telephone reservation. With some special exceptions, such as VIP reservations, the reservations department typically handles all incoming telephone reservation requests. Complete information is the key to successful completion of a telephone reservation. Figure 3–2 includes 19 points to use in evaluating the effectiveness of a telephone reservationist. Particular attention must be directed toward day and date of arrival; arrival time; departure date; name or names; requested rate; special requests; VIP data; and, if the company owns multiple hotels, confirmation of the location of the hotel.

The third source of hotel reservations is the central reservation system. A **central reservation system** is an independent company that charges the hotel a fee for each reservation it generates or a percentage of the revenue generated from the reservations it books. The amount due the central reservation system company is calculated by the reservations module of the property management system.

The fourth source of reservations, in-house reservation requests, are made by individual guests, or a representative, who comes into the hotel and asks for a reservation in person (a **walk-in**). In order to provide the best service possible, these reservation requests are usually handled by the employee contacted (i.e., the front desk agent, the assistant manager, etc.). All infor-

- ☐ Phone is answered within three rings, or call is placed in queue with recording to please hold.
- ☐ Department name and reservationist's name are stated.
- ☐ A choice of smoking or non-smoking room is offered.
- ☐ Asks if you are attending a group or convention and quotes applicable rate(s).
- ☐ Asks if you are a member of honors reward program.
- ☐ Pricing for each room type is offered.
- ☐ Features and description of selected room are offered.
- ☐ Asks to take reservation.
- ☐ Approximate arrival time is requested.
- ☐ Any special requests (e.g., feather pillows, top floor room) are acknowledged.
- ☐ Type of payment is requested.
- ☐ If payment is to be made by credit card, credit card information is requested.
- ☐ Cancellation policy is explained.
- ☐ Details of reservation are repeated.
- ☐ Confirmation number is provided.
- ☐ When reservation cannot be accommodated, alternative hotel suggestions are offered.
- ☐ Caller's name is used.
- ☐ Reservationist is courteous, polite, and easily understood.

Figure 3–2 Checklist for evaluating a reservationist

mation is then forwarded to the reservations department for final processing and confirmation.

Other Reservation Sources

Reservations sources can be categorized as direct, outside hotel representation, or marketing and sales. Any reservation taken from the four sources discussed in the previous section are considered direct reservations.

Hotels can contract with outside representatives to act as their agents in key markets such as a geographic location or a large corporation or association. These agents accept reservations remotely, that is, outside the city in which the hotel is located. The type of hotel using outside hotel representation is generally one with a well-recognized name and a large number of properties, such as the Marriott hotel chain founded by J. Willard Marriott (see Box 3–1).

A reservation that originates from marketing and sales usually involves some special instructions. Reservation requests of this nature usually must be handled with extra care. Guests holding this type of reservation are usually VIPs and may bring a great deal of business to the hotel.

Convention or Group Reservations

Conventioneers and/or group members are most often provided with reservation postcards by the marketing and sales department of the hotel. These cards, which are presented at check-in, show the name of the convention or group and the official dates when the convention or group will convene at the hotel. Occasionally, with approval from the general manager, the marketing and sales department may grant a flat rate to a convention or a group, which will be shown on the card. Otherwise, the card usually will indicate a range of rates from which the individual delegates choose. The reservation module of the property management system can generate a convention or a group report that reports by group the number of rooms booked, the number of rooms that are still available by rate category, and the name of the group.

Guaranteed Reservations

Requests for late arrival (usually after 6 P.M.) are only held with a deposit or, more commonly, a guaranteed reservation. A **guaranteed reservation** means that the individual guarantees payment for the first night's stay, regardless of whether or not the guest actually arrives. Guests who have reservations but for whatever reason do not arrive are called **no-shows**.

All guaranteed reservations are assured a room and the charge for the room is **credit card guaranteed**, by which the payment for the room is guaranteed should the guest not check in. The front desk assigns rooms to these reservations throughout the day as accommodations become available. On days when guaranteed reservations are on file and it has been determined that a sellout is possible, the front desk protects these reservations with rooms but does not actually assign them room numbers.

BOX 3–1
J. Willard Marriott

J. Willard Marriott. (Courtesy of the Hospitality Industry Archives and Library, University of Houston, Texas.)

J. Willard Marriott's (1900–1985) first successful businesses were the Hot Shoppes and an A&W Root Beer shop, which he opened in 1927. These prosperous ventures stemmed from Marriott's notion of providing inexpensive, quality food and services. With the onset of the Great Depression of the 1930s, Marriott saw how a low-cost restaurant could be successful even as luxury restaurants failed.

Marriott expanded his business opportunities by entering the airline and hotel industry. In 1957, J. W. Marriott opened his first hotel, the Twin Bridges Marriott in Washington, D.C. Subsequently, Marriott hotels were launched in Dallas, Texas; Philadelphia, Pennsylvania; and Atlanta, Georgia. As a result, by 1964, the Marriott Company earned $84 million in revenue and employed 9,600 people. In the late 1960s, Marriott acquired the Big Boy restaurant chain and the Roy Rogers fast-food restaurant chain.

Marriott's business ventures were not limited to the hotel and restaurant industry. A decade later, in 1976, J. W. Marriott entered the entertainment industry with the creation of the Marriott Great America Theme Parks, purveyors of wholesome family entertainment. The Marriott standard of quality and service also sailed the high seas with the company's acquisition of three luxury Sun Line cruise ships that sailed to the Caribbean and the Aegean and Mediterranean areas.

In the mid-1980s, the Marriott Company earned $4.5 billion in revenue and had 200,000 employees. In 1989, the company opened its 500th hotel in Warsaw, Poland. The tremendous success of the Marriott Company stemmed from Marriott's strong belief in community. He believed that, if you take care of your employees, they will take care of your guests.

Marriott International operates a broad portfolio of hotel brands, including Marriott, Ritz-Carlton, Courtyard, Residence Inn, Fairfield, Towne Place Suites, Executive Residences, New World, Ramada International, and Renaissance. Worldwide, Marriott International presently operates more than 324,000 rooms. Marriott also develops and operates vacation club resorts and senior living communities, and provides food distribution services to a multitude of clients.

Source: "J. Willard Marriott," Cathleen Baird, Hospitality Industry Hall of Honor Archives, Conrad N. Hilton College, University of Houston, Houston, Texas, 1996.

When a sellout is expected, the senior front desk agent on the evening shift registers all payment-guaranteed reservations by 6 P.M., using preprinted registration cards. The senior front desk agent writes "registered by [name of clerk], at [time]" in place of the guest's signature. He or she will assign an average-priced room of the type requested and set up a guest account, called a **folio**, which then will be used to charge all transactions incurred by the guest in the hotel that are not settled by the guest in cash.

A list of payment-guaranteed no-shows is compiled by the night auditor and sent to the accounting department for billing. The no-show rate is posted by the night auditor. A list of preregistrations is prepared by the evening senior front desk agent and left for the morning senior front desk agent. Any rooms that still show up as vacant on the next morning's housekeeper's report are held for a specified period of time or until regular checkout and then are checked out in the normal manner and sent to the auditing department, marked "preregistered no-show."

Reservation Processing

To maintain order, reservations are processed through a well-defined system. Regardless of the source or timing of the reservation, a single reservation form is completed for each individual request. No more than one reservation for one guest, excluding a Mr. and Mrs., is processed on each room reservation form. Whether a reservation is received by phone, fax, electronic mail, postal delivery, or in person, the following information should be collected:

1. Time stamps on all reservations
2. The names of all parties desiring reservations
3. Any convention or group affiliation
4. The type of accommodation required (double, king, suite, etc.)
5. The arrival date, arrival time, and departure date of each guest
6. The name and address of the party to whom the confirmation is to be sent
7. The form of payment to be used and the name and address of the party to whom the bill will be sent
8. The rate (i.e., **rack rate**, full rate with no discount or another rate) and whether the guest is on the **American Plan** (**AP**), in which the guest is provided a room and three meals or some meals, or a European Plan, in which the guest is billed for room and meals separately
9. Any special instructions or unusual requests, no matter how minor

All data should be verified before the telephone caller hangs up or the in-person registrant departs.

The reservations department generates a number of reports from the reservations module of the property management system, which are then forwarded to the front desk. These include the arrivals report, an alphabetical list of the day's expected arrivals, individually and by group; an overbooking report, a list of those with reservations who have been **walked** to other hotels, by identification number; a regrets report, the number of room requests denied; and a daily analysis report, which includes the number of reservations, arrivals, no-shows, and walk-ins by source and by room rate.

Reservation Revisions

Handling revisions and cancellations of reservations is equally as important as the careful handling of the original reservation to maintain happy guests and staff.

The reservationist must obtain complete information about the original reservation to speed up the processing of the revisions and cancellations. Procedures for revisions or cancellations for any day other than the current day typically include (1) removing the original reservation correspondence from the file and (2) removing the reservation from the future reservations file or inputting the new information into the future reservations file.

Revised or cancelled reservations for the current day are noted on the room reservation forms and are forwarded to the front desk once each hour. A cancellation and change report from the property management system reservation module lists reservations cancelled for the day or reservation changes and cancellations for later dates. This report in larger hotels is often generated hourly.

The front office manager and the reservations manager forecast arrivals and departures on future dates by using the estimated arrival and departure counts for a particular day. These counts are provided by the reservationist, who tallies every reservation prior to sending confirmations.

With automation of the reservation system, reservation software provides a confirmation of the guest's reservation information. However, it is still the practice of luxury and deluxe hotels to provide their guests with an individually typed confirmation in personalized letter form.

All guests are provided with a confirmation number that can be utilized to access their reservation details upon arrival. This is especially important if time does not allow a confirmation to be sent.

REGISTRATION

Front office staff members, such as valet parking attendants, doormen, bell staff, and front desk agents, are the first employees to have face-to-face contact with a guest. Their appearance, attitude, and manner of greeting and taking care of the guest all contribute to the impression the hotel leaves on the guest. Keep in mind that a satisfied guest may become what every hotel seeks—a repeat guest. Figure 3–3 provides a checklist for evaluating the arrival and registration experience.

Registration Department Staff

The registration department staff includes the assistant manager; the senior front desk agent; the front desk agent; and the message, mail, and information clerk. In the absence of the front office manager, an *assistant manager* may provide supervision to the "**front-of-the-house**" areas or those staff who have extensive guest contact: the front desk, and key, mail, and information desk. The assistant manager ensures that all guest services are performed properly, personally performs all VIP services, such as inspecting VIP accommodations before arrival and escorting dignitaries to their rooms, maintains proper records and reports on any unusual activities, grants rebates and approves checks, settles guest disputes on charges and other matters, and handles guest complaints. He or she also ensures adherence to all hotel and city regulations, coordinates with the security department on matters such as accidents, thefts, and lost and found, reviews and updates arrival lists and VIP lists, and coordinates with the front desk and the reservations office on all aspects of guests' needs and services.

The *senior front desk agent*, sometimes called the guest services representative, reports to the assistant manager. The responsibilities of this position include selling and assigning guest rooms, monitoring the **room status report** (a report that identifies the availability of rooms for arriving guests), assisting the reservations manager in maintaining the availability board, updating reservations statistics, and preparing daily forecasts and reports.

Like the senior front desk agent, the **front desk agent** is sometimes referred to as a guest services representative. He or she reports to the senior front desk agent or, in the absence of a senior front desk agent, to an assistant manager. The front desk agent processes registrations and room assignments for incoming guests; assists guests with any questions, needs, or problems; maintains a complete flow of guest records and details; describes and sells rooms, backed by a knowledge of each room, its features, and setup; answers guest questions concerning other areas of the hotel and the community; and learns the chief room clerk's duties and takes over this position when necessary. A qualified front desk agent may also take over the front desk in the absence of the senior front desk agent.

To serve the guest effectively, the front desk agent must be completely familiar with the hotel. Essential knowledge includes the floor plan of the hotel and what views, if any, are available; the number of guest rooms; the average size of guest rooms; hotel amenities (i.e., restaurants, entertainment, etc.); the different types of accommodations (single, double, etc.; see Figure 3–4); room rate structure (see Table 3–2); room variations, such as **adjoin-**

Courtesy Van Driver

- ☐ Van arrives within 15 minutes after call for pickup.
- ☐ Driver offers luggage assistance at airport.
- ☐ Driver offers luggage assistance at hotel.
- ☐ Driver provides directions to the registration desk.

Auto Valet

- ☐ Attendant provides a claim check and offers retrieval information.
- ☐ Clear and concise signage indicates valet charges.

Doorperson Services

- ☐ Doorperson opens car doors for arriving and departing guests.
- ☐ Doorperson offers to unload and load guest luggage.
- ☐ If luggage is tagged at the door, doorperson tells guest to present the claim ticket at check-in.
- ☐ Doorperson offers directions to registration.
- ☐ Doorperson is available and responsive to the guest.
- ☐ Doorperson greets each guest with a smile and eye contact.

Bell Staff

- ☐ Bellperson delivers bags to guest room within stated time after check-in.
- ☐ Bellperson provides guest with information about hotel features and services.
- ☐ Bellperson checks to ensure that the room and bathroom are in good order.
- ☐ Bellperson offers baggage placement assistance.
- ☐ Bellperson wishes the guest a pleasant stay.
- ☐ Bellperson uses a cart to provide fast, efficient service.
- ☐ Bellperson leaves the cart in the corridor when bags are brought in.
- ☐ Bellperson available and responsive to the guest.
- ☐ Bellperson uses guest's name when known.

Front Desk Check-in

- ☐ Agent confirms that spelling of the guest's name, number of nights the guest is staying, and the number of guests, and verifies payment.
- ☐ Agent asks for frequent traveler or frequent flyer numbers.
- ☐ Agent circles the rate on registration form [does not announce].
- ☐ Agent writes the room number on key packet [does not announce].
- ☐ If minibar is available, agent provides key.
- ☐ Agent offers luggage assistance.
- ☐ Agent wishes guest a pleasant stay.
- ☐ Agent advises guest of hotline numbers if available.

Figure 3–3 Checklist for evaluating arrival and registration

Front desk agents welcome guests to the hotel. (Courtesy of the Hospitality Industry Archives and Library, University of Houston, Texas.)

ing rooms (i.e., guest rooms that have an adjoining wall but no connecting door) or **connecting rooms** (i.e., adjoining rooms with individual entrance doors from the outside and a connecting door between) (see Figure 3–4); the availability of family accommodations (adding an extra bed to accommodate an additional person) and quiet rooms (rooms away from excessive street, pool, or other types of noise); and guest room features and amenities (i.e., VCR, DVD, computer, printer, fax, exercise equipment, etc.). Room rate structure is discussed in more detail in Appendix 3–1. Much of this information is available to the front desk agent with the typing of a few codes. Computers have all but made obsolete the paper rack with its stock cards and rack slips, which formerly held all of this data. (1)

The mail and information clerk reports to the senior front desk agent. The person holding this position provides information, advice, and recom-

Single or Twin

- One or two separate single beds; sold for single occupancy
- Bed measures approximately 36 inches by 75 inches

Double or Double Double

- One or two double beds; sold for single or double occupancy
- Bed measures approximately 54 inches by 75 inches

Queen

- One queen-size bed; sold for single or quad occupancy
- Bed measures approximately 60 inches by 80 inches

King

- One king-size bed; sold for single or double occupancy
- Bed measures approximately 78 inches by 80 inches

Suite

- A parlor or living room connected to one or more bedrooms with double or king beds

Figure 3–4 Types of guest room accommodations. (Photos courtesy of the Hospitality Industry Archives and Library, University of Houston, Texas.)

mendations to guests at the key, mail, and information desk or by telephone; supervises and assists in handling guest room keys, mail, and message processing; answers guests' questions concerning areas of the hotel, daily activities of the hotel and the community; distributes room keys to guests and bellmen in accordance with key control procedures; sells postage stamps to hotel guests; assists in the preparation of key inventory lists and orders; maintains the information rack of brochures on the hotel and the area; coor-

Table 3–2 Room Plans and Rates

Plan	
American Plan	Includes room and three meals
Modified American Plan	Includes room and two meals
European Plan	Includes room only
Rates	
Rack rate	Full-price room rate
Commercial rates	Reduced rates offered to frequent guests
Complimentary	Free or discounted as part of a special promotion
Group rate	Rate offered to a number of affiliated guests, i.e., members of a group
Family rate	Rate offered to parents and children staying in the same room
Day rate	Rate offered for less than an overnight stay or out by 5 P.M.
Package plan rate	Rate offered as part of an event, such as a local festival or a sporting event

dinates matters concerning guest mail with the hotel mail department and the nearest U.S. Post Office; establishes and processes changes in guest account folios; and is responsible for a cash bank. (2)

Arrivals Upon beginning a shift, the front desk agent should review the **arrivals report,** which includes the number of guests arriving by date and the type of room(s) that the guest has requested; the **departures report,** which includes the number of guests checking out on a particular date; and the **VIP report,** which includes the names and requirements of those guests arriving on a particular date who will receive special gifts and services. If a sellout is anticipated, an efficient front desk agent will call similar hotels in the area so that he or she has knowledge of alternative accommodations to offer guests. The first step in rooming a guest is greeting that guest. A friendly smile, a "Good Morning" or "Good Afternoon," and a "May I help you?" go a long way toward establishing a rapport with the guest. The guest may judge all other services during a stay by this first encounter. A poor first encounter will most undoubtedly result in the guest's close scrutiny and critical look at all other services. (3)

The next step is to determine if the guest has a reservation without making the guest feel uncomfortable. A question such as "Are we holding a reservation?" rather than "Do you have a reservation?" puts the emphasis on the hotel. If the guest does not have a reservation, the front desk agent must verify room status and availability in the hotel.

Once the presence or absence of a reservation has been established, the registration process should proceed smoothly. For an existing reservation, the front desk agent verifies the data taken by the reservationist, including the spelling and pronunciation of the guest's name, mailing address, rate, method of payment, and departure dates, and makes any necessary changes. From this point on in the registration process, the front desk agent should address the guest by the appropriate gender identifier or professional description (i.e., Mr., Ms., Dr., etc.) and the guest's last name. Before departing from the front desk, the guest must sign the registration card and is usually asked to initial the rate and date of departure should any questions or changes arise. At this time, authorization must be obtained for all forms of payment other than cash. Once the guest has registered, an **account** is created to handle all charges and financial transactions during his or her stay.

The third step in the arrivals process is the assignment of a room (recall from the section on reservations that specific rooms are not assigned by the reservationist). Prior to automation, hotels utilized a room status board, which showed whether a room was occupied, was being cleaned by housekeeping, or was available for immediate occupancy. The room status board now has been integrated into most property management systems and can be accessed through a front desk agent's terminal.

From the available inventory of rooms, the front desk agent selects and assigns a room. The guest copy of the registration card is printed and provided to the bell services representative, along with the room key. Once a guest registers, the telephone and housekeeping departments are notified, either manually or automatically, that the guest is "in the house." In addition, a guest history is created that may be used for future sales purposes.

In recent years, electronic locking systems on guest room doors have replaced the traditional lock and key system, reducing the security problems associated with lost or unreturned keys. The control center for the electronic locking system is the front desk. The issuance of a key to the guest is interfaced into the property management system. In a hard-wired system, the electronic lock on each guest room door is directly linked to the front desk through the property management system; as the guest is assigned a room, the code in his or her key is forwarded over the wires to the lock on the door. This code is programmed with the arrival and departure dates of the guest. The key becomes inactive at the checkout time on the date of departure, or, if the departure date changes, upon checkout.

If the lock on the door is not directly connected to the front desk, then the lock and the key are programmed in sequence, with the key being issued to the guest containing a code that is the next code in sequence in the memory of the lock on the guest room door.

Group Arrivals

You learned about group reservations in the previous section. Because group guests are already preregistered, they need only sign their card when they arrive; the room and folio numbers are added by the front desk agent as they are assigned. Should the hotel accommodate tour and convention groups frequently, the standard check-in procedures just described would result in tremendous delays for the group members and for any other guests arriving at the same time. Rooms should be blocked in such a way that the members of the group are close together, both enhancing group interaction and easing the trafficking of luggage. Group bookings are usually made well in advance, and the data, including number of arrivals and desired types of rooms, are shown on the arrivals report. On the morning of a group arrival, the following procedures should be followed:

1. Needed rooms are blocked off on the room rack.
2. Keys are sorted out for each room.
3. Individual or group registration cards are prepared in advance so that guests need only to sign in on arrival.
4. If group billing (no individual charges) is to be used, an account is opened.
5. If individual accounts have been arranged, they are generated in advance, along with information and room rack slips.
6. On arrival, a separate counter (or table) is set up in the lobby area away from the main desk, keeping congestion to a minimum and allowing the meeting planner or tour guide to handle the details.
7. Each guest receives an envelope containing a welcome note, key, charge instructions, tour or convention details, map of the city, and so on.
8. Bellmen stand by to move guests to their rooms in small groups.
9. The switchboard is informed of the arrival by individual slips or a tour list.
10. Any other departments that might be affected by the arrival of the group are informed, such as banquets, restaurants, room service, and housekeeping.

Mail, Messages, and Information

In recent years, the handling of mail by large hotels has diminished somewhat, because the average length of a guest's stay has become shorter. However, arrival time often is still an occasion for the guest to receive mail. In very large hotels, a separate key, mail, and information clerk handles the large volume of letters, parcels, telegrams, and messages, which are routed through the front office before arrival, during the guest's stay, and after departure. In most establishments, however, it is part of the front desk clerk's general function to handle these tasks.

The following procedures are suitable for most situations:

1. Incoming mail is routed to the front office manager, who then separates it into guest mail and hotel mail.
2. Guest mail arriving at the desk is time-stamped and sorted as soon as possible.
3. If the guest is registered, the mail is placed in the mail slot and a message is sent to the guest, either by personal contact or by illuminating the message light on the guest's room telephone.
4. If the guest has left the hotel, the cancelled registration card or the guest history file is checked to determine the guest's home address, and the mail is forwarded accordingly.
5. If the guest holds a reservation but has not yet arrived, the mail is placed in an alphabetically sectioned holding rack, and a note is placed on the reservation form.

Special mail (e.g., express delivery) should be delivered without delay by a member of the bell staff. If the guest is not in the room, a note is left in the room or the message light is illuminated.

Overbooking

It is the goal of every hotel or lodging establishment to achieve maximum room occupancy. A room that is not sold for a night is a financial loss that cannot be regained. In order to avoid such a loss, a hotel uses a standard formula to calculate the percentage of rooms that are left unoccupied. The average number of no-shows, cancellations, and early departures are added up and divided by the total number of rooms reserved to give the percentage of reserved rooms that typically are left empty. For example, if on the average there are 11 no-shows, 3 cancellations, and 2 early departures for 200 reservations, 8 percent of the reservations are not honored ($11 + 3 + 2 = 16$; $16/200 = 0.08$). Thus, the front office may accept 8 percent above their maximum number of accommodations, or 216 reservations. Occasionally, the unexpected happens; if all 216 guests arrive for the 200 available reservations, overbooking occurs. The front desk agent must be particularly attentive to the guest in what will most likely be a very difficult circumstance. First, the agent must rule out any possibility of space by looking for *sleepers*, rooms that have been checked out of but not properly inputted into the system, and *due outs*, guests that are expected to check out who have not done so. A savvy front desk agent also will check rooms listed as **out-of-order** (those rooms that have not been rented due to mechanical problems) to see if they are suitable to rent. If, after going through all of these possibilities, there is still no room available, the front desk agent must **walk** the guest to a hotel comparable in accommodations and features that has agreed to receive the guest. It is difficult to convince even a late arrival that a room was indeed held until 6 P.M. and that it is, in effect, because the guest is late that there is no room available. Many front desk agents have heard the following words from an irate customer: "A reservation is a reservation! What kind of operation are you running here, anyway?" In such a situation, a senior front desk agent, an assistant manager, or a front office manager should be called and introduced by title and name so that the guest knows that he or she is dealing with someone with authority. Relocation, perhaps to the front office manager's office, is also helpful in calming the guest and removing the conflict from public view. It also indicates to the guest that the situation is being taken seriously by the hotel.

If the guest being walked holds a confirmed reservation, the hotel initiating the walk covers the cost of the room and tax for the entire period of the guest's reservation. Alternatively, the hotel may cover the cost of the room and tax until a room becomes available. Depending on company policy, transportation to the alternate hotel may be arranged, usually at the hotel's expense. Should the guest be persuaded to return to the hotel when a room becomes available, return transportation should, of course, be arranged and paid for. If the company does not allow for the payment of the guest's stay in another hotel, a gesture of free transportation and a follow-up letter or a telephone call from the manager may repair the damage somewhat. The switchboard and bellman must be informed of the walk in order to handle forwarding of messages, telephone calls, and mail. (4)

GUEST SERVICES

The ability to respond to a guest's requests is critical to guest satisfaction. As the level of services to guests increases in volume or complexity, the creation of a separate department may become necessary.

The guest services department provides directions to points of interest, specialty shops, and shopping centers, recommendations for off-premise restaurants, tickets to the theater, reservations for tours, assistance with the purchase of airline tickets, help in locating the nearest religious service, assistance in setting up golf tee times, and other services. The **concierge** assists the guest with most problems concerning accommodations, handles their mail, and facilitates special requests with the front desk agent and other hotel personnel.

Guest Services Staff

The guest services department may consist of a single person, the concierge, or an entire department of employees who report to the concierge, including the concierge assistant, the bell captain, the bellmen and baggage porters, and the doormen.

The concierge reports to the front office manager. The concierge assistant, bell captain, and doorman report directly to the concierge. The concierge establishes policies and procedures and writes job descriptions, training manuals, and procedures for all areas of guest services, including bell service, doorman service, guest paging, baggage and package handling, guest tour and travel services, and special guest requirements. Additional responsibilities include assisting guests with the many unscheduled guest service needs (theater tickets, car rentals, sight-seeing tours, travel information, etc.); coordinating with the assistant manager, the senior assistant front office manager, and other departments; supervising and coordinating the parking of guest cars; and coordinating with the laundry manager to ensure quality guest laundry and valet service.

The *concierge assistant* works in cooperation with the bell captain under the direction of the concierge. He or she receives requests for service from front desk personnel and guests; immediately records requests for services and assigns bellmen to perform them; ensures that bellmen are on duty 24 hours a day; receives packages or other articles for or from guests and assigns bellmen to complete their delivery; brings any problems involving bellmen to the attention of the bell captain or concierge; assists the concierge and bell captain in evaluating all new bellmen; ensures constant and courteous answering and staffing of the bell captain's station; posts daily events on event boards located in the lobby.

The **bell captain** works under the direction of the concierge. The responsibilities of the bell captain include complete authority over the appearance, conduct, and activities of the bellmen; fast, courteous handling of all guest luggage during check-in and checkout; provision of advice to guests concerning hotel restaurants, facilities, and services; and close cooperation with the concierge assistant. The bell captain also must keep fully informed about events on the daily function schedule and make sure that the bellmen are similarly well informed; receive packages and other articles for guests and assign bellmen for delivery; receive requests for service by phone or personally from front desk personnel and immediately record them on a document called the bell captain's call sheet.

A *bellman* reports to the bell captain. He or she assists guests throughout their stay; transports and handles guest luggage to and from several areas of the hotel, but primarily from and to the main entrance; and obtains room keys, checks mail and messages, and takes guests to or from their respective rooms. Upon arrival in the room, the bellman makes sure all accommodations are adequately equipped with towels, soap, stationery, and other supplies; inspects luggage for damage after depositing it in a designated area; records evidence of recent luggage damage on a room slip in the event of a claim; and checks and explains the operation of the telephone, television, radio, air conditioning, and heating equipment, including setting the thermostat. Other responsibilities of the bellman include delivering packages, paging guests, and supplying information about the hotel and hotel functions; and maintaining the orderliness of the lobby or public rooms by picking up newspapers, emptying ashtrays, and straightening or properly placing furniture. The bellman also may process valet or laundry items on behalf of the valet or make arrangements for such service, operate the elevators, and assist in delivering room service items after hours.

The *baggage/luggage porter*, who like the bellman reports directly to the bell captain, is responsible for solving all guest luggage and transportation problems, and is in charge of the officially designated baggage room and other designated baggage storage areas. The person who holds this position also handles, stores, and distributes all heavy incoming and outgoing lug-

A doorman waiting to assist guests at the front door of a hotel. (Courtesy of the Hospitality Industry Archives and Library, University of Houston, Texas.)

gage; advises guests as to special requirements in response to unusual service requests, such as dealing with an airline on a guest's behalf over lost baggage; acts as an intermediary between guests and the freight agents of airlines, railroads, and bus lines, assuring proper shipping of any item sent on behalf of guests or the hotel; records time of arrival, name of sender, receiver, charges, and room number for items received or shipped; prepares package notice slips and forwards them to the key, mail, and information desk for delivery; and maintains waybills for all goods shipped or transported by freight or express.

Doormen, who report to the concierge, help guests enter and leave the hotel; assist guests with luggage; store and handle luggage; aid guests getting in and out of motor vehicles by opening and closing doors; make necessary arrangements for dispatching taxis; and direct and oversee traffic in the hotel driveway. Doormen also provide information concerning roads, local directions, and points of interest; cooperate with the hotel garage to have guest cars delivered and picked up; and observe the hotel driveway to prevent unauthorized parking or standing of vehicles.

TELECOMMUNICATIONS

The telecommunications department must provide in-room local telephone service, in-room long-distance telephone service, and the capability for in-room computer use by the guest, 24 hours a day. This department was formerly called the telephone or PBX department (the acronym **PBX** stands for private branch exchange). In early manual systems, all outgoing calls were made by the hotel operator. As telephone technology advanced, dial systems were introduced, in which guests could dial their own calls. The role of the hotel operator, sometimes referred to as the *PBX manager*, is now almost entirely limited to servicing incoming calls. Guests can direct dial all their local and most long-distance calls and **call accounting** automatically identifies guests' calls by their telephone number, date, and amount charged. In the United States, a guest also can dial out to most overseas locations. In-house guests also can call other guests (by dialing room numbers), room service, and other hotel departments.

As of January 1, 2000, hotels must provide telephones in each guest room, all meeting rooms, the lobby, and administrative areas that are hearing aid compatible and have volume controls for the handset and speakerphone.

While hotels may contract with a long-distance provider for their local and long-distance telephone services, federal regulations in the United States require that guests be allowed to use the long-distance service provider of their choosing.

Figure 3–5 illustrates a checklist of variables that might be utilized to evaluate telephone services.

Restriction of House Phones

- ☐ All house phones in the public areas and lobbies should be restricted from dialing directly to guest rooms.
- ☐ All house phones, while restricting direct dialing to guest rooms, allow calls to other hotel services, such as restaurants.

Telephone Dialing Rates

- ☐ In compliance with federal regulations in the United States, dialing information and rates are visibly displayed at the telephone.
- ☐ There is no service charge on any "0+" or "8xx" toll free calls placed from any guest room.

Telephone Faceplates

- ☐ Faceplate includes international symbols and written descriptions.
- ☐ Faceplate is equipped with a message waiting light.
- ☐ Telephone is equipped with two telephone lines with speaker capability.
- ☐ Faceplate has speed dial for hotel services.
- ☐ Emergency number is displayed on faceplate.

Incoming Calls

- ☐ Call is held for no more than 30 seconds.
- ☐ Held call recording is clear.
- ☐ Call is answered with the appropriate hotel message and greeting.
- ☐ Call is answered politely (i.e., "Good morning," "Good afternoon," "Good evening").

Internal Calls

- ☐ Call is put on hold for no more than 30 seconds.
- ☐ Call has a clear hold recording.
- ☐ Call is answered by hotel operator.
- ☐ Operator confirms name of guest before connecting a call.
- ☐ Phone is in good working order.
- ☐ Phone instructions are clear.
- ☐ Phone message light functions properly.
- ☐ Time of a call is included in the message.
- ☐ A guest's room number is not given out by the operator.
- ☐ Messages are accurate.
- ☐ If the guest does not answer, the phone mail engages are five rings of the phone.
- ☐ If a wake-up call is requested, the guest's name, room number, and time of wake up are repeated.
- ☐ Wake-up calls are made within five minutes of the requested time.

Figure 3–5 **Checklist for the evaluation of telephone services**

Night Audit

The audit of guests' accounts is the duty of the *night auditor*. At the close of business (usually 11:00 P.M.), the sales sheets of all departments are physically carried to the front office or transmitted electronically via the property management system so that the journal and vouchers for each department are available to the night auditor. The exact routine of the night auditor's work depends on the size of the hotel and the number of night auditors, and will be described in more detail in Chapter 7. In addition to performing the financial duties outlined in Chapter 7, the night auditor can function as a front desk agent, security officer, PBX operator and bellman, all in one eight-hour shift. (5)

Checkout

At **checkout**, the front office is responsible for settling guest account balances, updating room status information, creating a guest history, and promoting guest relations to enhance the possibility of a guest returning to the hotel or lodging establishment.

Settlement

A guest may pay his or her outstanding balance by cash, personal check, traveler's check, credit card, or, in special circumstances, by having the outstanding balance directly billed to a preapproved business entity. The type of payment is indicated at check-in. Once the account is settled, the front desk agent provides the departing guest with a final copy of the account folio. If the guest pays with cash, the front desk agent can zero the folio balance and mark it paid.

Most guests select a credit card to settle their accounts. Typically, a hotel prefers credit card (CC) payments over payment by personal check. The quicker, more efficient handling of CC payments in most cases is worth the service fee charged to the hotel by the CC company.

Traveler's checks are issued and guaranteed for payment by banks and credit institutions throughout the world in internationally recognized and accepted currencies such as U.S. and Canadian dollars, deutsche marks, Swiss francs, pounds sterling, and Japanese yen. When a customer purchases traveler's checks, he or she signs them in the upper left corner; when they are used as payment, the guest must then countersign the check in the lower left corner in the presence of the cashier, who then compares the countersignature with the existing signature. If the two signatures are the same, the traveler's checks may be accepted without further identification.

For the reasons indicated above, most hotels prefer not to accept personal checks for the payment of accounts. However, should a guest pay by check, the front desk agent should examine the check for the following features:

1. The check should be preprinted with the name and address of a legitimate bank.
2. The written amount and the figure amount should be the same.
3. The check should be dated for the date of checkout.
4. The hotel should be listed as payee and should be spelled correctly.
5. The guest should produce proper identification.
6. The signature on the check should match the guest's signature on some form of identification acceptable to the hotel.

Periodically, a charge comes in after a guest has departed. This is becoming less and less common with the use of automated property management systems, but the front desk agent should, as a matter of course, ask all departing guests whether any recent charges have been made in hotel restaurants or other outlets.

After the guest has departed, it becomes difficult, if not impossible, to collect unpaid amounts. Many hotels establish an amount under which they will not seek collection or address the uncollected charge upon a guest's return visit.

Room Status Change

Along with settling the guest account, the front desk agent must change the status of the guest room from occupied to **on change**, or a room from which the guest has checked out but is not ready for the next arrival or is not ready for cleaning, and notify the housekeeping department of the departure. With an integrated property management system, departure notification may be forwarded to housekeeping automatically. Because the room is not available until housekeeping is finished with it, the "on change" status should be for as short a time as possible in order to maximize room sales.

Preparation of Guest History

To successfully return current guests and strategically market to new guests with similar characteristics, a hotel must maintain and evaluate data on all of its guests. The record of a guest's stay, called the **guest history**, becomes part of a file that can be used to determine when a guest might visit in the future; the type of accommodation the guest prefers; dining preferences; use of amenities or recreational facilities; and other, more personal data, including home address and telephone number, spouse's and children's names, birthday, and so on. The guest history can be used by the hotel's sales and marketing department for promotional mailings soliciting repeat business or to target potential guests with similar profiles.

Guest Relations

For years, producers of musical productions have had one criterion of the success of their productions. When they can send the audience out of the theater whistling or humming a show tune, they know the show has succeeded. Similarly, if a hotel can send its departing guests away from the desk with a smile, it is certain that the hotel has made a positive impression. Figure 3–6 provides a checklist of the features of a successful checkout. This often begins with an **express checkout**, which involves providing the guest with a folio early in the morning of the day of the checkout in order for the guest to review the charges and perhaps speed up the checkout process.

Too often, checking out a guest is treated as if it were a disagreeable duty to be completed as quickly as possible in order to make room for the next guest. When this attitude radiates from the hotel side of the desk, it is usually due to the fact that the routine has become entirely mechanical. (Is it

Front Desk

- ☐ Time spent by guest in line did not exceed 10 minutes (unless customer requested additional assistance).
- ☐ Guest was acknowledged with a sincere greeting.
- ☐ Guest was offered a review of charges.
- ☐ Guest was asked about satisfaction with stay or visit.
- ☐ Folio disputes were handled courteously and efficiently.
- ☐ Guest was thanked for staying at the hotel.
- ☐ Front desk agent used the guest's name when appropriate.
- ☐ Front desk agent was attired in a neat, clean, and well-fitting uniform.
- ☐ Front desk agent was wearing a name tag.

Bell Staff

- ☐ Bellperson arrived at the guest's room within 15 minutes of call.
- ☐ Bellperson inquired as to guest's satisfaction with the hotel.
- ☐ Bellperson thanked the guest for staying at the hotel.
- ☐ Bellperson's uniform and shoes were neat, clean, and well fitting.
- ☐ Bellperson's name tag was worn.
- ☐ Bellperson used guest's name as appropriate.
- ☐ Bellperson used clean, polished equipment or cart in good working order.

Airport Courtesy Van Driver

- ☐ Driver acknowledged guest with a polite greeting.
- ☐ Driver offered luggage assistance at the hotel and airport.
- ☐ Driver thanked the guest for staying at the hotel.
- ☐ Driver's uniform and shoes were neat, clean, and well fitting.
- ☐ Driver wore a name tag.
- ☐ Driver operated a van that had a neat and clean exterior and interior.

Figure 3–6 **Guest relations departure checklist**

time for job rotation?) All front office staff members must remember that the guest is the raison d'être of the hotel business. One of the simplest, yet most effective, ways to pleasantly send the guest on his or her way is a simple, heartfelt "thank you." This little phrase can be made the conveyor of a high measure of appreciation and goodwill. Even if no response is received from the guest, the front office staff member should look directly at the guest and add a smile while speaking (a "step in the right direction," from *Bedknobs and Broomsticks*, The Walt Disney Co.), which will make the speaker feel good.

In Chapter 4, we move on to a much less visible, yet no less important, department of any well-managed hotel—the housekeeping department. This department often has more employees than any other department in the hotel, but it may have the highest turnover rate of employees if it is not managed properly; it also has more guest contact than most of the other departments in the hotel.

SUMMARY

The front office is the first and last contact that a guest has with a hotel. Key responsibilities of the front office include reservations, registration, guest services, PBX, and checkout. The responsibilities of the front desk are successfully accomplished by numerous staff members, including the following: front office manager; assistant front office manager; reservations manager; concierge; front desk agent; key, mail, and information clerks; bell staff; doormen; and baggage porters.

To accomplish the reservations function successfully, particular attention must be given to future room availability, identifying sources of reservations and reservation categories, guaranteeing reservations, processing and revising reservations, and processing statistics for decision-making purposes.

Effective registration of a guest includes adhering to standards of greeting, knowledge of the hotel's room inventory and facilities, and collecting pertinent information concerning length of stay and method of payment. Walking a guest due to overbooking is an especially difficult circumstance and must be carefully planned so as to minimize the potential for losing the guest's business.

In order to handle the various requests from a guest effectively, most hotels have established a guest services unit that includes a concierge who is skillful in effectively resolving the simple and the most difficult requests.

A critical service provided by the modern hotel is telecommunications. Careful consideration must be given to the telecommunications requirements of each hotel guest and to proper handling and fair allocation of costs.

During the lodging of a guest, a proper accounting of all charges incurred by the guest must be maintained in the guest's account folio. At the close of the business day, the night auditor for the hotel is responsible for posting outstanding charges, verifying and posting room rates and taxes, completing day's-end balances by department, compiling reports for distribution, preparing cash deposits, backing up the record of guest charges, and resolving room status issues.

The last contact that a guest has with the hotel, and the one that leaves a lasting impression, typically involves checkout at the front desk. Thus, it is critical that the front desk efficiently and successfully settle a guest's account balance, update room status, create a guest history, and promote guest relations.

References

1. Grace Paige and Janet Paige, *Hotel/Motel Front Desk Personnel* (New York: Van Nostrand Reinhold, 1989).
2. Paige and Paige, *Hotel/Motel*, p. 42.
3. H. V. Heldenbrand, *Front Office Psychology* (Chicago: American Hotel Register Company, 1944).
4. Paige and Paige, *Hotel/Motel*, p. 58.
5. Peter Franz Renner, *Basic Hotel Front Office Procedures,* 3rd ed. (New York: John Wiley & Sons, Inc., 1997).

Review Questions

1. In the last two hours, I've delivered the baggage of six incoming guests, routed messages to guests on three different floors, and helped four other guests check out. Who am I?

2. A guest arrives without a reservation. Explain the check-in procedure.

3. Name the functions of the front office.

4. Why does the front desk clerk depend upon the housekeeper?

ACTIVITIES

1. Visit a local hotel and prepare a diagram of the organization of its front office, listing key positions and the job responsibilities of the key positions. Compare your findings with the structure shown in Figure 3–1 and the duties and responsibilities of the key positions described in this chapter.
2. By telephone, make a reservation at a local hotel and then cancel the reservation. Evaluate the reservationist(s), using the checklist found in Figure 3–2.
3. Discuss with a local hotel front office manager the source and type of reservations typically received by the hotel.
4. Check in to a local hotel and evaluate the service provided by the courtesy van driver or auto valet, door person, bell staff, and front desk agents. Evaluate your experience using the checklist found in Figure 3–3.
5. Call a local hotel and evaluate how your call was handled, using the checklist found in Figure 3–5.
6. Observe the checkout of a guest at a local hotel and evaluate the checkout, using the checklist found in Figure 3–6.

Appendix 3–1

Projecting Hotel Occupancy, Establishing Room Rates, and REVPAR

Projecting Hotel Occupancy

Stabilized Occupancy

New hotels have an assumed two- to five-year buildup in occupancy (OCC). After that period, occupancy is considered stabilized. Stabilized occupancy refers to the level of occupancy that a hotel must achieve to be profitable over its economic life, including any stages of buildup, plateau, or decline.

Different types of travelers have different travel patterns (i.e., days of travel, length of stay, and seasonality of travel). The particular mixture of visitors will influence the hotel's occupancy. For example, a hotel that generates its occupancy from business travelers might have 100 percent occupancy Monday through Thursday, and 30 percent, 35 percent, and 45 percent occupancy on Friday, Saturday, and Sunday, respectively. Its weekly occupancy would be approximately 73 percent. This figure would become the stabilized occupancy figure unless a different market mix could be generated.

Fair Market Share

Fair market share is the ratio of a hotel's available guest rooms and the total number on the market. For example, if there are 1,600 rooms in the competitive market, with 300 belonging to the Stutts Hotel, the fair market share of the Stutts Hotel would be 300 divided by 1,600, or approximately 19 percent. The Stutts Hotel might achieve more or less than 100 percent of its fair market share, depending on its competitive strengths and weaknesses.

The **actual market share** is calculated by multiplying the number of rooms by the occupancy percentage and then dividing the number of occupied rooms by the total number of occupied rooms in the competitive room set. For example, if the Stutts Hotel achieved an 80 percent occupancy, it would have 240 occupied rooms. If the total competitive room set of 1,600 rooms was averaging 1,200 occupied rooms, the hotel would have an actual market share of 20 percent (240 divided by 1200).

Market Penetration and Competitive Indexing

While less valuable in projecting occupancy, market penetration and competitive indexing are useful in ranking the occupancy of hotels in a competitive market. *Market penetration* is a measure of how well a hotel is attracting occupancy of its rooms. Market penetration is calculated by dividing the hotel's actual market share by its fair market share. If the Stutts Hotel has an actual market share of 20 percent and a fair market share of 20 percent, it has a market penetration of 1.0. To be competitive, a hotel should aim to keep its market penetration above 1.0.

The *competitive index* of a hotel reflects the number of days per year that a single room in a hotel is occupied. For example, if the occupancy rate of Hotel A is 80 percent, that of Hotel B is 70 percent, and that of Hotel C is 81 percent, the three hotels can be ranked by multiplying their respective percentages by 365 days (number of days in an operating year). In the above example, the competitive index is as follows: Hotel C, 295; Hotel A, 292; and Hotel B, 255.

Establishing Room Rates

The following methods have been used to establish room rates.

Competitive Position

Room rates are established by comparing the rates of hotels that are competitive in terms of quality, room size, facilities and amenities, and location. The range of room rates by category of room utilized by a competitive hotel sets the general limits for the rates.

Hubbart Formula

Room rates should cover all operating costs, including a predetermined net income level, debt service, and development cost. The rate-setting process begins with a determination of the development and financing costs of the project and continues working upward from the bottom of an income (rooms, food, beverage, misc, etc.) and expense (payroll, benefits, goods, advertising, etc.) statement, which would be customized to the anticipated operating characteristics of the subject property. Since the described process does not take into account the local conditions and competition of the marketplace, it is often used to justify a project's feasibility rather than to set an actual room rate.

Rule-of-Thumb Method

The rule-of-thumb method is based on the premise that every dollar of average room rate should support $1,000 of total hotel value, including land, improvements, and furniture, fixtures, and equipment (FF&E) on a per-room basis. For example, a total hotel value of $50 million, divided by 450 available rooms, equals an average value per room of $111,111.11; dividing by $1,000 gives a room rate of $111.00.

Market Segmentation Method

In the market segmentation method, you multiply the average room rate per market segment by the anticipated number of occupied room nights for each of the respective market segments that produce revenue for the hotel. The average daily rate is calculated by dividing the total room revenue by the total number of occupied rooms. The resulting number is a weighted average room rate, which if reviewed daily, can reflect the price sensitivity for each segment of lodging demand that is critical to the hotel's success.

REVPAR

The revenue per available room, or REVPAR, is the best way a hotel has to compare its competition and is a reflection of the way occupancy and average daily rate (ADR), which is an occupancy ratio derived by dividing net room revenues by the number of rooms sold, are being managed. REVPAR can alert the manager to how well the reservations department is selling during slow periods and/or how successfully reservationists are upselling hotel guests to higher rated rooms or packages during peak periods.

To obtain REVPAR, the ADR is multiplied by the OCC for a specific period. The property management system, which is the computer software package that supports a variety of applications (i.e., reservation, registration, checkout, charges to a guest room), including revenue forecasting, can be used to effectively maximize the hotel's available rates. Forecasts can be generated instantly for a single day, a week, a month, or 90 days with the REVPAR module. The more intricate the occupancy and rate mix are, the more important the forecast becomes.

When a reservationist is speaking with a guest, the REVPAR module in more advanced systems can instantly sort through the myriad of rates and packages and provide the reservationist with instructions on how to sell the guest (i.e., give rates for differing time periods) in a manner that will maximize hotel revenue and occupancy.

Hotel revenue is a function of rate and occupancy. Initially, managers look at either rate or occupancy as a measure of success and realize too late that they are misleading and that only when the concepts of rate and occupancy are analyzed together is the true revenue picture fully understood. Thus, you must understand REVPAR to understand revenue, and to understand REVPAR, a clear understanding of ADR and occupancy is essential.

Chapter 4

Housekeeping

CHAPTER OUTLINE

- **Housekeeping Staff**
  - Executive Housekeeper
  - Assistant Housekeeper
  - Inspector
  - Houseman
  - Laundry Supervisor
  - Guest Room Attendants
  - Runners
  - Linen Room Supervisor and Attendants
- **Scheduling**
  - Turnover
- **Guest Room Cleaning**
- **Public Area Cleaning**
- **Inventory and Control**
- **Employee Safety**
  - Responsibility, Reputation, and Quality of Service
  - Economics
  - Accident Prevention

Appendix 4–1 Sample Housekeeping Routines

BOX 4–1 Curtis Leroy Carlson

Curtis L. Carlson. (Courtesy of the Hospitality Industry Archives and Library, University of Houston, Texas.)

The first business venture for Curtis L. Carlson (1914–1999), the son of a Minneapolis grocer, was selling newspapers at the age of 12. Carlson became an entrepreneur when he recognized the profitability of managing additional paper routes. He organized a network of routes and employed his brothers to make the deliveries. After earning a BA in economics in 1937 from the University of Minnesota, Carlson began a promising career with Procter and Gamble, winning the Number One Salesman award in 1938. He also started Gold Bond stamps, the first use of trading stamps in the food business. The grocers who supplied Gold Bond stamps to their customers saw their business increase by 60 percent. By 1953, Gold Bond trading stamps had became a household word. Today's frequent flyer and frequent guest programs are extensions of the trading stamp concept and have the same objective—to spur sales and to command consumer loyalty.

Carlson's extraordinary success in the customer incentive business eventually enabled him to diversify his capital. In addition to purchasing real estate, he purchased a 50 percent interest in the downtown Minneapolis Radisson Hotel in 1960, acquired the remaining shares two years later, and began adding new hotels.

Today, Curt Carlson's entrepreneurial and leadership skills are legendary. His companies, which encompass the entire spectrum of the hospitality industry, include Carlson Hospitality Worldwide, with Regent International Hotels

Housekeeping is essential to an efficient and effective hotel's operations. There is not one department in a hotel or a lodging enterprise that can exist without housekeeping service. A strong working relationship between housekeeping and other departments is absolutely essential but can become extremely complicated. The timing of housekeeping activities is affected by the requirements of other departments. For example, a convention involving multiple locations may take place in the morning and afternoon, and a wedding reception using one of the same spaces may be scheduled for that same evening. The function of the housekeeping department as a service unit for every department in a hotel can become difficult in terms of staffing and Resorts, Radisson Hotels Worldwide, Radisson Seven Seas Cruises, and Country Inns & Suites by Carlson. These lodging operations include over 470 locations in 42 countries and four cruise ships that sail worldwide. Carlson Marketing Group is a worldwide marketing services company. Friday's Hospitality Worldwide has more than 460 restaurants in 350 cities and 40 countries. In addition, his five different operations in the travel industry (Carlson Wagonlit Travel, A.T. Mays, Travel Agents International, Carlson Vacations, and Carlson Leisure Group) have 5,300 offices in 140 countries. His other companies include Carlson Hospitality Worldwide Procurement Group, Carlson Real Estate, and the newest venture—Gold Points Plus.

Spanning six decades, Carlson's privately held business, one of the largest in the United States, comprised over 100 corporations, with a worldwide workforce of more than 145,000, representing 125 different countries. At the end of 1996, the company generated system-wide revenues of more than $13.4 billion. Carlson Companies' brands earned more than $20 billion.

The ultimate entrepreneur, Curt Carlson was a firm believer in the free enterprise system. He considered profit to be an essential and an honorable ingredient to a successful business. He gave immeasurably to his community through the economic growth of companies that provided jobs and good salaries, with opportunities for advancement, education, and prosperity. He believed firmly that, if a company is to be successful, its employees must move forward. He believed that, if every year an employee feels that he or she is better off than a year ago, the employee will be satisfied and work hard. He also noted that, if this is not the case, the company will fail.

Source: "Curtis Carlson," Cathleen Baird, Hospitality Industry Hall of Honor Archives, Conrad N. Hilton College, University of Houston, Houston, Texas 1997.

and standards of quality, and it demands a well-organized and well-trained staff. (1)

The complexity and unpredictability of the housekeeping department's schedule makes it essential that the department head communicate to staff members that cooperation and flexibility are essential in the effective performance of their jobs. Good attitude, cooperation, and coordination eliminate many problems. Hotel management must reinforce these qualities if it wants to retain high-quality, talented staff. Hotelier Curtis Carlson believed that, if employees are satisfied and work hard, the company will succeed; if they do not, the company is doomed to failure (see Box 4–1).

HOUSEKEEPING STAFF

Figure 4–1 illustrates the organizational structure of a housekeeping department in a full-service hotel. The housekeeping staff includes the executive housekeeper, assistant housekeeper(s), inspector, housemen, laundry staff, room attendants, runners, and linen room supervisor and attendants.

Executive Housekeeper

The **executive housekeeper**, sometimes called the director of housekeeping, may work under the direction of the rooms manager or the general manager in a smaller property and the resident manager or an assistant general manager in a larger hotel. He or she is responsible for the cleanliness and order of the entire hotel. Key responsibilities include hiring housekeeping personnel; maintenance of accurate records on equipment, inventory, and personnel; and the organization of all cleaning schedules. On a daily basis, the executive housekeeper makes inspection tours of all areas of the hotel, establishes and revises staffing requirements, and researches new products and equipment.

The housekeeping department is usually the largest in the hotel; excluding food service employees, it can comprise 75 percent or more of the total permanent staff. The housekeeping department also has more unskilled workers on its staff (room attendants, cleaners, and housemen) than any other department. At one time or another, housekeeping employees may come into personal contact with the guests, and all are directly involved in a very important phase of guest relations—servicing the guest rooms. The training of these employees in their duties and in their relationships with

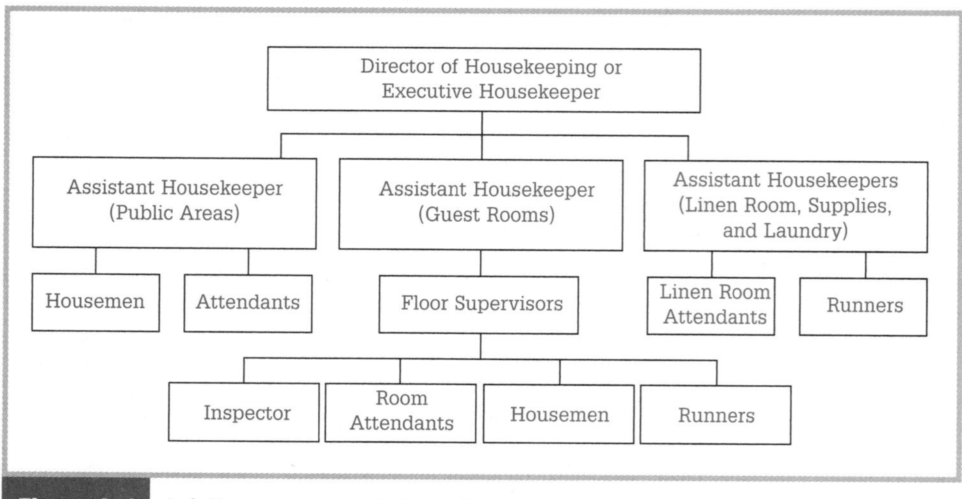

Figure 4–1 A full-service hotel's housekeeping department

each other, with staff members in other departments, and with guests is a very important responsibility of the executive housekeeper.

Another major function of the executive housekeeper is the inventory and control of the many housekeeping supplies. Guest room supplies and those required in public areas must be replenished daily in order to maintain hotel standards. The room attendants and housemen need adequate supplies and proper equipment (rags, pails, carpet sweepers, hand and floor vacuums, etc.) in good working order to clean and service the guest rooms, corridors, and other public areas of the hotel. The sheer volume of supplies necessitates a strong inventory system. There are so many employees and guests handling and using these supplies that distribution control is difficult, if not impossible. Rather than trying to keep track of how many bars of soap are used each day, the executive housekeeper, in cooperation with the controller, establishes a *pattern of consumption*, a ratio between the volume of business and usage of supplies. Ratios can be established for major items, particularly the more expensive ones—guest stationery, soap, facial tissues, and postcards. By keeping a record of each order (a simple work sheet showing date, quantity, and price), any variation from the established pattern can be spotted and investigated. (2)

Effective control of the equipment is easier to maintain. Selected items, such as the maids' carts, carpet sweepers, and hand and floor vacuum cleaners, should be carefully inventoried, kept under lock and key when not in use, and, wherever possible, assigned to a specific employee, who assumes the responsibility for the safety and condition of the appliances.

The final major area of the executive housekeeper's responsibilities is reporting, and record keeping. Organized control of payroll, which is vital for all departments, is essential due to the volume of employees in the housekeeping department.

Assistant Housekeeper

A full-service hotel may have one or more assistant housekeepers. There may be one for public areas, another for guest floors, and yet another for the linen room, laundry, and supplies. The assistant housekeepers work under the supervision of the executive housekeeper and must schedule, train, and supervise personnel, prepare weekly schedules in accordance with occupancy, and make periodic reports on the condition of their respective areas.

An assistant housekeeper for public areas makes regular inspections of all public areas and executive offices and forwards a written inspection report to the executive housekeeper. On the inspection tour, the assistant housekeeper must make sure that all rooms scheduled for use are in perfect condition at the time they are needed and inspect public area restrooms with the housemen.

The assistant housekeeper for guest rooms is responsible for all guest

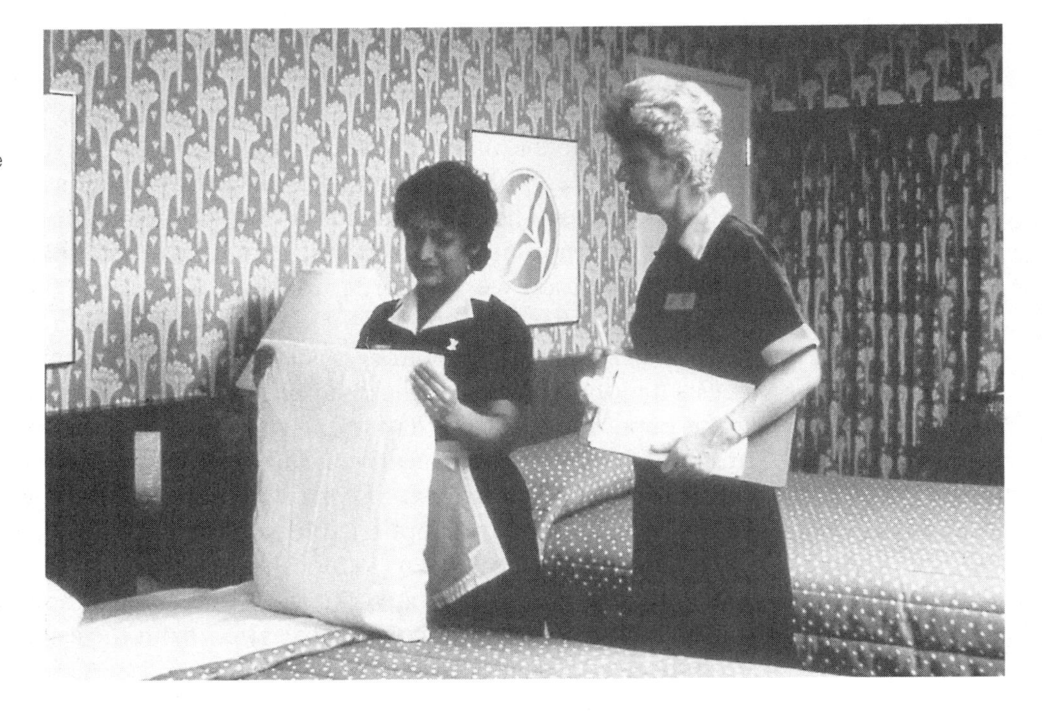

A housekeeping floor supervisor observing a guest room attendant's work. (Courtesy of the Hospitality Industry Archives and Library, University of Houston, Texas.)

room floor linen closet and service areas, as well as the training and direction of guest room floor supervisors and attendants.

The assistant housekeeper for linen room, supplies, and laundry trains the linen room attendants in caring for, shelving, and distributing linens; checks the supply inventory regularly, noting items to be reordered or requisitioned; processes supply requisitions; trains the runner in the correct methods of shelving and stocking linens; and makes sure the established controls are rigidly enforced.

Linens for the food and beverage department are often stored in the linen room on shelves separate from the bed linens. In smaller hotels, they are cared for by the same personnel who are responsible for the housekeeping linens. Since each dining area may have its own table sizes and color scheme, the linen must be separated by room. The system of management for the linens and the activity in the linen room itself will depend largely on whether the hotel has its own laundry facility.

Inspector

The **inspector** typically works under the direction of the assistant housekeeper for guest rooms. Responsibilities of this position include training guest room attendants, organizing the work of guest room attendants, controlling equipment and supplies, evaluating the job performance of the guest room attendants, and providing feedback to improve the efficiency and effectiveness of the guest room attendants. In addition, the Inspector is responsible for assuring that the hotel's standards of cleanliness, consistency, and comfort are upheld.

Houseman Under the general direction of an assistant housekeeper or, in some cases, the executive housekeeper, the **houseman** is in charge of carpet repairers, wall washers, window washers, drapery cleaners, shampooers, vacuumers for deep cleaning of carpeted areas, chandelier cleaners, and furniture movers.

Laundry Supervisor The **laundry supervisor** reports directly to an assistant housekeeper. He or she is responsible for the careful training of laundry workers in the care of uniforms, as well as the care of beds, bath, table, and other linen. Proper training in the presorting, pretreatment, and use of correct formulas makes the process more efficient and prolongs the life of the linens. The laundry supervisor also monitors the quality of linens and takes any necessary remedial action. The sooner a rip in a drapery, stain on a sheet, or spill on a bedspread is attended to, the easier it is to take care of, and the less likely that permanent damage will occur.

Guest Room Attendants Historically, there are three categories of **guest room attendants**—day, bath, and night guest room attendants. The day guest room attendant makes beds, supplies each room with clean linen and prescribed amenities, and cleans the guest room. The bath guest room attendant thoroughly cleans the bathroom, washing the wall tiles and floor fixtures. The night guest room attendant services the rooms in the case of late checkouts, is on call for extra

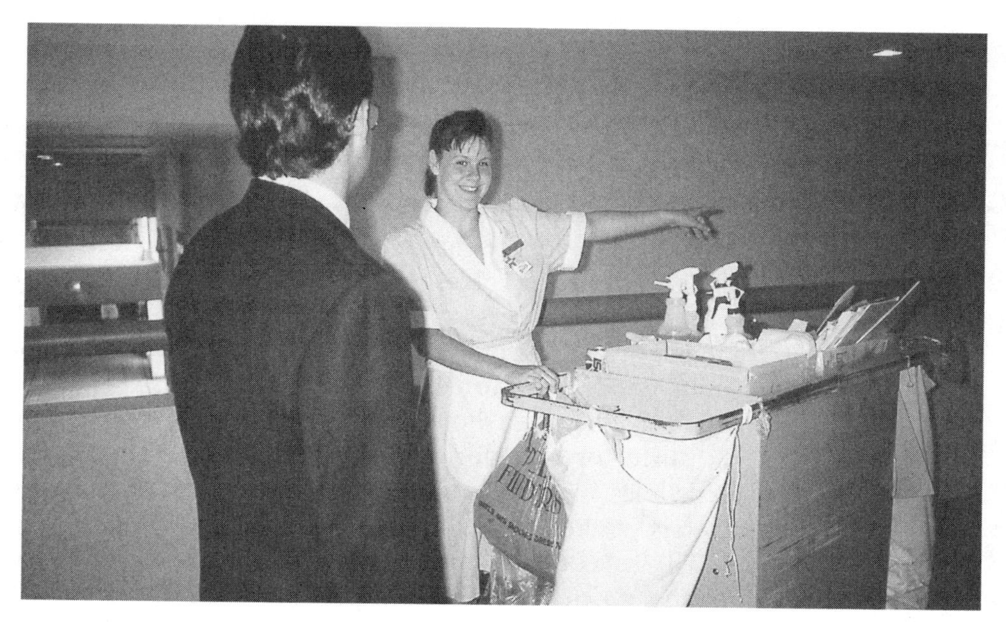

A guest room attendant with a housekeeping cart providing directions to a guest. (Courtesy of the Hospitality Industry Archives and Library, University of Houston, Texas.)

supplies or other requests by the guest, and, in hotels offering the service, "turns down" the beds. Each guest room attendant typically works under the direction of an inspector on an assigned floor and is responsible for the care of 15 rooms. In addition, the guest room attendant is responsible for the care and maintenance of all equipment, including the housekeeping cart.

Runners The guest room attendants require a constant supply of clean linens to make up their assigned rooms. Supervised by an inspector or assistant housekeeper, a runner shelves linens on a linen truck in the laundry and delivers the clean linens to the guest floor linen closets, keeping a specified number of each type of linen in the closet. The runner then returns the linen truck to the laundry to be reloaded.

Linen Room Supervisor and Attendants Under the direction of an inspector or an assistant housekeeper, the linen room staff must keep a careful count of the linens sent to and returned from the laundry each day. The linen room supervisor does periodic spot checks, counting linens as they go out in a hamper from a floor or a section of the building or as they come through the central linen room. Adjustments are made to any shortages or overages to ensure that the guest room attendant has an adequate number to prepare the rooms.

The linen room attendants are responsible for issuing linens to the floor housekeepers and for receiving linens from the laundry. The linen room attendants are also charged with inspecting linens for quality and ensuring that a stock of various sizes and types of linens is available to meet housekeeping requirements.

SCHEDULING

The cost of labor involved in preparing a guest room can become one of the highest costs for a hotel. As you saw in the last section, preparation of a single guest room involves the activities of attendants and linen room, laundry, and inspection personnel. One way to reduce these costs in a hotel is to adjust the employees' work schedules to fit demand, which in this case is the number of rooms to be cleaned.

The executive housekeeper typically schedules personnel 15 days in advance for the morning, afternoon, and evening shifts. However, these schedules are subject to change if the house count changes or if a large function is booked at the last minute.

To schedule the staff effectively, the executive housekeeper must have on hand a written weekly rooms forecast; a revised three-day rooms forecast; a forecast of group and convention bookings; weekly function sheets; a list of occupied rooms; and a list of daily checkouts.

The number of rooms that a room attendant is expected to clean is calculated as follows: the number of minutes required to clean a room (the standard is about 30 minutes) multiplied by the number of rooms to be cleaned, divided by 60 (i.e., the number of minutes in an hour) (see Figure 4–2). On average, each room attendant is expected to clean 14 to 16 rooms in an eight-hour shift. Each room attendant works an eight-hour day, with 30 minutes for lunch and two 15-minute breaks (one in the morning and one in the afternoon).

However, different hotels may have different expectations. The rooms in a luxury hotel, which may have special furnishings and amenities, may require more than 30 minutes to clean. The attendant may be able to clean only 8–10 rooms in an eight-hour shift. On the other hand, the rooms in a hotel with small, simply decorated guest rooms may take less time to clean; in this type of hotel, the guest room attendant may be able to clean more than 14–16 rooms in that same eight-hour shift.

Guest room attendants typically arrive by eight in the morning, get their keys, check the schedule board, and go to their usual floors. Before they begin, the inspector or floor supervisor informs them if they are expected to work in other areas after they have finished cleaning their assigned rooms. In resort hotels, the guest room attendants are usually scheduled later in the day, as the guests arise later in the day. In a commercial hotel, the majority of the guests are business travelers who may arise much earlier than eight in the morning; in this situation, earlier staffing of the morning shift may be required.

Figure 4–3 illustrates a **master staffing sheet** for a hotel housekeeping department. The master staffing sheet provides a complete breakdown of the various work stations in the hotel of the guest room attendants, housemen, supervisors, and assistant housekeepers. This is a permanent record of the division of labor and in narrative and graphic form indicates where each station is located, the days off assigned to the area, the person whose permanent station it is, and the regular relief. Typically, changes to the master

Projected occupancy × Total number of rooms = Total occupied rooms = 0.8 (80 percent) × 200 = 160

Cleaning time required per room × Total occupied rooms =
Total cleaning time = 30 min/room × 160 rooms = 4,800 min (80 hr)

Total cleaning time ÷ Work shift per employee = Personnel required = 80 hr ÷ 8 hr/employee = 10 employees

Figure 4–2 Staffing decision for guest room cleaning (scheduling guest room attendants)

		Sunday		Monday		Tuesday		Wednesday		Thursday		Friday		Saturday	
Employee Name	Station	A.M.	P.M.	A.M.	P.M.	A.M.	P.M.	A.M.	P.M.	A.M.	P.M.	A.M.	P.M.	A.M.	P.M.
JoAnn Davis	Lobby	X		X		X		X		X					
Jeri Jones	Lobby						X		X		X	X		X	
Kathy Light	Lobby		X		X								X		X

Figure 4–3 Master staffing sheet

staffing sheet can be made only by the executive housekeeper. With the master staffing sheet as a guide, the assistant housekeeper of guest rooms makes up the weekly and daily work schedules according to occupancy and availability of the guest room attendants. These schedules are generally posted in a common employee area and are subject to change with changes in forecasted occupancy.

Turnover

Another variable that has an impact on scheduling is turnover. **Turnover** is the measure of the number of new employees and the number of employees who leave. The new employees can be new hires or rehired employees. Employees leave for a number of reasons, including layoffs, resignations, dismissals, and retirements. The turnover rate is especially high in the housekeeping department, with its large number of unskilled workers. The turnover rate is calculated by adding together all employees hired or rehired during a particular month and all employees separated from the payroll for any reason during that month (3):

$$[(\text{Hires/rehires} + \text{payroll separations}) \div \text{Average number of employees}] \times 100 = \text{Turnover rate } (\%)$$

For example, if the housekeeping department had an average of 50 employees during the month, but 2 were hired and 3 were laid off, the turnover would be 5. The turnover rate would be $5 \times 100 \div 50 = 10$ percent per month. If that rate persisted throughout the year, annual turnover would be 120 percent!

Guest Room Cleaning

Of all the housekeeper's responsibilities, the one that appears to be the simplest is the preparation of the guest rooms—all it seems to entail is cleaning the room, changing the linens, and making the bed. Because it appears to be so easy a task, guests will not tolerate an imperfectly made-up room. This attitude makes this function one of the most difficult in the hotel, as it is performed by a comparatively unskilled employee—the room attendant.

Each guest room attendant is assigned a **room attendant cart** to carry cleaning supplies, linens, and amenities for the guest room. Because these room attendant carts are left in the halls, visible to every guest, each morning they must be thoroughly cleaned before being equipped with linens and other supplies. In most hotels, each floor has a large housekeeping closet that houses the linen carts and supplies. The supplies, which are replenished each evening by a houseman or a runner, include sheets, pillowcases, bath towels, washcloths, and bath-mats. In addition, each floor closet contains a reserve of mattress pads, bedspreads, blankets, and shower curtains to replace any that have been stained, badly soiled, or otherwise damaged. A great number of other items are also needed to properly equip a guest room.

Housekeeping procedures typically require that checkouts (vacant rooms occupied the preceding night) be serviced first, unless a guest who is staying over requires early service.

Figure 4–4 identifies those minimal standards that should be considered when evaluating the housekeeping services in a full-service guest room. In brief, the procedure is as follows (see Appendix 4–1 for a more complete sample housekeeping routine):

1. Turn on all lights to determine whether there are any burned-out bulbs.
2. Turn off unnecessary lights.
3. Inspect the closets, dresser drawers, and the back of the bathroom door for any articles that might have been left behind.
4. Remove soiled linens from the bathroom.
5. Strip the bed(s), inspecting the spreads and blankets for stains, burns, or tears.
6. Remove and shake out sheets and pillowcases (guests have been known to store cash and other valuables overnight in their beds).
7. Carefully remove trash from the wastebasket to insure that valuables of the guest have not been mistakenly thrown away and that no glass or other items that might injure the room attendant are contained in the waste.
8. Empty ashtrays onto a newspaper, to guard against a lighted cigarette.
9. Clean and vacuum the room and bathroom.
10. Check the fixtures and faucets when cleaning the bathrooms to make sure that they are operating properly and have no sharp or broken edges.

Guest Room

- Bed linen and covers clean
- Bed in good condition
- Sheets fresh; no stains, holes, or rips; not damaged
- Bed pillows sufficient for bed size and in good condition
- Mattress in good condition; no tears in quilting or uneven areas
- Foot pocket made and neat
- Bed frame clean
- Room smells fresh and is free of odors
- Carpet/floor clean and well vacuumed
- Furnishings clean
- Drawers clean
- HVAC controls and vent clean
- Lamps clean
- Lamp seams face wall
- Walls clean
- Ceilings clean
- Wall hangings clean
- Baseboards clean
- Closets clean
- Windows clean
- Window treatment clean and in good repair
- Emergency instructions posted
- Door locks clean
- Telephone clean
- Telephone faceplate applied with correct room number
- Following materials are present and not dirty or worn:
  - Hotel services directory
  - Local telephone books
  - "Do not disturb" card
  - Stationery: single sheets and envelopes
  - In-room movie information where applicable
  - Room rate card posted
  - Signage posted indicating nonsmoking room if applicable
  - Room service menu
  - Doorknob menu
  - Ice bucket and glasses
  - Wine glasses (if minibar in room)

Guest Bathroom

- Free of odors
- Vanity clean, no hair
- Mirrors clean
- Sink and faucet clean, no hair
- Toilet clean
- Fixtures spot free
- Bath/shower clean, no hair
- Grout not discolored or stained
- Bath/shower curtain liner and/or door clean
- Floors clean, no hair
- Walls clean, no hair
- Ceiling clean, no hair
- Vents clean, no hair
- Doors and frames clean, no hair
- Towel bars/towel racks clean
- Guest bathroom amenities include the following:
  - Multiple rolls tissue
  - Facial tissue
  - Multiple glasses with caps
  - Amenities display tray
  - Facial soap
  - Shampoo or shampoo and conditioner
  - Deodorant soap
  - Mouthwash
  - Shower cap
  - Bath linen:
    - Washcloths
    - Hand towels
    - Bath towels
    - Bath mat

Figure 4–4 Evaluating housekeeping services in a full-service hotel guest room

The room attendant never moves a heavy piece of furniture or turns a mattress larger than a twin size. If the mattress is scheduled to be turned or if a piece of furniture needs to be moved, the room attendant turns to the houseman for help (no pun intended!). The key to the successful training of room attendants is establishing standardized cleaning routines that do not vary from day to day. (4)

As you have already learned, housemen also are directly involved in servicing the guest rooms. In addition to the daily cleaning performed by the guest room attendants, each room is given a thorough and **deep cleaning** by the housemen every three to eight weeks, depending on the established hotel policy. This periodic cleaning includes high wall dusting, cleaning the tile in the bathroom, dusting pictures, and vacuuming the drapes, blinds, sofas, cushions, and mattresses, as well as the carpet. Housemen also carry furniture to and from storerooms and from one guest room to another as needed.

In smaller hotels, housemen also may help set up a banquet room for a dinner, dance, or meeting and strip the room after the affair is over. Larger banquet and convention hotels have a separate department to do this task, with its own head houseman, who is directly responsible to the catering manager. One task formerly handled exclusively by housemen is shampooing rugs in the guest rooms, halls, and other public places. Many hotels give this time-consuming job to an outside contractor.

The final responsibility for the condition of the guest rooms rests with the inspector. In luxury hotels, there may be one inspector per floor, but it is more typical to find one inspector for three or more floors. It is also becoming more common for the assistant housekeepers to fulfill this responsibility. The assistant housekeeper also distributes room assignments and **floor master keys**, which are returned at the end of each day. They supervise, check, and approve the room attendants' work and make periodic inspections of the physical condition of all rooms on their floors for serious damage or deterioration requiring decorating or refurbishing. Any damage, such as leaking or broken faucets, out-of-order lamps, broken toilet seats, or improper operation of air conditioning units, is referred to the chief engineer for appropriate action.

Renovation is usually a top-management decision. The executive housekeeper makes the renovation request and, unless an interior decorator is hired, assists in the selection process, giving input on the colors of the paint, patterns for the upholstery, and so on. When a painting schedule is set up, the housemen are responsible for stripping the room and preparing it for the painters, who report to the chief engineer. Close cooperation and coordination between the executive housekeeper and chief engineer is necessary to keep to a minimum the amount of time that the room is out of order. In between paintings, members of the housekeeping staff, called wall washers, are assigned to keep the rooms clean and attractive.

Public Area Cleaning

Figure 4–5 identifies the minimal standards that should be considered when evaluating the housekeeping services in public areas of a full-service hotel guest room. The lobby cleaner is a houseman whose sole duty is to keep the lobby reasonably clean and in order during the day. Since the lobby is the most used public area in a hotel, this is a demanding job. In a large city hotel, thousands of people, both guests and nonguests (restaurant, bar, banquet, and convention guests; shop and concession customers; employees, visitors, and the general public), all congregate in or pass through the lobby. Without the constant attention of the lobby cleaner in picking up loose papers, cigarette stubs, and other litter, and cleaning the ashtrays and sand jars, the lobby would be in deplorable condition before the night cleaners arrived to clean it thoroughly.

Lobby and Banquet Area

- Carpet/flooring clean
- Wall and light fixtures clean
- Doors and frames clean
- Service entrance doors clean and closed
- Furnishings clean
- Telephones clean
- Walls clean
- Ceiling clean
- Plants/flowers dust free and in good condition
- Ashtrays/urns and trash cans clean
- Signage clean

Guest Corridors and Elevators

- Carpet/floor clean
- Wall and light fixtures clean
- Doors and frames clean
- Service entrance doors clean
- Interior windows clean
- Window treatments (drapes/blinds) in good repair
- Furnishings clean
- Walls clean
- Ceilings clean
- Baseboards clean (if applicable)
- Plants/flowers clean and in good condition
- Ashtrays/urns and trash cans clean
- Vending area signage clean and in good repair
- Vending/ice areas clean and in good repair
- All elevators clean

Public Restroom

- Restroom free of odors
- Floor clean (free of papers, no standing water)
- Commodes/urinals clean and spot free
- Sanitary seat covers are in each stall
- Sinks clean and spot free
- Interiors/vanities clean
- Soap dispensers filled
- Paper goods and supplies in adequate quantity
- Paper goods and supplies dispensers clean
- Trash receptacle not overflowing
- Lighting clean
- Walls clean
- Ceilings clean
- Doors clean

Figure 4–5 Evaluating housekeeping services in public areas of a full-service hotel guest room

Lobby cleaners play a critical part in maintaining a hotel's public appearance. This attendant is cleaning a crystal chandelier. (Courtesy of the Hospitality Industry Archives and Library, University of Houston, Texas.)

Inventory and Control

Maintenance and control of the linen supply is the key aspect of inventory and control in housekeeping. The linen room often has been called the heart of the housekeeping department. The executive housekeeper's office is either a part of the linen room or adjacent to it. The storerooms for reserve linen, cleaning, and other supplies is also in close proximity. The day linen room attendant counts and sorts the soiled linen, preparing it for the laundry. The night linen room attendant counts and distributes the clean linen and all supplies to the room attendant's storerooms on each floor. Washable uniforms for all hotel departments are generally issued from the linen room, and minor repairs are made on them by the seamstress, who also repairs drapes, curtains, and other linen products. Many employees are responsible for washing their own uniforms. Those requiring dry cleaning, although under the control of the room attendant, are usually cleaned, stored, and repaired by the house valet, who can be a concessionaire or an employee of the hotel. Linen inventory control and laundering are among the executive housekeeper's major responsibilities.

Overstocking can lead to waste and unnecessary expense, and understocking, to loss of time. If the room attendant does not call the linen room for additional supplies when he or she is short, understocking can even lead to guest complaints. It is the responsibility of top management, in cooperation with the housekeeping department, to establish an **operating par stock**, which is the number of items necessary to supply a room according to the hotel and/or brand standard for a specific number of days. The ideal level of operating par stock for room linen is five times the daily amount in use; this obviously depends on the number of beds and bathrooms in the hotel. This level allows for one set of linens in the rooms and one each in the laundry, the room attendants' floor closet, the linen room, and in transit. Few hotels have—or for that matter, can afford to have—that much linen in circulation. A factor of 3 to 3½, or even 2 to 2½, if the hotel has its own in-house laundry, is more common. Operating at these levels presents no problem, except during peak periods of occupancy, particularly during weekends and holidays. Commercial laundries usually provide 24-hour service, with pickup and delivery every day except Sunday and holidays. When a holiday falls on a Monday, as many now do, there are no deliveries of clean linen for two days. If the hotel is fortunate enough to have 100 percent occupancy over that weekend, the room attendant will have three complete changes of soiled room linen on Tuesday morning. Hotels with in-house laundry facilities can arrange for coverage on these holidays, but only on a costly overtime basis. Few executive housekeepers can truthfully say that their room attendants never had to leave a bathroom without its full supply of linens or a bed unmade until clean linens were delivered after a busy weekend or holiday. To avoid the outlay of funds needed for the initial setup and annual replacements, some hotels rent all their linen. Many that have their own bed, bath, and restaurant linen still rent uniforms for the room attendants, housemen, cleaners, and maintenance staff, and most items used by kitchen personnel, such as coats, aprons, caps, and dresses.

Establishing a **circulating par stock**, or the number of items that are part of the operating par but are in use and will be reused, for restaurant linens, which also is the housekeeper's responsibility, is more difficult. The highest turnover of guests during any one meal is usually in the coffee shop, but most coffee shops do not use linen tablecloths or napkins. The daily requirements for regular dining rooms can be estimated and a par can be established. Banquets pose a real problem, because functions vary greatly in size and requirements, not only in table setups but also in the color of the linens—one bride might want rose and another, light blue. Hotels must therefore have in stock a sufficient quantity of tablecloths and matching napkins, in at least three or four basic colors, to properly service the number of people that can be accommodated at any one time in their largest banquet room. The alternative is to rent them from a linen supply company as needed. Many hotels use a combination of the two methods, purchasing a smaller quantity of colored linens and renting when more are needed. (5)

In many hotels, the colored linens are not kept in circulation but are returned to the permanent storeroom after each use. This storeroom also holds all guest room and restaurant linens that are purchased but never put into use, but nevertheless are carried on a hotel's inventory and can become part of the circulating par stock.

Control of the reserve linen is very important. The storeroom must be securely locked, with access given to only authorized personnel; no items should be removed without a requisition approved by the room attendant. A **perpetual inventory system** should be in place, reflecting additions to the storeroom (purchases), removals from the storeroom (items issued to room attendants), and balance on hand. Frequent spot checks should be made by the linen room supervisor to verify the balance. Semiannually or annually, a physical count of every item in stock should be taken and compared to the perpetual inventory. A representative of the accounting department should be present to supervise the count and test-check the accuracy of the calculations in the perpetual inventory book, verifying opening balances, comparing purchases to vendors' bills, and comparing issues to approved requisitions.

Because linen represents a major operating expense, bulk buying reduces the unit cost, and since immediate deliveries are almost impossible to obtain, it is the normal procedure for the executive room attendant and the food and beverage manager in a hotel to estimate their annual requirements in advance and present them to the general manager for approval. When a decision has been made, an order is issued for the full quantity, with partial shipments arranged at convenient intervals.

Keeping track of the circulating linen is difficult, and with their busy schedules, room attendants have little time to do so. There are four ways in which linen can be taken out of circulation: (1) normal wear and tear, (2) improper use or carelessness in handling, (3) losses in the laundry, and (4) theft. The following paragraphs outline procedures that should be part of a hotel's normal operating routine for controlling the supply of linen in circulation. If serious shortages are uncovered through spot checks or periodic physical counts, these procedures should be reviewed and strengthened, if only through improving the employee training program and more active supervision of the daily routine.

Of the four causes for replacing linens, wear and tear is the only one that is unavoidable. After being used and washed over and over again, linens inevitably will wear out. A reasonably accurate estimate of the expected number of linens needing replacement for a given period may be established by calculating the average life expectancy of each article—the number of washes that linens can be put through before they wear out. The number may vary according to the quality of the linen and the commercial laundry used. The replacements required for any given period are calculated by dividing the total washes for the period by the wash use expectancy figure. The number of washes and the number of linens are both itemized on the laundry bills; to calculate the total, the accounts payable clerk extracts these figures from all invoices received during the period of interest (usually one month). For example, if a standard of 120 washes were established for double-size sheets and 2,400 were washed during the month, 20 would need to be replaced during that month (2,400 divided by 120). If this calculation is done every month and replacements are made as computed, the number in circulation should remain constant at the established par stock.

A second way that linens are removed from circulation is through improper use or carelessness in handling by either the hotel's employees or the hotel's guests. Some more common misuses of linens are as follows: using them in the kitchen to clean utensils, countertops, greasy stoves, and floor spills; using them in the dining room to pick up and wrap broken glasses or dishes; using them to clean floor spills and to wipe ashtrays containing lit cigarettes or burning ashes; and using them to shine shoes. Napkins so used must be discarded, because they are too badly stained for regular use. In the guest rooms, room attendants might use face towels instead of rags to dust and clean the guest rooms if they are out of rags. Also, linens can catch and tear on the sharp edges of the soiled-linen chutes if the room attendant tries to pack too many in at one time. Training is a never-ending task, requiring constant repetition of proper procedures for both the staff and supervisors.

Losses in a laundry should be the easiest to ascertain. To check against the number of pieces charged for on the laundry bill, most executive housekeepers instruct their linen room personnel to carefully count and record the clean linen as it comes from the laundry. However, many do not undertake the much less pleasant task of counting the dirty linen before it is sent out. Before dirty linen can be counted, it must be sorted by type, a tedious and even a difficult job. Linens with minor tears must be removed and turned over to the seamstress for repairs, as minor tears can develop into major ones in the wash; such articles may be discarded by the laundry. Another difficulty in keeping track of linens in the laundry is that the batch that is sent out is rarely the same as the batch that comes back the next day. Some items may be held back for rewashing or proper folding, or merely because they were not finished in time.

An accurate count and record of all linens going to and from the laundry must be kept, both to control shortages and to avoid double billing. To record an accurate count requires only a simple work sheet. Across the top, a list is made of all the sizes and types of linens. Two columns are needed for each item, one for soiled and the other for clean linen. Each day the linen supervisor enters the number of items sent out and the number returned. At the end of each month, the work sheet is sent to the accounting department to be totaled and reviewed by the controller and the executive housekeeper and, if serious shortages are shown, by the general manager. The laundry should also be notified of any shortages, and an attempt should be made to collect for them. The actual settlement is typically a negotiated amount, possibly 20 to 50 percent of the total claimed by the hotel, usually covering a period of six months to one year.

Torn, badly stained, or poorly ironed pieces are all too often part of the clean linen deliveries. Because the room attendants are the ones who see the clean linens when they make up the rooms, their role in quality control is essential. Many executive housekeepers have had guests complain that a bed appears to have been slept in because poorly ironed sheets were used to make it up. Timely deliveries are also important, particularly for a hotel operating with a limited par circulating linen inventory. Unfortunately, laundry employees are no different from hotel employees; they need the same constant training and supervision. This is out of the hands of the executive housekeeper, who can only make the laundry's top management aware of deficiencies in the quality of the service rendered and keep doing so until the desired results are obtained.

Losses due to theft generally are accepted as a normal operating expense in many businesses, and hotels are no exception. Controls and surveillance can minimize these losses, but they cannot be avoided completely. Many guests like to return home with souvenirs, which can be anything not nailed down in the guest rooms, public areas, or restaurants. In theory, stopping the souvenir hunter is easy: just inspect the room after the guest checks out but before he or she leaves the hotel. In practice, this is virtually impossible in most hotels and can lead to ill will and passing blame to the employees. Room attendants should be trained to report to their inspector any major missing items (blankets, spreads, pictures) and any damage to the guest room. If the loss or damage is serious, it should be reported also to the general manager, who can then take the necessary action.

Guests are not singularly responsible for the loss of hotel property. Employee theft is also a problem. However, it is easier to control, or at least to minimize, these losses. The most effective steps are the use of time cards;

employee package passes; inspection of the contents of all packages brought into or taken out of the hotel by employees; a separate employee entrance/exit through the timekeeper's office; and preventing employees from loitering in the hotel before or after working hours. Because of the number of employees involved, most large hotels require the housekeeping staff to punch two time cards, one at the timekeeper's station as they enter and leave the hotel, and the other in or near the linen room, as they start and finish their shifts.

EMPLOYEE SAFETY

Employees are a company's most valuable asset. Hotel accidents and injuries in all departments have a very serious impact on the hotel's ability to offer adequate service to its guests. This is particularly true of the housekeeping department because of the large number of employees involved in keeping guests happy. The Occupational Safety and Health Act (OSHA), which covers most of the employees working today in the United States, makes it mandatory for every employer to keep the place of business free from any hazards that might cause injury to an employee. In 1989, the U.S. National Institute for Occupational Safety and Health (NIOSH) conducted a study of large hotels and determined the most frequent types of injuries to employees occurring in hotels (see Figure 4–6). The five elements involved in most accidents are:

1. A harmful agent such as a caustic chemical
2. Contact with extreme temperature or a burn
3. An unsafe act, such as a room attendant hurrying from the housekeeping closet to a guest room with her hands full of clean glasses for all of the guest rooms on the floor
4. An unsafe condition, such as a water spill in the laundry
5. Personal factors, such as a room attendant thinking his rubber-soled shoes will not slip on the wet floor
6. **HAZCOMM**, or Hazard Communication Standards have also been developed by OSHA and must be communicated by employers about possible hazards related to chemicals they use on the job.

Responsibility, Reputation, and Quality of Service

Hotel management has a moral obligation to provide a safe, secure place for its guests and employees. It also has a legal obligation to meet national, state, and local safety regulations applicable to the hotel industry. The image of a hotel can be severely damaged by one major incident. Accident prevention enhances guests' perceptions of comfort, safety, and security and results

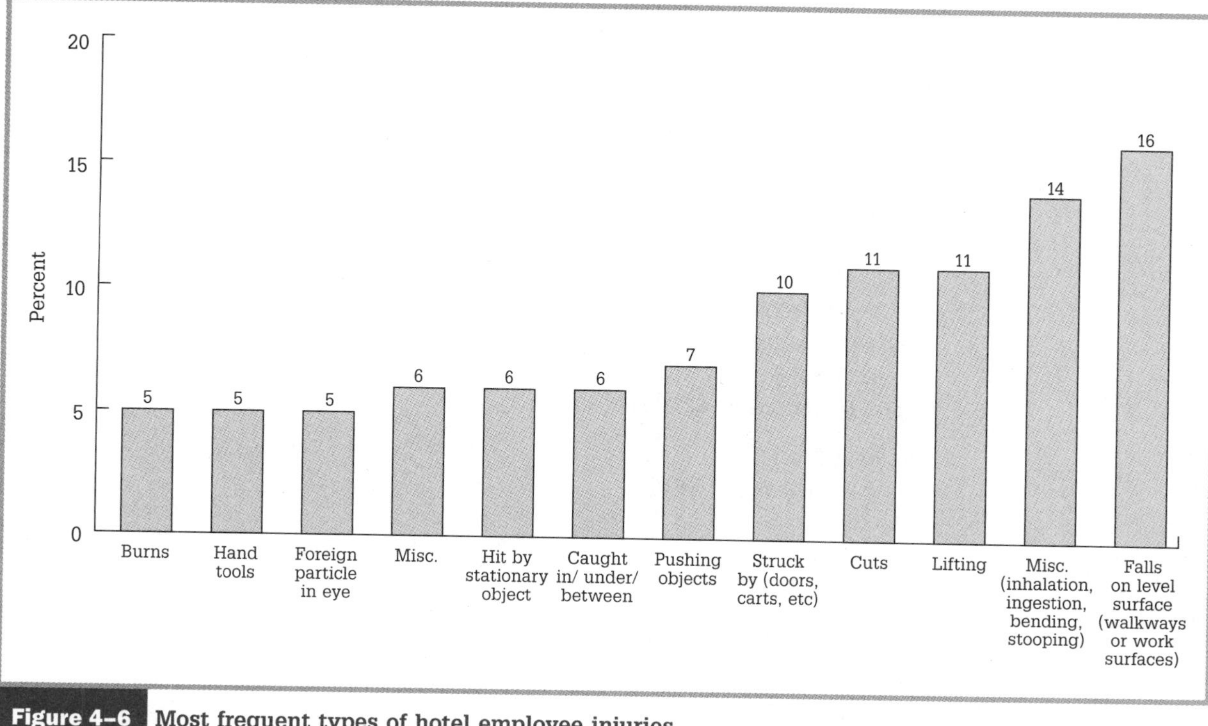

Figure 4–6 **Most frequent types of hotel employee injuries**

in better business. Accidents adversely affect a hotel's ability to serve its customers and, thus, reduce its quality.

Economics Increasing numbers of workers' compensation claims increase insurance costs and reduce hotel profits. Many unsafe acts are carried out without consequences. For example, for every 330 unsafe incidents of the same type, no injury might occur in 300 instances, minor injury might occur in 29, and a major injury might occur in 1 instance. Because no one can predict which of the incidents will result in injuries, accident prevention must be incorporated within the busy activities of serving the guests. For example, if a member of the housekeeping department slips on standing water in the laundry, falls against a storage cabinet, and breaks a shoulder, the direct costs are the employee's hospitalization and absence from work. However, these are not the only costs involved (see Figure 4–7).

Accident Prevention Injuries in the housekeeping department can be minimized by carefully training room attendants and others to be alert to hazards and observant in hazardous situations. For example, all guest room attendants should wear

Direct Costs

Medical:

X-ray	$150
Physician	500
Hospital	300
Drugs	50
Therapy	150
Miscellaneous	200
Total medical	$1,350

Compensation (for six weeks' pay) at 40 hr/week × $6.50/hr at the rate of 0.666 (66.6 percent) = $1,039.00

Total Direct Costs $2,379.60

Indirect Costs

Patient's lost salary = $521.00

Supervisory time on this case might include:

At the scene of the accident	0.5 hr
Going to the hospital with employee	0.5 hr
Waiting at the hospital	3.0 hr
Visiting the hospital during second day	1.0 hr
Investigating the accident	2.0 hr
Completing the forms	2.0 hr
Training a replacement during six weeks	15.0 hr
Calling employee, insurance company, etc.	3.0 hr
Total	27.0 hr × $9/hr = $243.00

Lost production time:

Employees assisting at the accident
Employees talking about the injured during the six weeks
Less efficient new employee
Lack of total reduced efficiency when the injured employee returns to work
= 53 hours × $6.50/hr = $344.50

Miscellaneous:

Flowers, cost of gas and mileage for hospital visits by company and employee's wife
Employee's babysitting costs
Clerical costs for processing forms
= $151.00

Total Indirect Costs $1,259.50

Total Direct and Indirect Costs $3,639.00

Figure 4–7 Costs associated with a hotel employee injury

rubber-soled, closed-toe, low-heeled shoes and should not wear jewelry or loose-fitting clothing that might snag on objects in the room. In training, the safe and proper use of the various chemicals should be emphasized. For example, room attendants must know not to mix bleach and other chemicals. Another example is the proper use of linen carts. Linen carts should be packed with the heaviest linens on the bottom and should not be overloaded. Carts should be pushed slowly, and hands should be placed on the handles, not on the side of the cart. Earlier in the chapter (and in Appendix 4–1), we discussed the safe cleaning of ashtrays and disposal of trash.

In this chapter, we touched briefly on the problem of laundry loss through theft. In the next chapter, we will cover other types of theft, as well as loss prevention and security.

Summary

The housekeeping department, which is essential to the successful operation of every department in a hotel, may have more employees than any other department. The head of the housekeeping department, the executive housekeeper, is responsible for inspecting all public and guest areas, employee training, inventory and control, and reporting and record keeping.

In scheduling the staff, the executive housekeeper must have a knowledge of forecasts, occupied rooms, checkouts, and turnover. If a hotel is adequately staffed with properly trained employees, the activities of the housekeeping department become a series of routines that provide hotel guests with a high level of quality and service.

Inventory and control is particularly important in handling the linen inventory. If improperly handled, the damage and/or loss of linens can become a considerable expense. Employee injuries, with their direct and indirect costs, can also result in considerable cost to a hotel. A well-organized and consistently implemented safety program is particularly important for the housekeeping department, with its large number of unskilled employees.

References

1. Robert J. Martin, *Professional Management of Housekeeping Operations*, 3rd ed. (New York: John Wiley & Sons, Inc., 1998), p. 23.
2. Madelin Schneider and Georgina Tucker, "Who Does What in Housekeeping," in *The Professional Housekeeper*, 4th ed. (New York: John Wiley & Sons, Inc., 1998), p. 60.
3. Lester R. Bittel, *What Every Supervisor Should Know*, 3rd ed. (New York: McGraw-Hill Book Company, 1974), p. 437.
4. William S. Gray and Salvatore C. Liquori "Housekeeping," *Hotel and Motel Management and Operations*, 3rd ed. (New York: Prentice Hall, 1994), p. 138.
5. Gray and Liquori, *Hotel and Motel*, p. 149.

6. Margaret M. Kappa, Aleta Nitschke, and Patricia B. Schappert, "Safety and Security," *Managing Housekeeping Operations* (East Lansing, MI: Educational Institute, American Hotel and Motel Association, 1990), p. 140.

Review Questions

1. If a housekeeping department with 25 employees hired two new housekeepers in one month, what would the turnover percentage be for the month? If this rate continued similarly for the remainder of the year, what would the annual turnover percentage be?
2. I give the guest rooms a general cleaning every three weeks, including high wall dusting, cleaning the bathroom tile, and vacuuming the drapes, blinds, and sofas. Who am I?
3. Outline the tasks that a guest room attendant needs to do in order to properly clean a guest room.
4. Describe the type of person that should be recruited for the position of housekeeper.
5. Describe a plan that might minimize loss of linens due to actions of employees and guests.

Activities

1. Interview an executive housekeeper in a hotel in your local community and describe the primary responsibilities of the job as related to you in the interview.
2. Compare the organizational chart in Figure 4–1 with that of a housekeeping department in a hotel in your local community. How are they different? How are they similar?
3. Visit a local hotel and inspect a guest room. Use the checklist provided in Figure 4–4 to evaluate the condition of the room. After your inspection, develop a routine for cleaning the guest room. Compare your routine with that utilized by the local hotel.
4. Evaluate the condition of the public areas of a local hotel, using the checklist provided in Figure 4–5. What improvements could be made?
5. Interview a local executive housekeeper and discuss the linen control policy for the hotel. How does it compare with what was described in the chapter?

Appendix 4-1

Sample Housekeeping Routines

Checking Rooms

1. Before knocking on the door, check whether the maid lock-out pin is showing in the doorknob (indicating that the room is double-locked from inside). If it is showing, mark the room as occupied and recheck it at 12 noon. The same applies to doors where there is a "Do Not Disturb" card on the outside doorknob. If the "Do Not Disturb" card or the lock-out pin is still in place at 12 noon, notify your supervisor immediately. He or she will take the proper steps to find out when the guest wants the room serviced. Also report any strange odors, sounds, or other irregularities you observe either in the guest rooms or anywhere in your working area.
2. To enter: if there is no pin showing and no "Do Not Disturb" sign, knock lightly with your fingers, *never your key*. When a guest answers your knock, tell the guest that you are the maid and that you are taking a room check. Ask the guest when he or she wants the room serviced. The guest may give you a time or may reply that he or she is checking out. Report any checkouts to the housekeeping office, along with the time, if known.
3. If a guest has his or her belongings in the room but has not used the room to sleep, mark your work sheet with the symbol "Sb." This situation is called a "sleep out."
4. *Even if you believe a room to be vacant or checked out, be sure to knock*. If there is no answer, quietly unlock the door and enter. When you have made absolutely sure that there is no baggage in the room, closet, or bathroom, mark the room vacant.
5. Once you have completed checking your assigned area, return your check sheet to your supervisor.

6. Go to the linen room and check your cart to be sure you have sufficient linen and cleaning supplies. Check your work sheet to determine in which of your rooms you should start.
7. Make up rooms that have been checked out first, so that they may be resold, unless a guest in another room has requested immediate service.

Making a Room

1. When entering a vacant room, leave the door wide open, hang your maid sign on the doorknob, and leave it that way until you have finished. If there is a guest in the room who requests that the door be closed, be sure and place your maid sign on the corridor doorknob *outside*.
2. Turn on every light to check for burned-out lights. Replace needed bulbs and turn unnecessary lights off.
3. Take a *good look*! Report any damage to furniture or equipment immediately. In a checked out or vacant room, look through all drawers, closets, and doorknobs for any articles that may have been left behind. If you find some, call them in to the housekeeping department immediately. It might be possible to return these items to the guest before the guest leaves. If not, put them in a bag marked with date, time, and room number, and give them to your supervisor, who will see that they are sent to the housekeeping department and filed in the lost and found.
4. Open window draperies and remove empty bottles and glasses.
5. In an occupied room, hang all articles of clothing found on the bed, chairs, or furniture neatly in the closet, making sure that all hangers are on the rod in the same direction and that the front of all suits, dresses, coats, and so on, are facing the same way.
6. Printed material, newspapers, magazines, and any other books and papers, if they are not in the wastebasket, should be placed neatly on the desk, dresser, or table.
7. Empty partially filled glasses found in the room and in the bathroom into the toilet and flush the bowl. If there is a room service tray or cart in the room, take it to the service area and phone room service to pick it up.
8. Once you have made sure that there are no burning cigars or cigarettes, empty the ashtrays before putting them in with the trash (see number 7 in the next section). Never throw cigar or cigarette butts in the toilet bowl (they will stop it up). Then clean the ashtrays.

9. Shake blankets and covers over the bed so that any clothing or articles left in the bed won't be lost, reading glasses won't get broken, and so on. Do the same with the top sheet and then spread it on the floor. Pull the bottom sheet, pillowcases, and all soiled bath linens and put them in the middle of the sheet. Gather up the entire bundle and put it in the soiled linen bag on your cart. If the sheets are stained, rinse them out in cold water in the bathroom sink and add them to the regular soiled linen. Bring fresh linen from the housekeeping cart.

Cleaning the Bathroom

1. *Bathroom fixtures.* While waiting for the bed to air, start cleaning the bathroom. First, wash the toilet seat, back, and sides of the entire fixture with warm water and detergent and *wipe them dry with a soft cloth to prevent water spotting.* Next, put cleanser in the toilet bowl and leave it there until you are finished with the rest of the bathroom. Clean the light fixtures and door frames. Open the medicine cabinet; clean the inside walls, door, and shelves with a damp cloth and *wipe them dry.* Do the same with any recessed area or open shelf. Clean the bathroom mirror and mirror frame. *Wipe them dry.* Clean the soap dish and glass rack. Pay particular attention to the washbowl and counter, making sure the chrome taps and faucets are polished and free of water spots.
2. *Bathroom walls.* Wipe down tile with a scrub cloth and polish it with a soft cloth. Do the same with the glass shower doors, paying particular attention to the chrome trim. Test and polish the showerhead, faucets, and drain. Scrub and polish grab bars, the soap dish, and the tub. Release the clothesline if there is nothing on it (do not let it snap back).
3. *Toilet and bathroom floor.* Before cleaning the floor, flush the clean toilet bowl, making sure the toilet flushes properly. Using your bowl mop, swish the water around the entire bowl, paying particular attention to the area just under the lip of the rim.
4. *Floor.* Remove the rug, bathroom scale, hamper, stool, and wastebasket from under the counters. With clean, warm water and detergent, using a sponge and scrub cloth, wash the floor and dry it while it is damp with a scrub cloth. Always work from the back of the bathroom toward the door. Keep your rubber mat outside the bathroom door. As you exit the bathroom, place your pail on this mat so that dripping water or wet pail bottoms won't damage or spot the carpeting.
5. *Closet and preliminary sweeping.* While your bathroom floor is drying, sweep (broom) lightly the carpet in the corners of the room and

the baseboards (areas that your electric sweeper won't pick up). Sweep the corners and the baseboard as well; dust the closet shelf, hangers, and rod daily, and clean it with a damp cloth once a week. There should be 12 hangers in each closet—four ladies' and eight men's. Be sure two laundry bags, with lists attached, are on the closet shelf. Remove all hangers that are not standard equipment. Vacuum the closet floor, wipe the door, turn off the light, and close the door.

6. *Drawers.* If the room is vacant, open all dresser drawers and wipe them with a damp cloth. If the room is occupied, check only the desk drawer to determine if supplies are needed. The desk should contain the following items: stationery folder, ballpoint pen, room service menus, house directory, telephone directory, special information, notepad, ashtrays, and matches (in a smoking room only).
7. *Trash basket.* Dump the trash basket on an open sheet of newspaper. Never put your hands in the basket, as you run the risk of cutting your hands on broken glass or razor blades. Wipe baskets and reline them with trash bags.
8. *Dusting.* Starting at the entrance door, dust the door and door frame, pictures, lamps (shades, bases, and bulbs), lamp cord, baseboard, and the furniture in all areas of the room. Use polish where and when instructed. Wipe the telephone mouthpiece and receiver with a cloth wrung dry in a mild detergent solution. *Wipe them dry.* Note and report any frayed or defective wiring and broken wall plugs.

Making the Bed

1. Make sure that bedspreads are clean and not stained, spotted, or frayed. Fold any discolored or torn linens with the defective area showing, and take them to the linen room when you finish your shift.
2. Divide the bottom sheet evenly with the wide hem at the head of the bed, *right side up*; tuck the sheet securely and smoothly under the mattress at the head of the bed, and make mitered or tight-fitting corners. Tuck in one side, making sure the sheet is all the way in, without pulling on the sheet. At the bottom of the bed, taking the width evenly in both hands, *pull* as tightly as possible, miter the corners, and tuck in one side. On the remaining side, pull the sheet as tightly as possible and tuck in, mitering the upper corner. The sheet should be smooth, even, and tight enough to "bounce back" if it is sat upon.
3. Put the top sheet on evenly, leaving at least 8 inches of the wide hem *right side down.* (The finished hem will then show when it is turned back over the blankets at the head of the bed.)

4. The beds should be made up with white blankets. Extra blankets, put in the room only at the guest's request, should be green. When guests have checked out, the green blankets must be returned to the linen room. Place a white blanket on the bed, leaving the top about 6 inches from the top of the mattress. Now put on the blanket cover. Be sure it is straight and the top is even with the top of the blanket. Turn back the top sheet over the blanket and the blanket cover, making sure they lie straight across the bed.
5. Next, holding the bottom sheet with your left hand so that it won't come loose, turn all your bedding under at the bottom at one time, and miter or tightly fold the corners, making sure they are tucked in as far as possible. *Tuck the bedding in at the sides.*
6. Place the spread on the bed evenly, making sure it just misses the floor at the foot and both of the sides. Single beds should have one of two types of pillows: 100 percent white goose down (blue ticking) or 50 percent white goose down and 50 percent goose feathers (blue ticking, different pattern). Double beds should have two of each type. Non-allergic foam or latex pillows should also be available at the guest's request. If latex pillows are requested, put the other pillows on the closet shelf. When the guest checks out, the latex pillows should be returned to the linen room. Put the pillows in place, hem side to the outside of the bed and seam to the headboard. Cover the pillows neatly with the spread. With practice, this entire process should not take you more than five minutes.

Completing Work on the Bathroom

1. The bathroom floor should now be dry. Replace the rug, wastebasket, hamper, and scale. Be sure the floor is not wet when you replace the scale, as this will make rust marks, which are very difficult to remove. Make sure that the following articles are in the bathroom: four bath towels; three hand towels; four facecloths; one wastebasket; one bath mat; one hamper; two large soaps; two small soaps; one bath scale; one retractable clothesline; one box of facial tissue; two rolls of toilet tissue (one on roll, one in cabinet); one stool. If everything is in order, close the bathroom door.
2. Vacuum, including under the beds and behind the furniture. If anything is moved, be sure to put it back in its proper place. Vacuum from the far side of the room toward the door.
3. Check the electric alarm clock; be sure it is working and shows the correct time. Test the electric shoe polisher.

4. Check both the radio and television to be sure they are working; however, never play either while making up a room. If they are on when you go in, turn them off.
5. *Turn the thermostat to 72 degrees.*

Checking Your Work

Are the lamp shades straight; are seams to the rear? Are the bedspreads straight and even? Are the drapes in their correct position? Is the furniture all back in its proper position? Is there a fresh pack of matches with each ashtray? Are there sufficient ashtrays? If you have answered "Yes" to all of these questions, your work is done. Close the door and make sure it is locked. Mark your work sheet. Your supervisor will then inspect the room.

Chapter 5

Loss Prevention and Security

CHAPTER OUTLINE

Guest safety and security are an integral part of the hospitality industry. Another term for safety is "loss prevention." A loss prevention and security program is also a means of protecting a hotel's resources—both people and property—from accidental loss, damage, or injury. With the exception of large convention hotels, loss prevention and security was not part of the hotel departmental structure until the 1960s. However, by the mid-1970s, most hotels either had established loss prevention and security programs or were contracting with outside firms to provide full-time security. (1)

LOSS PREVENTION

Guest Room Safety

Generally, guests suffer the same types of injuries as the staff (see Table 5–1). A good safety program can prevent the most common types of injuries to both employees and guests. One that involves all employees can have a great impact on public safety.

The most common accident that guests have is a slip or a fall in the bathroom, particularly in the bathtub or shower. This occurs not only because the area is slippery, soapy, and wet, but also because the shower handle, towel rack, or soap dish sometimes do not remain fixed when the guest grabs them for support.

Table 5–1 Sources of Guest Injuries in a Hotel

Bathrooms	Tubs and showers
	Sharp hardware
Guest room	Unstable objects
	Unidentified glass
	Rough edges
	Defective carpeting or flooring
	Defective furniture
Public and internal areas	Damaged carpeting or flooring
	Defective lighting
	Broken glass
	Water on hard-surface flooring
	Elevators
	Obstacles in passageways
Public and external areas	Defective lighting
	Cracks in sidewalks and curbs
	Water, ice, and snow
	Trash on walking surfaces

In the past, chemical etching of the tub's ceramic surface was recommended in order to provide a firmer grip. However, laboratory tests have indicated that this is of little value when the tub is wet or coated with a slight soap residue. Because of the potential for tripping on their edges, rubber bath mats contribute to falls and should not be used. Sticky sprays, good only for one shower or bath, are impractical for hotel use.

Although safety strips are not appreciated by some guests, who feel that they are unsanitary or can collect bacteria, they are the only known practical solution for tub surfaces. Negative reactions can be reduced by properly cleaning them, periodically replacing them, and selecting attractive colors and designs.

Alerting the guests to hazards by printing safety messages on soap wrappers, urging guests to be careful of falls in the bathroom and explaining that abrasive strips have been installed to promote safety, also may assist in minimizing the risk of a fall.

The installation of sturdy soap holders and grab bars is also important. Soap holders should do two things: (1) allow drainage and (2) keep the soap from sliding out. They should be fabricated and installed to withstand a 300-pound pull or push from either direction. Soap holders that do not meet these requirements should be phased out.

The next most common accidents are cuts received on sharp metal shower edges, burns from hot water, and bumps and bruises involving children. Some guest accidents happen because a guest is unfamiliar with the hotel surroundings. Guest accidents also may occur because of unstable televisions, unidentified glass doors, rough furniture edges, tripping hazards (oversize bedspreads, dangling extension cords, etc.), defective furniture, and loose furniture parts.

These accidents suggest the need for consistent vigilance in two departments—housekeeping and engineering. The executive housekeeper should encourage room attendants to look actively for potential hazards as they clean and to suggest safety improvements. As you learned in the last chapter, the housekeeping department is responsible for replacing torn linen; housekeeping staff should also be on the lookout for oversize bedspreads, broken or loose furniture, frayed cords, or other unsafe conditions in the guest rooms. Cords should be secured or positioned out of the major lanes of traffic in the room. Room attendants also should check for loose, damaged, buckled, or frayed carpeting as they vacuum. Faulty lighting, burned out bulbs, trash, uneven floor surfaces, loose tiles, and cracked plate glass are other hazards.

The **engineering department** must establish standards for safety and must develop a system to identify, log, and correct emergency and nonemergency situations. For example, the engineering department should make sure that all large panes of glass are marked with safety decals and that all identified defects are taken care of promptly.

Safety in Public Areas

Injuries occurring where guests congregate are primarily falls due to loose carpets, separated seams, poor lighting, ice and water, and tripping hazards, such as vacuum cleaners, carts, and cords.

Water and ice spills on uncarpeted floors should be cleaned up immediately. Warning signs must be used while floors are being mopped in public areas. Rubber runners both inside and outside the lobby in rainy or snowy weather can reduce slipping hazards.

Elevator safety is also essential. Establishing an inspection schedule for elevator safety maintenance and putting "Out-of-Order" signs on or near elevator doors on each floor at the first sign of elevator trouble are important steps in maintaining guest safety.

Obstacles must be removed from passageways and attendants' carts, and other obstructions must be kept as near the hallway walls as possible. All personnel should be on the alert for people in front if they are pushing a cart. Ladders, toolboxes, and other equipment must be removed immediately after repair work is finished to avoid creating additional hazards.

Most guest accidents out-of-doors involve falls. Typical accidents include tripping over curbs; stumbling in holes, cracks, or rough areas of pavement; and slipping on ice or snow. The engineering department can prevent many of these accidents by replacing burned-out bulbs immediately; repairing damaged pavement, sidewalks, and curbing as quickly as possible, and clearly marking those areas that need attention; keeping outside areas clean and free of trash; and clearing ice and snow as soon as possible.

Safety in Banquet Areas

Many accidents in banquet areas happen because preparation for such a function involves many critical steps in a very short period of time. The major types of accidents in banquet areas are falls over carpeting and chairs. Other types of accidents include falls off platforms, down stairs, and over wires, and on food or liquid spills. Figure 5–1 provides a safety checklist that should be used after a banquet area is prepared, before the guests arrive.

Swimming Pool Safety

Accidents in the hotel swimming area include slipping on wet tile; head injuries due to diving into the shallow end of the pool; drowning; cuts from broken beverage glasses on pool steps and sharp metal edges on railings; and allergic reactions to chlorine. Good housekeeping practices for the pool area include proper cleaning, posting and enforcement of safety rules, prompt repair, and regular maintenance. A safety option is to employ a trained and certified staff of lifeguards. This option provides for consistent cleaning, enforcement, and repair of the swimming pool.

Loss Prevention Committee

Loss control is the development of standards and procedures that are designed to protect the guests and the assets of the hotel from unnecessary loss. A key component of loss control is a loss prevention committee. The

- ☐ Check carpeting and rubber runners frequently for worn or frayed areas, curled edges, buckles, and seam separations.
- ☐ Treat linoleum and tile with nonskid cleansers and waxes; inspect chairs periodically for "metal fatigue" at the joints, missing nails and screws, protruding bolts, and severely worn seats.
- ☐ Check platforms and that stair platforms are placed against the wall, with no gaps, and that portable platform sections are set together carefully so that there are no separations between them.
- ☐ Examine temporary stairs for wear and signs of damage.
- ☐ Stairs with three or more risers should have a handrail on at least one side.
- ☐ Tape down loose wires and cords.
- ☐ Check glassware before use for breakage and contamination.
- ☐ Position carts where they won't become a hazard.
- ☐ Do not overload trays.
- ☐ Wipe up spilled food immediately.
- ☐ Servers should wear low-heeled, rubber-soled footwear.

Figure 5–1 **Banquet room safety checklist**

responsibilities of the **loss prevention committee** include, but are not limited to, a review of past accidents and security problems; an evaluation of present hazards and security problems, and development of policies and procedures to control them; and prevention of future hazards through attention to employee suggestions and new technology. See Table 5–2 for a more complete list of responsibilities. It is important that a cross section of employees participate in the committee's monthly meetings and that the committee have management authority. The committee should include at least five members, each of who is a representative from each of the following categories: management, supervisory personnel, and hourly employees (see Table 5–3).

In the interest of safety program coordination, the general managers of larger properties often appoint one committee member as a safety manager—usually the chief engineer or director of security. The selection should be based on organizational and technical skill, as well as availability.

The most important function of the safety manager is to be acquainted with all required codes, laws, and regulations in order to ensure complete compliance throughout the property.

Committee meetings should be limited to one hour, and an agenda should be prepared and distributed in advance to ensure that the meeting is well organized and productive. As an ongoing follow-up procedure, each member of the loss prevention committee should communicate pertinent information to superiors and employees.

Table 5–2 Functions of the Loss Prevention Committee

Review past accidents and security incidents, and develop corrective actions and follow up.
Provide overall guidance and direction to the hotel's loss control and prevention program.
Identify existing hazards and security problems peculiar to the hotel and implement policies and procedures to control them.
Review reasonable employee and guest suggestions regarding safety and security suggestions, and develop plans for possible implementation.
Monitor inspection reports to ensure that corrective action is taken promptly.
Participate in monthly meetings to discuss accident prevention, safety and security problems, and inspection reports.
Promote safety awareness programs for employees.
Implement safety training programs for employees.
Evaluate new as well as existing facilities, equipment, or procedures for safety concerns prior to use, purchase, or implementation for accident potential.
Establish standards for safe operating procedures for existing equipment and equipment to be purchased in the future.
Maintain committee activity records in a three-ring binder.

A successful loss prevention and control program depends on full commitment from management. If the general manager actively participates in loss prevention and control, prevention, other employees will follow suit. It is the general manager's responsibility to integrate safety, security, and property conservation into all areas of hotel operation.

The department head or supervisor is responsible for implementing a loss prevention and control program. Depending on the size of the hotel, the

Table 5–3 Loss Prevention Committee Membership

Position	Duties
General manager	Chairs meetings
Human resources department	Keeps employee accident records
Assistant manager	Keeps guest safety and accident records
Chief engineer	Keeps maintenance records
Director of security	Keeps hazard reports
Executive housekeeper	Keeps maintenance records
Food and beverage manager	Keeps hazard reports
Controller	Keeps record of claims paid
Secretary	Takes minutes
Insurance representative or outside consultant	Keeps claims information
One or two employees selected monthly	Bring awareness of employee concerns to management

department head or supervisor may be the only management-level person dealing with employees on a daily basis. This makes the supervisor the most knowledgeable person about employees' attitudes, work habits, and equipment use, and gives him or her the best opportunity to observe employees in action. Like the general manager, the supervisor must demonstrate commitment to the loss prevention and control program in order to implement it successfully.

Hotel Inspection

To keep guest and employee accidents to a minimum, it is essential to detect unsafe actions and conditions in advance. You learned in Chapter 4 that inspectors in the housekeeping department perform daily inspections of the guest rooms. While this is not necessary in every department, a department head or a supervisor in each department of the hotel should perform inspections of their areas at least once a month.

An **inspection** should include the physical structure (floors, doorways, etc.); equipment in the laundry and kitchen areas; power tools in the engineering department; cleaning and transportation equipment in the housekeeping department; observation of any unsafe work practices or poor work habits by employees; and conditions of all public areas, such as lobbies, function areas, and so on.

The department heads conduct inspections with a checklist developed by the department and approved by the safety and security committee. The checklist should emphasize the high accident areas of housekeeping, food and beverage, and engineering. Typically, the checklist focuses on tips for the safe operation of equipment; proper lifting; keeping the working area clean; wiping up spills; wearing safety equipment; sanitation; careful packing of moving equipment; and tripping hazards. A tips list should be developed for each group of employees that includes food service; food preparation; housekeeping; banquet service; stewarding; laundry; engineering; receiving; parking; bell staff; door staff; front desk; and clerical areas. Upon completion of the monthly inspection, each department should begin correcting the identified hazards, and the checklist should be submitted to the safety and security committee for follow-up purposes.

Accident Investigation

An accident can be defined as an unforeseen and unplanned event or circumstance. Although every accident may not result in an injury, accidents stop the work flow and have some economic impact on the hotel's business. The purpose of an accident investigation is to examine the cause of an accident and to prevent the occurrence of similar incidents in the future. Each accident should be treated as a signal that the potential exists for greater damage or injury and should be investigated thoroughly.

Accident investigation also demonstrates management's concern for guest and employee safety; pinpoints areas in current operations or safety

- **Who** is responsible for reporting an accident?
- **What** training should department heads and supervisors receive in for an accident investigation?
- **Where** can proper forms be obtained?
- **When** should employees notify their supervisors of accidents?
- **Where** can proper forms be obtained?
- **Why** is the timely and proper handling of an accident important?
- **How** should the accident data be reported and used at safety and security loss prevention and control committee meetings?

Figure 5–2 **Questions an accident investigation and reporting policy should answer**

programs that need revision or strengthening, and provides education regarding safety. All hotels should have a written policy regarding accident investigation and reporting. Figure 5–2 provides an overview of the questions such a policy should be able to answer.

An accident investigation should be completed within 24 hours, when the facts are still fresh in the minds of those involved, witnesses haven't had time to influence each other, the physical conditions are unchanged, and corrective action can be initiated to prevent others from being injured. The only exception to this 24-hour rule would be if a person has been injured and needs immediate medical attention or is too emotionally upset to discuss the incident. If the accident is severe, the hotel's insurance representative should be advised immediately.

When conducting an accident investigation, the investigator, who usually is the department head or supervisor, should keep several points in mind:

1. Let the injured party tell the story.
2. Take the injured party back to the scene of the accident.
3. Determine what the injured party was doing just before and at the time of the accident.
4. Although verbal reenactment of the accident can be valuable, never allow anyone to repeat an unsafe act physically.
5. Avoid placing or accepting blame.

While allowing the participants in the investigation to talk freely, keep them focused on the issues but don't ask leading questions.

There are typically separate forms and considerations for employee accidents and for public liability accidents. When properly completed, each form should give department heads and supervisors key information that they will need to stay informed and to plan future action. It is most important to record all incidents that could result in claims, that could recur, or that could result in another incident involving a guest or an employee. If no injury is reported, in many cases a hotel will assume that no further action needs to be taken. For example, a guest falls while taking a shower. He reports the fall to the front desk. Since no apparent serious injury resulted from his fall, the front desk takes no action and the guest continues on his travels. Three months later, the hotel receives a claim for hip surgery, based on the guest's fall in the hotel. Without any report, documentation, or investigation of the incident, defense by the hotel against the claim could be difficult.

All incidents—both those reported formally to management and those learned of indirectly by management—should be documented for two reasons: (1) to identify what action needs to be taken by the hotel in order to prevent recurrence and (2) to provide a defense for the hotel against groundless allegations of negligence.

THE SECURITY DEPARTMENT

The role of the security department is a difficult one. Incidents often involve on-the-spot decisions made under stressful circumstances. The rapport established by a security department employee with an upset guest can profoundly affect the guest's perception of the hotel and may affect the course of subsequent legal action. A minimum standard of reasonable care, as defined by management, must be maintained at all times. (2) A professional and effective security department ensures the comfort, safety, and security of guests, employees, and the corporation's assets, and provides an indirect contribution to the hotel's financial success.

Director of Security

The director of security, who reports to the general manager or resident manager, is responsible for implementing hotel security policies and procedures in coordination with the general manager and all department heads. Depending upon the size of the hotel, the director of security is usually supported by a staff that may include an assistant director and security officers. (3) For more details on the responsibilities of a director of security, see Table 5–4.

Security Planning

Every hotel must assess its vulnerability in order to tailor a security plan that will meet its needs. There are multiple factors to consider, such as limiting access; monitoring activity; misappropriation of assets; employment guidelines; guest relations; contracts with outside security firms; use of force;

Table 5–4 Responsibilities of the Director of Security

Administration

Advise the general manager of loss control procedures for the various departments throughout the hotel.

Review, revise, and update security procedures as necessary.

Plan and organize the security department's staff and activities.

Assist the personnel department with preemployment checks on employees who have been hired in critical areas when consulted.

Administer the employment and termination of all security personnel.

Ensure that the timekeeper and contract security personnel are in proper uniforms and are performing their duties in a professional manner.

Supervise semiannual key inventories in all departments.

Be familiar with the provisions of the various labor contracts, state and federal laws, and union regulations that may apply.

Develop job descriptions for supervisors, security officers, and timekeepers, with the assistance of the general manager.

Training

Train all employees in security responsibilities.

Give specific training to supervisors and security officers.

Supervise continuous training through seminars and training sessions.

Continue his or her own professional training through seminars and training sessions.

Participate in orientation program for new employees.

Reporting

Keep the general manager fully informed of all security-related matters.

Supervise the daily processing and distribution of security reports to management.

Maintain a chronological log of all incidents.

Prepare monthly and quarterly major incident reports.

Maintain complete and accurate records of all safety and security incidents.

Keep all records and reports concerning security matters and hotel business confidential.

Be a liaison between management personnel and all employees, and assist with security problems and loss control; hire outside law enforcement and fire and safety officials.

Notify outside law enforcement and fire and safety officials.

Other responsibilities

Attend and participate in safety loss prevention and security committee meetings and other staff meetings as determined by the general manager.

Be fully trained and prepared for all emergency procedures.

arrest; employee locker control; guest room security and safety notices; bank deposits and escort of funds; lost and found; baggage storage; key control; unregistered guests; reporting incidents; and record keeping. (4) To keep track of these various factors, hotels generally conduct a security audit, such as the one shown in Appendix 5–1.

Unruly Guests. When using hotel facilities, guests and visitors should be required to practice standards of conduct that will not interfere with the comfort, safety, and security of others. This is especially important in lounges and other public facilities. Unruly guests or visitors should be handled politely and firmly. Every effort should be made to remove unruly persons from public areas before prolonged discussions or interviews can occur. A private office or a secluded area should be used both to avoid exposing other guests and visitors to any confrontations or unpleasant scenes, and to avoid any possible allegation of failure with respect to the unruly person's right to privacy.

Use of Outside Security Firms. In some cases, such as with VIP guests or exhibits of valuable merchandise, patrons or guests may request the services of an outside security firm or armed security guards. Management should secure a special release in such cases. The release covers security firms hired directly by exhibitors, conventions, and show management. The presence of gaming facilities in a hotel, like those that contributed so much to Barron Hilton's success (see Box 10-1), present very specialized security issues.

The outside security firm must provide the hotel with satisfactory evidence of liability coverage in the amount of not less than $2 million per occurrence, including, but not limited to, premises, operations, personal injury (including assault and battery), contractual liability, and professional liability.

The outside security firm also must agree to indemnify and hold harmless the hotel from any liability involving the security firm (including specific incidents involving weapons), and from any and all legal fees and costs.

Key Control. While disposable key cards and electronic guest room locking devices have eased some of the security problems inherent in the hotel industry, key control is still a concern. The security department must coordinate with the front desk department to ensure that guest room keys are issued only after identification and registration have been verified. Strict control of **master keys**, or those keys providing access to all guest rooms that are not double-locked, and **emergency keys**, or keys that open all guest room doors, even when they are double-locked, is a concern of the security department.

Another way to enhance key control is to make sure that, upon check out, a conscientious effort is made to retrieve guest room keys by all persons having contact with the departing guest, including the bellman, the cashier, the doorman, the maids, security personnel, and the garage attendant.

Emergency Plans

Emergencies such as bomb threats, floods, earthquakes, tornadoes, fires, hurricanes, gas leaks, loss of utilities, riots, and elevator evacuations, while unexpected and, in most cases, out of the control of the security department, can and should be anticipated. (5)

BOX 5–1
Gerard Ferdinand Pélisson and Paul Jean-Marie Dubrule

Gerard Pélisson and Paul Dubrule. (Courtesy of the Hospitality Industry Archives and Library, University of Houston, Texas.)

The cofounders of the Paris-based hospitality company Accor SA have made it grow so that it has become one of the world's largest conglomerates, comprised of hotels, restaurants, travel agencies, car rental companies, and restaurant voucher firms.

In the 1960s, Gerard Pélisson (1932–) and Paul Dubrule (1934–) were both living in the United States, working for major computer firms. The travel industry in France was experiencing a surge in growth, and there was a clear need for new lodging facilities. Most of the new properties being developed were concentrated in major urban areas such as Paris. Paul Dubrule decided to do something different. Noting the success of American lodging properties located in suburban areas and along major highways, Pélisson and Dubrule opened their first Novotel hotel outside of Lille in northern France. The success of this hotel allowed the duo to continue exploiting the undervalued and underdeveloped highway marketplace in Europe, and soon the company began to expand their ventures to include airports and popular vacation sites along seasides and in mountain regions. This was only the beginning of what would become one of the largest hotel and hospitality companies in the world.

Pélisson and Dubrule served as cochairmen of the company, sharing all responsibilities and making all management decisions. In 1973, one of their decisions was to form Sphere SA, a holding company for a new chain of two-star hotels, called Ibis. At about the same time, the two elected to purchase a chain of roadside steakhouses, Court Paille. By the end of the 1970s, the company had also purchased Mercure, a hotel chain dedicated to the metropolitan business traveler, with 240 properties in Europe, South America, Africa, and the Far East.

Beginning in 1979, Accor brought Novotel, Ibis, and Sofitel brand hotels, as well as the seafood restaurant chain, Seafood Broiler, to the United States. In 1982, Novotel and its holdings were incorporated under the name Accor. The purchase of Sofitel was instrumental in this transformation, as these hotels were primarily located in international cities and business centers, near airports, and in the most prestigious tourist areas.

In the mid-1980s, Accor invested in a chain of Italian restaurants, Pizza del Arte, and entered into a partnership with the bakery and catering company Lenotre. Accor also entered the travel industry by investing in AfricaTours, the largest tour operator to the African continent. With the subsequent purchases of Americatours, Asiatours, and Ted Cook's Island in the Sun, Accor expanded its travel businesses into North and South America, Asia, and the South Pacific.

In 1985, a subsidiary of Accor (Hotec) introduced Formule 1, a new idea in the hotel industry. The Formule 1 hotels were one-star budget properties marketed toward vacationing young people and travelers with limited financial resources. Also in 1985, Accor took control of Britain's Luncheon Voucher. In a few short years, Accor became the world leader in restaurant vouchers for employees.

In 1987, Accor entered into the market of homes for elder care and created the Parthenon chain of residential hotels in Brazil. In 1988, the company launched the Free Time fast-food chain, and invested in Cipal-Parc Asterix, a theme park north of Paris.

In 1990, Accor made a major move into the U.S. market with its purchase of the Motel 6 hotel brand. In 1992, Accor purchased controlling interest in Wagon-Lits, the dominant railroad sleeping car business and second-largest hotel chain in Europe, which established Accor as the world leader in the hospitality industry, with 2,100 hotels, 6,000 restaurants, and 1,000 travel agencies.

In 1993, Accor purchased 51 percent of the hotel company Pannonia from the Hungarian government. This move expanded the company's holdings into Hungary, Germany, Austria, Bulgaria, Romania, Slovakia, the former Soviet Union, and Yugoslavia.

Throughout the 1990s, Accor developed conference centers, offices, and hotels in cities and towns under the subsidiary label, Atria. Accor also continued expansion of its restaurant businesses with L'Arche cafeterias, L'Ecluse winebars, Boeuf Jardinier steakhouses, Café Route cafes, Actair airport restaurants, train station cafes, and Meda's Grills in Spain. In its car rental ventures, the company shares control of Europecar Interrent International with Volkswagen in 89 countries in Europe, Africa, and the Middle East. In March 1994, Accor merged its Wagon-Lits travel-related business with Carlson Companies (see Box 4–1) to form a network of 4,000 travel agencies in 125 countries.

Source: "Gerard Ferdinand Pélisson and Paul Jean-Marie Dubrule," Cathleen Baird, Hospitality Industry Archives, Conrad N. Hilton College, University of Houston, Houston, Texas, 1999.

Table 5–5 Components of an Emergency Plan for Disasters

Identifying possible types of disasters that may occur, including natural disasters if likely in the geographic area (i.e., hurricanes, tornadoes, floods).

Layout of the current hotel floor plan with any modifications that have occurred in renovation or remodeling.

Identifying who should be notified for each and/or all emergencies, and what method(s) (i.e., phone, fax-in another state, other audible devices) will be used.

Establish specific duties and responsibilities of key individuals.

Establish emergency shut-down procedures for designated parts of the building (i.e., higher floors, rooms with considerable glass) or building systems (i.e., natural gas, electrical, etc.).

Develop evacuation routes, including directional signs both in the hotel to emergency shelters and from exterior areas of the building to safe areas.

Insure locations of shelters that have been determined to be secure based on the type of emergency (i.e., fire requires evacuation from a building, while a natural disaster, such as a tornado, may require moving guests and employees to secure areas within a building).

Prepare systematic floor evacuation plan for high-rise buildings.

Secure participation by, and cooperation with, other mutual aid organizations.

Depending on its location, a hotel is at higher risk for certain disasters, such as an earthquake or civil unrest. In such cases, the general manager, in coordination with local authorities, should develop an emergency plan tailored to the specific hotel. Different plans should be developed for different emergency situations. One of the most important features of an emergency plan is the delegation of specific responsibilities so that hotel staff know who to turn to and what is expected of them in the case of an emergency. Table 5–5 outlines the components of an effective emergency plan.

In the following chapter, several departments are covered that are important to the success of a hotel. Typically, these departments are covered in courses in a hotel management curriculum and thus are only considered briefly in this text.

SUMMARY

A loss prevention and security program is a means of protecting a hotel's resources—both people and property. Generally, injuries to the public mirror those among staff. The most common guest accident in the bathroom is a slip or a fall. The next most common accident is a cut from a sharp object or a burn from hot water. Injuries can occur in the guest room because of unstable appliances, glass doors, rough edges on furniture, and damaged carpet. The prevention of injury to the guest must extend to the internal and external public areas as well.

The loss prevention committee can be used to improve safety for both employees and guests. A key component in any loss prevention program is regular inspection of the facilities. If an injury to an employee or a guest occurs, a thorough investigation of the accident must take place as soon as possible. Employee injuries can be minimized through employee training.

The head of the security department is the director of security. Key to the responsibilities of the director of security include the security audit, implementation of hotel security policies and procedures, and preparation of emergency plans.

References

1. The Sheraton Corporation, *Employee/Guest Safety* (Boston: The Sheraton Corporation, 1983), p. 3.
2. Raymond C. Ellis, David M. Stipand, "Setting Up the Security Program," in *Security and Loss Prevention Management,* Second Edition (East Lansing, MI: Educational Institute, American Hotel and Motel Association, 1999), p. 6.
3. Raymond C. Ellis, David M. Stipand, "Department Responsibilities in Guest and Asset Protection," in *Security and Loss Prevention Management,* Second Edition (East Lansing, MI: Educational Institute, American Hotel and Motel Association, 1999), p. 15.
4. Raymond C. Ellis, David M. Stipand, "Security Programs and Guest Concerns," in *Security and Loss Prevention Management,* Second Edition (East Lansing, MI: Educational Institute, American Hotel and Motel Association, 1999), p. 165.
5. Raymond C. Ellis, David M. Stipand, "Emergency Management," *Security and Loss Prevention Management,* Second Edition (East Lansing, MI: Education Institute, American Hotel and Motel Association, 1999), p. 291.

Review Questions

1. Name three functions of the loss prevention committee.
2. Discuss the areas to be included in a hotel loss prevention inspection.
3. Discuss the role of the director of security in maintaining hotel security.

4. A guest has just slipped on wet tile in the lobby and has fallen and hit her head, while other patrons looked on. She appears to be just shaken up, but she is bleeding slightly from a cut on her forehead. Describe the steps you would take to handle this situation.

ACTIVITIES

1. With the permission of a local hotel general manager, attend a loss prevention committee meeting and summarize the events that transpired.
2. Review and critique the employee safety program of a local hotel.
3. Conduct a security audit of that same hotel, using the form included in Appendix 5–1.
4. Interview the general manager of a local hotel about the hotel's emergency plan. Based on your interview, provide a critique of the plan.

Appendix 5–1

Hotel Security Audit

I. Personnel

A. Number of Employees: Permanent ______ Temporary ______

B. Names of Executive Staff:

General Manager: ____________________________
Resident Manager: ____________________________
Controller: ____________________________
Human Resources Director: ____________________________
Chief Engineer: ____________________________
Executive Housekeeper: ____________________________
Food and Beverage Manager: ____________________________
Purchasing Manager: ____________________________
Director of Safety: ____________________________
Director of Security: ____________________________

If there is no director of safety or security on premises, name and title of executive responsible:

Safety: ______________________
Security: ______________________

C. Personnel Procedures:

1. Is Human Resources office located for direct access by prospective employees?
Yes _____ No _____

2. Do all applicants for employment complete a standard hotel application form?
Yes _____ No _____

3. Which of the following preemployment checks are conducted?
a. Two most recent previous employers contacted:
Yes _____ No _____

b. Termination cause/reemployment eligibility:
Yes _____ No _____
c. Personal references contacted: Yes _____ No _____
d. Schools attended: Yes _____ No _____
e. Physical examination: Yes _____ No _____

4. Are employees hired on a probationary basis?
Yes _____ No _____

5. Is there a security orientation program for new employees?
Yes _____ No _____

6. Is there a safety orientation program for new employees?
Yes _____ No _____

7. Are employee photo identification cards used?
Yes _____ No _____

8. Are timekeepers in full view and in attendance at the time clock and employee entrance?
Yes _____ No _____
Other (specify): ____________________

9. Are nonmanagement level employees required to use the employee entrance?
Yes _____ No _____

10. Are employee locker inspections conducted?
Yes _____ No _____
a. If yes, how often?
b. By whom are locker inspections conducted?
c. Are inspection dates posted? Yes _____ No _____

11. Are terminated employees' lockers inspected before they leave the property?
Yes _____ No _____

12. Does the hotel have a property pass system with authorized signatures?
Yes _____ No _____

13. Are staff members allowed to bring personal packages into the hotel?
Yes _____ No _____

14. If packages are checked, give location where checked and person responsible for them:
Location: ____________________
Person responsible: ____________________

15. Is a checklist maintained to ensure recovery of hotel property from terminated employees?
Yes _____ No _____

16. List the person responsible for recovery of the following items from terminated employees:
    Photo I.D.: ____________
    Keys: ____________
    Uniforms: ____________
    Tools/Equipment: ____________

II. Physical Plant

A. Type of Hotel

1. Transient _____ Resort _____ Convention _____
   Residential _____ Other (specify) _____
2. Number of guest rooms: _____ Floors: _____
   Number of guest room floors: _____ Number of function rooms/floors: _____
3. Number of outlets/concessions: _____
   Please list each outlet/concession below:
   ____
   ____
   ____
   ____

III. Hotel Operations

A. Front Office

1. Is guest identification verified before key is issued?
   Yes _____ No _____
2. Who is responsible for recovery of keys from departing guests?
3. Is there a partition between the front office rooms clerk and the front office cashier's area?
   Yes _____ No _____
4. Do front office cashiers have holdup alarms?
   Yes _____ No _____
5. Are safe deposit boxes available 24 hours a day?
   Yes _____ No _____
6. Are safe deposit boxes alarmed? Yes _____ No _____
   If yes, specify type of alarm used: ________________
7. Describe safe deposit box security procedures:
   ____
   ____
   ____
   ____

B. Engineering

1. Are records kept of engineering job assignments in guest rooms?
   Yes _____ No _____
2. Are all supplies and/or materials issued to the engineering department authorized by requisition?
   Yes _____ No _____
3. Do engineers turn in their assigned keys at the end of the day?
   Yes _____ No _____

C. Housekeeping

1. Are linen closets and supply closets secured when not in use?
   Yes _____ No _____
2. Are rubbish and linen chutes secured when not in use?
   Yes _____ No _____
3. Does housekeeping handle lost and found?
   Yes _____ No _____
   If not, who does: ______________________________
4. Outline the procedure that is followed when maids find property in unoccupied rooms:
   ____
   ____
   ____
5. Do guest room attendants keep doors open or closed when working in guest rooms? Open _______ Closed _______
6. Is a record maintained of all keys issued to housekeeping personnel?
   Yes _____ No _____
7. Who is notified if key is not turned in? _______
8. Are maids allowed to leave hotel with section master keys during their meal period?
   Yes _____ No _____
9. Outline the procedure for handling money, jewelry, or other valuables turned in by maids from guest rooms:
   ____
   ____
   ____

D. Food and Beverage

1. How often are random checks made of incoming supplies by the food and beverage controller? _______

2. Are requisitions reviewed on a random basis by the food and beverage manager?
   Yes _____ No _____
3. Identify general liquor store room security controls, including bar stock control:
   ____
   ____
   ____
4. Is all garbage and trash inspected before disposal?
   Yes _____ No _____
5. Are random checks of garbage made by the security staff?
   Yes _____ No _____
   If yes, how often? ______________________________
6. Are all room service materials removed from guest rooms and corridors as soon as possible?
   Yes _____ No _____
7. Who is responsible for hotel silverware, china, glassware, etc.? ______________
8. Who is immediately notified of food and beverage losses? ________________
9. Outline the controls used to reduce losses:
   ____
   ____
   ____

E. Sales

1. Are arrangements made for the protection of guest's exhibit equipment during large functions?
   Yes _____ No _____
2. If outside security is hired by exhibitors, is there a corporate policy in place regarding liability?
   Yes _____ No _____

F. Public Relations

1. Are all inquiries from representatives of the news media referred to the general manager or the resident manager?
   Yes _____ No _____
2. Does the general manager contact the corporate public relations director regarding any incidents which may adversely affect the reputation of the properties?
   Yes _____ No _____

G. Laundry and Dry Cleaning

1. Are records maintained of all room keys issued to valets each day?
   Yes _____ No _____

2. Are records maintained of all room deliveries, including the valet who made the delivery?
   Yes _____ No _____
3. Are clothes delivered to the valet checked for valuables?
   Yes _____ No _____
4. What action is taken if valuables are found? ______________________________
   ____
   ____
5. Is outgoing linen inspected on a random basis by housekeeping or security?
   Yes _____ No _____

H. Receiving

1. Does the receiving clerk check all incoming goods upon receipt against delivery tickets or copies of purchase orders?
   Yes _____ No _____
2. If a discrepancy is found, what action is taken?
3. Is incoming merchandise transferred without delay to the appropriate storeroom?
   Yes _____ No _____
4. How often are scales checked for accuracy?
   ____
5. Does a security employee visit the receiving area periodically, or is a security employee assigned there permanently?

I. Purchasing

1. Does the hotel use a competitive bid system?
   Yes _____ No _____
2. Does the purchasing manager visit suppliers monthly to verify prices?
   Yes _____ No _____
3. Does the general manager review all purchase orders?
   Yes _____ No _____
4. Outline the purchasing system:
   ____
   ____
   ____
   ____

J. Security

1. Does the hotel maintain a security staff?
   Yes _____ No _____
2. Number of personnel in the security department: ______________________

3. List security staff and positions:
____
____
____
____
____

4. Are security personnel armed?
Yes _____ No _____

5. Are security personnel in uniform or civilian dress?
Uniform _______ Civilian _______
If uniform, describe: ___________________________

6. Are employees union or nonunion?
Union _______ Nonunion _______

7. Is security in-house or contracted out?
In-house _______ Contracted out _______
If contract, name and address: ___________________________
____

8. Is security on duty around the clock?
Yes _____ No _____

9. How many shifts are employed? _____________________

10. How do security personnel communicate?
____
____

11. Are radio codes used to keep the communications confidential from the public?
Yes _____ No _____

12. Is liaison with local law enforcement and fire and safety officials maintained?
Yes _____ No _____

13. What procedure is followed in the event of a death on the premises? __________
____

a. How is the property of the deceased inventoried and secured?
____
____
____
____

b. Is a written report submitted to the security department?
Yes _____ No _____

14. Does the hotel practice effective procedures to keep undesirable persons off the premises?
Yes _____ No _____

15. If a known undesirable person is seen on the premises, is the person asked to leave? Yes _____ No _____
    Is documentation made of this action? Yes _____ No _____

16. If guests are seen entering their rooms with a known or suspected undesirable person, is a written notation made for future reference in case of subsequent allegations of theft? Yes _____ No _____

17. Are major incidents reported promptly?

    Incident:

a. Arson/fires	Yes _____	No _____
b. Natural disasters	Yes _____	No _____
c. Bombs/bomb threats	Yes _____	No _____
d. Crimes of violence	Yes _____	No _____
e. Suicide	Yes _____	No _____
f. Employees terminated for theft	Yes _____	No _____
g. Loss of hotel property through larceny or fraud ($1,000 and over)	Yes _____	No _____
h. Civil disorders, strikes	Yes _____	No _____
i. Major guest property losses ($1,000 and over)	Yes _____	No _____
j. Loss of proprietary information	Yes _____	No _____
k. Incidents that may reflect on the integrity of the hotel	Yes _____	No _____

18. What procedures are followed for visits by ranking government officials, dignitaries, controversial figures, and/or proponents of highly emotional political or business issues?
    ____

19. To whom is the director of security responsible? ____________________

20. When was the last security survey conducted? ____________________
    By whom? ____________________

IV. Access Control—Internal

A. Alarms

1. Are all fire alarms reported simultaneously to local fire departments and the hotel?
   Yes _____ No _____

2. Are all alarms reported immediately to the security office and then to the police?
   Yes _____ No _____

3. Are alarms tested periodically as per the loss prevention and control manual?
   Yes _____ No _____

B. Alarm Locations:

Alarm	Location
General cashier	
Front office cashier	
Safe deposit boxes	
Executive offices	
Engineering storeroom	
Food/beverage storeroom	
Controller's office	
Computer room	

C. Does the hotel have a station check-in system for foot patrol guards? Yes ___ No ___
Is a garage included? Yes _____ No _____

D. Elevators

1. Number of elevators:
   Guest _______ Service _______ Freight _______
2. How are elevators operated and/or monitored?
   Automatic recall _______ Manual _______ CCTV _______

E. Telephones

1. Are office phone dials locked after office hours?
   Yes _____ No _____
2. Are records kept of all outgoing calls made by employees in each department?
   Yes _____ No _____
3. Are telephone operators trained to handle emergency and threatening calls?
   Yes _____ No _____

V. Access Control—Perimeter

A. External Perimeter Doors

1. Please list:
   ____
   ____
   ____
   ____
2. How are external doors and emergency doors secured?
   Locks _______ Panic Bars _______ Guards _______

B. Loading Dock or Receiving Area

1. Is area monitored? Yes _____ No _____
   If yes, how? ______________________

2. Is area secured after delivery hours? Yes _____ No _____
   If yes, how? ____________________

C. External Lighting System

1. Type used: _______

D. Garage

1. Public _______ Concession _______ Hotel Owned _______
2. How many floors? _______
3. Does the garage entrance go directly into hotel lobby?
   Yes _____ No _____
4. Does the garage entrance go directly to guest room floors?
   Yes _____ No _____
5. What security precautions are in place at garage entrances into the hotel?
   Panic Doors _______ CCTV _______ Alarms _______
   Other (specify) ____________________
6. Are notices posted as to charges/liability?
   Yes _____ No _____
7. Name and address of garage owner: ________________________________
8. Is garage open 24 hours, with an attendant or supervisor on duty?
   Yes _____ No _____
9. Is the area patrolled by security or a fire watch?
   Yes _____ No _____

VI. Key Control

A. Locking System

1. Identify the lock manufacturer, type of lock (i.e., mortise, key-in-knob, etc.), and what areas are mastered:

Area	Lock Manufacturer	Type of Lock	Mastered
Guest rooms			
Function rooms			
Offices			
Computer			
Storage			

2. Can lock cylinders be rotated on all guest room floors?
   Yes _____ No _____
3. List hotel's key assignments: ____
   ____

4. Does reproduction of all back-of-the-house or guest room keys require a written authorization?
   Yes _____ No _____
   If so, who authorizes reproduction? ______________________
5. Is a locksmith kept on the premises? Yes _____ No _____
   Name: ____
6. To what department is the locksmith assigned? ________________
7. Where are key blanks secured? ________________
8. Who maintains a written record of key reproduction?
9. Who inspects the key inventory?
10. Who has access to the key-making machine or key blanks?
11. Do employees turn in keys at end of the work day?
    Yes _____ No _____
    If no, explain why: _______
12. What action is taken in the event of a lost key? ______________________
    ____
    ____
13. When combination locks are used, who has a master key or combination to open them?
    ____
    ____
    ____
    ____
14. Are combinations changed on safes/vaults whenever an employee no longer needs access?
    Yes _____ No _____
15. Are records of combinations kept? Yes _____ No _____
    Where are they secured? ________________
16. List guest key drop boxes throughout the property:
    ____
    ____
    ____
    ____

VII. Emergency Plans of Action

A. Explain briefly hotel's emergency plan of action for the following:

1. Fires: ________________
2. Bombs/bomb threats: ________________

3. Natural disasters: ____________________
4. Civil disorders, strikes: ____________________
5. Blackout: ____________________
   a. Who decides to evacuate? ____________________

B. Beyond the emergency plan, does the hotel have a written security program?
   Yes _____ No _____

Chapter 6

Marketing and Sales, Food and Beverage, Engineering, and Human Resources Departments

CHAPTER OUTLINE

The marketing and sales, food and beverage, engineering, and human resources departments are just as important as the departments we already have discussed. Our coverage of these departments is, of necessity, just an overview; each of these topics could fill a chapter or indeed a book. Another important department, the accounting department, is the subject of its own chapter (see Chapter 7).

The Marketing and Sales Department

The marketing and sales department is a relative newcomer to the hospitality industry. It has been only in recent years that the hospitality industry has learned the lessons of other businesses and has adopted the tools of persuasion and sales to influence revenue. For the most part, the emphasis of this department is on sales—probably 90 percent of its effort. Marketing plays a lessor role, being directed at a corporate or regional plan that directs the sales force.

The sales staff may be the first contact many individuals have with a hotel. Also, it is with the sales staff of the hotel that a convention or a corporate executive first establishes contact. The individual's first impression, especially for those who are not familiar with the hotel, is formed entirely by the appearance, personality, bearing, and conduct of the hotel's sales staff.

The sales staff's efforts directly affect everyone in the hotel, from room attendants to managers. The old adage "nothing happens until someone sells something" fits the hotel industry perfectly. If no one stays at the hotel, there are no rooms to clean, no meals to serve, and no guests to attend to.

The sales staff is most closely associated with the housekeeping, front office, and food and beverage departments. Indeed, the definition of group sales is bringing a group into the hotel, housing and feeding it, and planning its meetings.

The sales staff spends many months securing a convention and is able to do so by promising a flawless performance. To deliver this flawless performance, effective communication between the sales and other departments is essential.

The Sales Staff

The sales staff consists of a director of sales, along with as many sales managers and sales representatives as are necessary to effectively cover the files of previous guests and groups booked by the hotel, develop potential leads, and solicit business for the hotel. (1) Table 6–1 outlines the key responsibilities and reporting relationships of the sales staff. Sales secretaries—one for

Table 6–1 Key Responsibilities and Reporting Relationships of the Sales Staff

Director of sales	Reports to the general manager Establishes and coordinates all efforts to obtain group business Makes commitments to a convention or a group function with regard to room commitments Works closely with advertising agencies in the development of all printed matter and promotional programs
Sales manager	Reports to the director of sales Has responsibility for a specific market segment
Sales representative	Reports to a sales manager with responsibility for a specific market segment Has a specific area of sales responsibility
Sales secretaries	Greets clients, takes messages, files client information

the director and others for the sales managers and sales representatives—complete the sales staff.

The division of work among the sales managers is usually based on the type of customers a hotel is attempting to attract. A sales manager may specialize in corporate accounts, conventions, or tour and travel markets.

Characteristics of a Successful Sales Department

A salesperson uses his natural instinct to seek out and identify prospects and to convert those prospects into guests. A **prospect** is a potential purchaser of a hotel's room and/or meeting space. A room cannot be sold to someone who doesn't need one; similarly, food cannot be sold to someone who is not planning a banquet. A particular hotel's product or service is sold for one of three reasons:

1. It is better.
2. It is different.
3. It is cheaper.

An effective salesperson is able to determine the guest's need and depict the hotel's product or service as the one best able to satisfy that need.

The personality of most good salespeople is forceful, extroverted, success oriented, and self-assured. Successful salespersons condition themselves for affirmative decisions by a positive orientation to all aspects of their day. Successful salespersons are guest oriented and realize that guests not only buy rooms on the basis of the food, rooms, and beverages, but also take into account satisfaction, prestige, competency, courtesy, decor, mood, location, as well as many other factors. Thus, price is only one consideration among many when trying to sell rooms.

A successful sales department usually contains a fully stocked reference library that contains the following: copies of booking reports from other hotels in the chain; research of past conventions in the city from the Convention and Visitor's Bureau; state and local association directories; city and state manufacturer directories; pertinent telephone directories; city directories; world convention dates; a directory of associations; and a standard directory of advertisers.

In order for a sales department to generate prospects successfully, the hotel should be a member of the following: the Chamber of Commerce; the Convention and Visitor's Bureau; and local, state, and national hotel sales manager's associations. These affiliations should be used in networking, which is key to the success of sales. **Networking**, the exchange of information or services among individuals or groups that will prove valuable in selling guest rooms or meeting spaces in a hotel, should include local Convention and Visitor's Bureau personnel; local general managers and sales managers at competing hotels; press contacts; out-of-town corporate representatives; local association executives; state and regional association executives; and national association executives and those coordinating future citywide conventions.

The Telephone Survey

Periodically, the sales staff should conduct a telephone solicitation campaign or a telephone survey to collect all possible local business leads, making use of the contacts mentioned earlier. Telephone calls are made by the sales representatives and the sales managers. The goal is to develop as many bona fide corporate leads as possible in the local market. This procedure eliminates the necessity of cold calls (random, unsolicited calls), which are typically a waste of effort; makes the local community aware of the hotel; and creates a reference list, which can be used in the future to explore group business and banquet business.

Call reports should be used to document the information collected in a telephone survey. Figure 6–1 illustrates the information that should be included in a call report. Call reports are grouped into seven categories that reflect the type of business that might be sold: (1) group, room, and banquet; (2) group and room; (3) group and banquet; (4) group only; (5) room and banquets; (6) room only; and (7) banquet only. It should be noted that, while it may be more profitable for a hotel to attract groups that **book** sleeping rooms and banquet rooms in advance, in some local markets, a group may only require banquet space, and thus it becomes critical to track the number of such groups, since they are essential components of the total revenue picture for the hotel. These seven categories are further divided according to the number of persons in a potential group.

Once the telephone survey is completed, follow-ups are assigned as follows: group leads, in order of priority, are divided among the sales staff;

Sales Representative

From ______________________ City ______________________

Date ____________ Telephone Number ______________________

Regarding ______________________

Person Contacted ______________________

Title ______________________

Remarks ______________________

Figure 6–1 **Call report**

room leads are recorded on mailing lists that are then forwarded to the front office manager for consideration; and banquet leads are generally turned over to the catering manager.

The Sales Call

In addition to the time spent on telephone surveys, a sales manager spends many hours calling on potential customers in person. The manner in which a sales manager makes a personal call can either help or hurt in securing the business. Table 6–2 provides some guidelines that a sales manager should follow when making personal calls.

After a call is completed, the results should be written up as soon as possible, to capture the essential points covered and to allow the sales manager to make a better impression during the next contact. For example, on the

Table 6–2 **Guidelines for Making Personal Sales Calls**

Ask for a specific person by name when entering the office.

Always present your calling card to the receptionist.

Always say, "May I please see Mr. M?" rather than "Is Mr. M in?"

Should the secretary indicate Mr. M is unavailable, leave your card and ask that it be given to the party.

Should the wait be prolonged, ask the receptionist if it might be more convenient to see Mr. M at another time.

When shown into the office of the prospect, shake hands, make eye contact, smile genuinely, and announce your name and company clearly.

Give the impression that the only purpose for your being in the area is to see Mr. M.

Be brief.

At the conclusion of the call, end by saying something like, "I certainly took more of your time than I had promised to take. Thank you so much, Mr. M."

next call, the sales manager might say, "I certainly remember the day I was in your office. You seemed to feel so strongly about our individually decorated rooms." Should the customer have forgotten this part of the conversation, this technique has the added benefit of reinforcing a positive reaction to the sales manager's product.

Convention Bookings

A key component of most full-service hospitality businesses is the conventioneer large-group booking on **block**, which is an agreed-upon number of rooms set aside for members of a group. Because of the complexity of such events, a hotel should have established procedures for convention bookings that are designed to prevent any misunderstanding between the sales office and other affected departments, such as the front office.

Convention planning formally begins with the arrival of the association executive, the representative of the group that is holding the convention. Preliminary planning materials should include an accurate history of previous conventions and a detailed record of arrangements, prices quoted, promises made, and so on. The sales manager accompanies the association executive to the catering manager, who becomes the association's "one-stop" service contact. The catering manager makes all the arrangements. At this point, the sales manager becomes less involved but is still responsible for coordinating the efforts of the catering manager and association executive, and for ensuring that all arrangements offered and confirmed are fully understood.

In addition, the sales manager is still the association executive's host when the executive is in the hotel and makes sure that he or she sees the right people for the assistance needed and that it is given with the warmth, hospitality, and service promised.

Nothing can damage a hotel's reputation more than for an association executive to believe that he or she is important to the sales manager only until the convention is definitely booked. A good personal relationship between the association executive and sales manager is essential.

Convention bookings should include a tentative program, indicating the types of function space required; availability should be checked at the time the space(s) are reserved in order to avoid conflicts. Although the exact convention program has most likely not been established at the time of booking, no savvy association executive will book a hotel for a convention until he or she is satisfied that it meets the requirements of the event.

The practice of reserving all banquet rooms, meeting rooms, and guest rooms in a hotel for a convention, called "hold all space," should be avoided, to minimize the amount of unused space. In most cases, the association executive will know the basic program requirements one year in advance. If a customer does request that the hotel "hold all space," the final program requirements should be submitted at least six months in advance, the required public space and rooms should be booked, and the "hold all space" should be lifted. This said, the key to successful convention booking is flexibility. Because events are so different, bookings cannot be handled by any one set of regulations. Only after an event has been booked do the general manager, food and beverage manager, and director of sales develop the procedures for handling the function.

Program entries are recorded in the hotel's **function book**, which lists all group business and the guest rooms, meeting space, and other items that the hotel has committed for a particular time period. These entries are the responsibility of the sales manager who is booking the function. Like the availability board and so many other aspects of hotel record keeping, the function book is becoming an automated module of the property management system, so the need for manual entries is disappearing. Manual entries are to be made in pencil and should include the following information: date(s) (tentative or definite); type of function; starting and ending times; estimated number of persons; group name; contact name and phone number; date booked; and the initials of the person booking the function. If housing is being handled by the Convention Bureau, this should be noted in the client's file.

Confirmation Letter. Once a convention has been booked, a confirmation letter is sent to the association executive. The letter typically states the dates in question, alternate dates, and the days of the week; the number of rooms, suites, and meeting rooms reserved; any abnormal arrival patterns; and a review of the function space reserved for the program. The function space should be acknowledged, but not mentioned specifically by name in case changes are necessary.

The catering manager generally will follow up the confirmation letter with a brief note inviting the association executive to call at any time to discuss the arrangements.

Booking Follow-up. With the automation of the property management system, a file on a group booked several years in advance automatically comes up just before the current year's convention. It is important to address correspondence to the office, wishing them success with the current year's meeting and indicating that the hotel is looking forward to serving the group at a later time. Specifying the year and date (if known) of the anticipated service in such a letter has the added benefit of reminding the association executive of the commitment, which may prompt him or her to call the hotel with any changes. Many convention groups do not think of their past year's decision as a binding contract.

A future booking might be affected by the results of the present year's convention. The preconvention contact could bring any such changes to the sales manager's attention early enough to avoid a hotel being empty. More than one seemingly "sure" booking has been lost through complacency of the sales staff.

A letter to the hotel that is hosting the present year's convention, asking for information that might enable the hotel to better serve the group, is also a useful tool. Sometimes such information is not available, or the hotel may not cooperate. In these cases, data can be obtained from the Convention and Visitor's Bureau of the host city, which is typically sponsored by dollars generated from hotel room taxes and is created to promote the city or locale for group business.

The Weekly Report. Near the actual convention dates, the front office provides a weekly report to the sales department. The report, covering the next six weeks, shows all room blocks reserved and the actual count of reservations received against that block. Each week, a form letter is sent to the association executive the day the report comes out, reiterating the number of rooms blocked and providing an update on the number of reservations received. For example, the letter might say: "We are holding a block of 350 rooms, for arrival on Sunday, May 20, 2000, and as of today, April 15, 127 reservations have been received against this block."

The progress of guaranteed reservations received against the number blocked out is called the **room pickup**. Should the room pickup be below standard for the reserved block, the sales staff should make immediate contact to determine if all rooms in the block are needed.

All group bookings, including conventions, are subject to a two-week cutoff date. The hotel has no obligation and issues no guarantee on reservations received after the cutoff date. In addition to being noted at the time of booking, the cutoff date information must be made specific on all convention confirmations and must be clearly printed on all reservation cards.

Unused portions of the room block revert to the hotel. As stated above, the hotel is not responsible to the association for the balance of the block but will show its members preference whenever possible. On the day of the cutoff date, the association executive should be contacted to determine whether any rooms should still be held, such as for VIPs who have not yet responded. Rooms held after the cutoff date become the responsibility of the association.

The convention history will show the pattern of reservations and can be used to estimate the number of last-minute reservations.

Once the cutoff date has passed, the "final" numbers and any special instructions are relayed to the front office.

Cancellations. Cancellations on a tentative or a definite booking should carry the notation, "This has been removed from the function book," and the name of the person who removed it. Sales managers should erase the function book entry and make it a point to initial the cancellation form using the function book as a "desk." This procedure prevents the initialing of any cancellation form until the booking has been removed from the function book.

Sales managers are also responsible for checking the function book at the end of each month, making note of the next month's events. This procedure serves as a double check on entries and cancellations. The director of sales typically spot-checks the function book as well.

The Monthly Forecast. A monthly forecast is issued on the first of each month, showing all tentative and definite convention bookings for future dates. The booking forms are collected and checked against the forecast at the end of the month, to determine that all bookings have been entered correctly. Then the forecast is retyped and an up-to-date copy is widely distributed. Recipients of the monthly forecast include: the general manager; the food and beverage manager; all sales personnel; the catering manager; the front office manager; housekeeping; and engineering.

The forecast becomes the basis for three additional reports:

1. A report representing the month's business that has been confirmed and that still remains tentative.
2. A cumulative report, showing all bookings for the year, including those of the past month.
3. A month-by-month listing of all definite bookings for the next three years.

During the month, the sales copies of all booking forms, definite and tentative, are circulated to the entire sales department and then to the director of sales. Each sales manager has a copy of the monthly forecast and is responsible for updating the forecast with his or her bookings. For example, if one of your bookings changed from tentative to definite, you would need to add one definite booking and delete one tentative booking from your copy of the forecast. At the end of the month, the modified forecasts are collected by the director of sales and a new, up-to-date copy is issued.

Convention Instruction Memos. A convention instruction memo is issued to each department head for each convention that is booked. The memo should outline all of the information that each department needs to contribute to the overall success of the convention. Instruction memos are usually the responsibility of the catering department, but much of the information will come from the sales office. Table 6–3 lists the information included in a typical convention instruction memo. (2)

Table 6–3 Information Included in a Typical Convention Instruction Memo

Group Title	Convention Dates
Title and name of primary contact	
VIP names	
Billing instructions	
Housing commitment and room pickup	
Complete convention program	
Instructions to each department head	
Discussion of any functions outside the hotel that might increase or decrease the volume of business in bars, lounges, or restaurants	
Departures and arrivals of tours during the convention	

The Food and Beverage Department

As you probably already know and as we mentioned in Chapter 2, the primary function of the food and beverage department is to provide food and drink to the hotel's guests. Today's full-service hotel may have a coffee shop, a gourmet restaurant, a poolside snack bar, room service, two banquet halls, ten banquet rooms, a bar and lounge, and a nightclub. On a busy day (or night), it's quite likely that each of these outlets will have functions booked, with additional servers and stewards adding to the already heavy kitchen traffic. Furthermore, more than one function may take place in an outlet during a 24-hour period (e.g., a convention during the day and a wedding reception at night). A successful hotel must be able to manage its food and beverage operations successfully. No one knows this better than Lord Charles Forte, whose career in the hospitality industry began in the restaurant business (see Box 6–1).

Structure and Staffing of the Food and Beverage Department

The functions of the food and beverage department fall into two main categories: production and service. The food production, or kitchen department, is headed by the executive chef, a position that requires years of training and experience. Reporting to the executive chef are a variety of culinary specialists who are responsible for different aspects of food preparation.

The food service department, headed by the assistant food and beverage director, is responsible for customer service in all restaurants and food outlets. Employees in this unit include the individual restaurant and outlet managers, maitre d's, and servers, all of whom must have good interpersonal skills in order to be able to serve a wide range of guests.

Many larger hotels have yet another subunit that is responsible only for room service and another that is responsible for all outlets where alcoholic

BOX 6–1
Lord Charles Forte

Lord Charles Forte. (Courtesy of the Hospitality Industry Archives and Library, University of Houston, Texas.)

Charles Forte was born in 1908 in the village of Monforte Casalaticco, Italy. In 1913, he and his mother joined his father in Scotland, where the family opened a successful restaurant and ice cream parlor. After completing his education in Scotland and Italy, Forte managed a large family food service business. However, his vision was to have his own restaurant. Within five years, he opened the Meadow Milk Bar at an exceptional location in central London. In spite of the dismal economic conditions in Britain after World War II, the Meadow Milk Bar's success enabled Forte to expand his company to include nine additional restaurants, as well as numerous government catering contracts and all of the airline catering for Heathrow Airport. One of his biggest coups was the exclusive contract to cater the 1951 Festival of Britain, an exhibition on the South Bank in London that received nearly 8.5 million visitors in four months.

Charles Forte purchased his first hotel, London's Waldorf, in 1958. In 1962, Forte PLC, entered the London Stock Exchange. His was the first company to recognize the importance of highway travelers by opening the first motorway service area in Britain, providing motorists with a place to obtain food and beverage while in transit. Three prestigious hotels in Paris made up the company's first major international hotel acquisition in 1968: the George V, the Plaza Athenee, and the Tremoille. Lord Forte became the founding member of the London Tourist Board.

The 1970 merger, with Trust Houses PLC and the 1973 purchase of the U.S.-based Travelodge properties, helped to establish Forte PLC as a major force in the hotel and food service industry of Great Britain and around the world. In 1995, Forte PLC had 940 hotels with 97,000 rooms and more than 600 restaurants, including the original Meadow Milk Bar.

In 1970, Forte received knighthood and became Lord Forte. He is a Knight of the Grand Cross of the Italian Republic and was personally presented with a special Papal Medal by Pope Pius XII.

Margaret Thatcher once observed that Charles Forte is a man whose vision has never dimmed. When he founded his business, he was equipped with two vital strengths—a clear sense of right and wrong that he inherited from his parents and a sound education from his childhood in Scotland. By adding to these his own enterprising spirit, determination, and leadership, he has built a company that has provided billions of pounds in foreign earnings for the United Kingdom and jobs for tens of thousands of people throughout the world.

Source: "Lord Charles Forte," Cathleen Baird, Hospitality Industry Hall of Honor Archives, Conrad N. Hilton College, University of Houston, Houston, Texas, 1997.

Food and beverage departments provide a variety of services to hotel guests. (Courtesy of the Hospitality Industry Archives and Library, University of Houston, Texas.)

beverages are sold, including bars, lounges, and service bars. Because of the high value and profit margins associated with the sale of alcoholic beverages, control and accountability are important attributes for a beverage manager.

As you learned in the previous section of this chapter, most full-service hotels do considerable convention and catering business. The typical convention will use small function rooms for separate meetings, larger rooms for general sessions, and even larger facilities for banquets. Individually catered events include local parties, wedding receptions, business meetings, and other functions held by local groups. To provide for the unique needs of these particular kinds of customers, hotels often organize separate catering and convention departments. Organization and efficiency are two vital attributes of a convention and catering department.

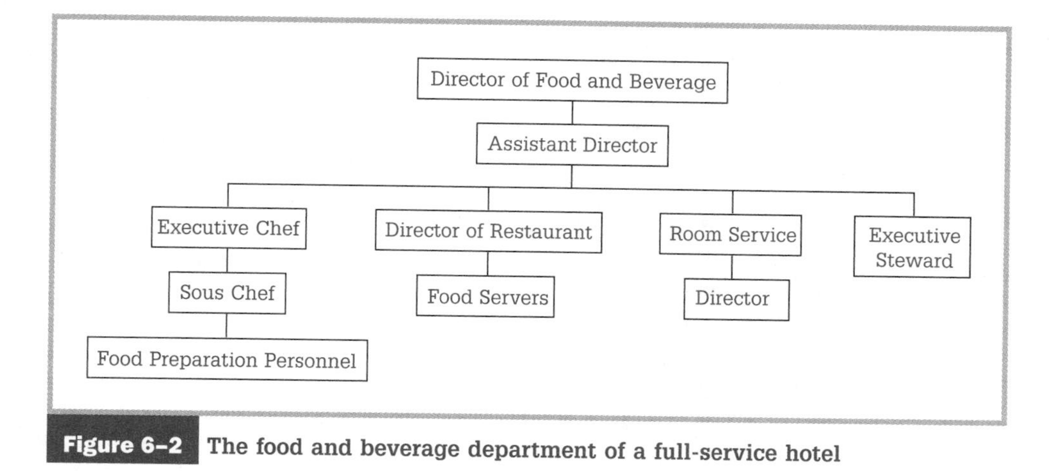

Figure 6–2 **The food and beverage department of a full-service hotel**

Finally, the job of cleaning the spaces of the food and beverage department, dish and ware washing, and general food and beverage expediting is often delegated to a separate subunit known as the stewarding department. For a summary of the organization of the food and beverage department of a full-service hotel, see Figure 6–2.

Coordination and cooperation among these various departments is essential to the successful operation of the food and beverage department. A guest who is dining in a hotel's restaurant requires the services of a maitre d', one or more chefs, one or more servers, a bartender, and a steward. On a larger scale, a convention banquet cannot be held without the efforts of the convention and catering, kitchen, food service, beverage, and stewarding departments. Cooperation and coordination are more important in the food and beverage department than in any other department in the hotel. A meal must be prepared in a certain order and time frame to ensure that the soup is still hot and the ice cream has not melted by the time they reach the table.

Convention Services

As you learned in the previous section, the convention and catering department takes over from the sales manager once a convention has been booked. The catering manager acts as a direct liaison between the hotel staff and the current conventions in the hotel, giving association executives a single person to go to with questions or concerns.

The convention services representative must be familiar with all hotel facilities and limitations of available building space. He or she also must have knowledge of, and experience with, the following areas: hotel policies and the law; the sales department; hotel architecture; the public address system; audio-visual facilities (screens and projectors); and all facilities booked by the convention (see Figure 6–3).

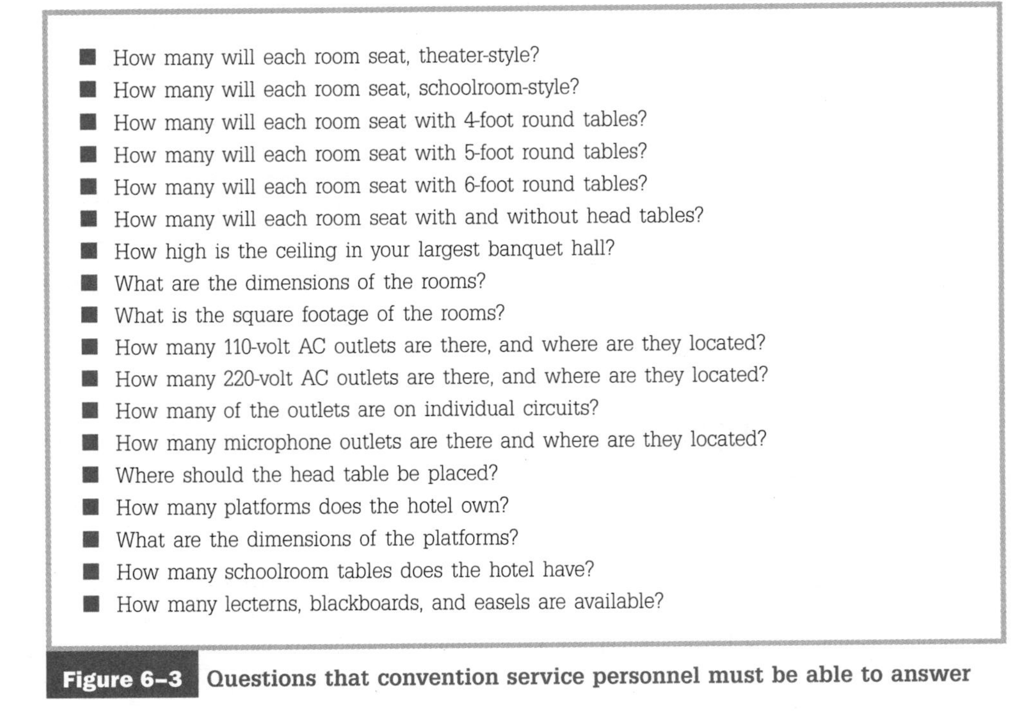

- How many will each room seat, theater-style?
- How many will each room seat, schoolroom-style?
- How many will each room seat with 4-foot round tables?
- How many will each room seat with 5-foot round tables?
- How many will each room seat with 6-foot round tables?
- How many will each room seat with and without head tables?
- How high is the ceiling in your largest banquet hall?
- What are the dimensions of the rooms?
- What is the square footage of the rooms?
- How many 110-volt AC outlets are there, and where are they located?
- How many 220-volt AC outlets are there, and where are they located?
- How many of the outlets are on individual circuits?
- How many microphone outlets are there and where are they located?
- Where should the head table be placed?
- How many platforms does the hotel own?
- What are the dimensions of the platforms?
- How many schoolroom tables does the hotel have?
- How many lecterns, blackboards, and easels are available?

Figure 6–3 **Questions that convention service personnel must be able to answer**

Regarding hotel policies, convention services personnel must be familiar with management's flexibility in dealing with convention guests. The attitude of many hotels that are driven by convention business is, "If we have it, they can use it; if we haven't got it, we'll rent it. If they don't break the law, destroy the building, or disturb other guests, let them do it."

Convention service personnel must have an excellent knowledge of the physical advantages and disadvantages of all areas of the building. Ideally, they should be able to respond to any of the questions listed without having to check on them.

Before final discussions with the association executive are held, all documents and correspondence must be studied carefully to make sure the needs of the convention are met. Any special arrangements that may have been made by the sales manager at the time of the booking, including room rates, exhibit hall fees, public address system fees, food and beverage function prices, and number of complimentary rooms, should be reviewed. Put yourself in the customer's place: nothing is more annoying than to have to discuss an issue again when you thought it was already settled.

Convention service personnel must also exercise discretion in making any changes to the arrangements that already have been made between the association executive and the sales department. Improvements should be

This hotel chef is preparing a dish for banquet service. (Courtesy of the Hospitality Industry Archives and Library, University of Houston, Texas.)

suggested as *alternatives*, and their advantages should be pointed out. Here is an example. Let us say that a customer has requested a stage setup as follows:

Stage measurements of 36 feet × 12 feet × 32 feet
A standing lectern (3 feet wide) at stage right
A head table of 8 feet for four persons at stage left
A screen (15 feet × 20 feet) in the center of the stage
A laser pointer and a gooseneck mike at the lectern

At first glance, this looks like an excellent plan. When you evaluate it further, however, you discover that the screen (20 feet long), the head table

(8 feet), and the lectern (6 feet) just fit on the stage. The stage is large enough, but the setup is not good. Since 80 percent of all people are right-handed, the lectern should be at stage left so that, when the speaker uses the laser pointer, he or she has to turn only a few degrees to direct the light onto the screen. The head table should be at stage right, angled at 45 degrees to the screen so that the people seated at the head table do not have to turn their heads completely around to see the screen. Furthermore, if the speaker is using a gooseneck mike and turns to look at the screen, his or her voice runs the risk of not being picked up. If a lavaliere microphone attached to the speaker is used, then this problem is eliminated and the speaker can cross the stage and still be heard clearly.

A server puts the finishing touches on a room service order. (Courtesy of the Hospitality Industry Archives and Library, University of Houston, Texas.)

Many hotels cater to the convention market by offering meeting facilities and equipment. (Courtesy of the Hospitality Industry Archives and Library, University of Houston, Texas.)

An alternate arrangement includes these and other improvements to the original plan:

Stage measurements of 36 feet × 12 feet × 32 feet
A standing lectern at stage left
A small table to the right of the lectern for ice water and glasses
A skirted head table for four persons, angled toward the screen, at stage right, with ice water, glasses, and ashtrays
A screen (15 feet × 20 feet) in the center of the stage
A laser pointer and a lavaliere microphone at the lectern
Two table microphones at the head table

Elaborate hotel ballrooms can be the ideal setting for banquets and other celebrations. (Courtesy of the Hospitality Industry Archives and Library, University of Houston, Texas.)

It is the details that the association executive and the conventioneers will remember. Another nice touch is to have someone hang the association banner on stage without being asked to do so.

Conventions are often times of celebration. Thus, liquor laws and other legal restrictions must be understood fully by all convention service personnel in order to ensure that a convention runs smoothly. In addition, laws governing fire exits, aisles, draperies, flameproof materials, floor load, fuels, gases, automobiles in the building, and any local restrictions must be understood and followed to ensure safety. For example, all floor plans of the hotel supplied to convention attendees should have fire exits marked with a larger dot and a note explaining that these doors cannot be blocked or locked under any circumstances.

A detailed resume of all of the meeting's needs must be distributed to all hotel departments at least seven days prior to the *first day* of the meeting, the day the executive director of the association and/or the conven-

A. Contact authorized to make major decisions on behalf of the group:

Name

Address

Telephone number, fax number, e-mail address

B. Billing:

1. Name and address of party to whom bills should be sent
2. List what the association will pay for and what the convention attendees are expected to pay for.
3. Any special instructions, such as check guarantees, and whether the association needs a bank to start registration.

C. Complimentary accommodations: list the party or parties getting free rooms and for how long.

D. Special attention: identify the party or parties that should receive special attention, and give details of the expected attention.

E. Room rate, commitment, and pickup:

1. Number of rooms that were blocked.
2. Number of rooms picked up (list all hotels involved in a city-wide convention) rate quoted to group (flat or special).

F. Major arrival and departure dates.

G. Room check-in and check-out pattern.

H. Breakfast pattern in restaurants.

I. Attendance versus guarantee of functions.

J. Expected telephone/in-room computer use.

K. Garage: expected changes in local vehicle traffic.

L. Exhibit information:

1. Set-up days and hours.
2. Show days and hours.
3. Dismantle days and hours.

M. Security: list the security provider (hotel or outside contractor) and any special security concerns (VIPs, valuable merchandise).

N. Special information: special requirements during meetings and coffee breaks.

O. Room setup

1. Include diagrams if available.
2. Setup style and expected number of attendees.
3. Location of aisles.
4. Location, number, and size of head tables.
5. Should the head tables be skirted (term used for the way the fabric will be attached to the table, with skirting being clipped on with a much smoother appearance)?
6. Height, length, and width of risers.
7. Should risers be carpeted and skirted?
8. Is a lectern required?
9. If a lectern is required, where should the lectern be placed?
10. How many blackboards, chalk, and erasers should be made available?
11. Are pads, pencils, ashtrays, ice water, and glasses needed?
12. Number and type of microphones.
13. Are television monitors required and for how long?
14. Are spotlights and spotlight operators required?
15. Is a record player required?
16. Will the session be taped?
17. Size and type of audio-visual equipment.
18. Location from which audio-visual equipment will project.
19. Will a projection platform be required?
20. Any special electrical equipment.
21. Any other special orders.

Figure 6–4 A sample convention resume

tion representative (association executive) arrive (the convention attendees may arrive later). The convention resume must include, but need not be limited to, the information shown in Figure 6–4. As already stated, each event is unique, and any special considerations or unusual circumstances also should be included in the convention resume so that there are no surprises.

THE ENGINEERING DEPARTMENT

The services of the engineering department, which consists of specialists qualified in various fields, form an integral link in the chain of services that are necessary to operate and maintain the physical plant. The **physical plant** refers to all mechanical, electrical, air-conditioning, and related equipment in the hotel's building. (3) Figure 6–5 provides a checklist of the essential features of a hotel's well-organized engineering department.

Maintenance of the physical plant is an absolute necessity: without it or any major portion of it, service to the guests would be reduced dramatically. The engineering department staff typically is headed by the chief engineer. The assistant chief engineer, building engineers, plumbers, electricians, carpenters, painters, and custodians all report directly to the chief engineer. The duties assigned to each member of the engineering department depend on his or her unique skills.

Plans and specifications issued for the construction of the building are available to all engineering department personnel and are kept in the chief engineer's office. All new engineering personnel should become familiar with the plans and specifications, and existing personnel should study them from time to time as well.

Engineering personnel are called on to fix broken windows, repair malfunctioning elevators, coordinate the sound systems for conventions and

- A technical and operations manuals library on all equipment and systems on property
- Building plans maintained in a single area in the hotel
- A building systems information file
- Systems operating schedules
- A preventive maintenance program
- A building and facilities maintenance program
- An energy conservation program
- A property conservation program
- A lockout procedure to be followed while repairing electrical and mechanical equipment

Figure 6–5 Essential features of a successful engineering department in a full-service hotel

banquets, and assist in plans for remodeling. The five major areas of responsibility include:

1. Preventive maintenance
2. Repair
3. Replacement
4. Improvement
5. Modification

Preventive Maintenance

Preventive maintenance is any work performed on equipment or the facility so that it can continue operating at proper efficiency without interruption. Manufacturers typically recommend the timing of preventive maintenance for best results. Alternatively, regular measurement of a piece of equipment

Established schedules for cleaning and preventive maintenance are a necessary component of successful hotel operations. (Courtesy of the Hospitality Industry Archives and Library, University of Houston, Texas.)

or facility component's output or efficiency in its use of a utility, such as water or electricity, will show the level of performance. A program of routine inspection and equipment service is an essential component of a smoothly run engineering department.

Repair To avoid any interruptions in the hotel's service to its guests, repairs must typically be made immediately, at the expense of other scheduled activities. Except in the case of emergency repairs, such as an out-of-order elevator with an agitated guest inside, repairs must be prioritized in order of importance. Usually those that directly affect guests and/or the use of rooms are of higher priority than, say, a broken door handle in the basement storeroom.

Replacement Replacement is performed when a piece of equipment or a facility component has reached the end of its useful life, that is, when it can no longer perform effectively and repair is no longer cost-effective. The most cost-effective way of handling replacement is to implement a program of planned replacement of major facility components, the retirement of failing equipment, before failure, with new or rebuilt components that have lower life cycle costs.

Improvement The goal of all improvement projects initiated by the engineering department is the enhancement of proper operation or reduction in operating costs. Such projects might include the installation of energy- and utility-conserving devices or the replacement of properly operating but maintenance-intensive equipment with similar but less demanding products. Sometimes it is difficult to identify whether an improvement project is worthwhile; one standard is to determine whether a payback of the initial investment will occur in three years or less.

Modification Modification is the alteration of the basic facility or its components to accommodate a new function. These can include the remodeling of existing space or the addition of new space. Unlike improvement projects, modification projects are initiated outside the engineering department. However, because modification projects are, in large part, driven by estimated costs and because engineering is the department of the hotel that is most familiar with the type of costs involved, the engineering department should be heavily involved in any modification project.

THE HUMAN RESOURCES DEPARTMENT

Like any other department, the human resources department directs its activities toward providing the hotel's guests with excellent service by a staff of well-trained professionals. Its objective is to staff the hotel with the best qualified personnel in the industry. Once employees become part of the hotel family, the human resources department becomes responsible for servicing one of the most important assets of the hotel—its employees. The responsibilities of the human resources department fall into three basic categories:

Recruitment and employment

Training and placement

Compensation and employee relations

It serves the hotel's executives, department heads, and employees in each of these areas. (4)

A successful human resources department must take the initiative and exercise creativity in developing labor sources. The staff must be alert to changes in the labor market.

Monitoring and encouraging the professional growth of employees is another responsibility of the human resources department. To fulfill this responsibility, the human resources staff coordinates all employee training, participating in planning, scheduling, and execution. There are three types of training involved in initiating a new employee: (1) induction training, or introducing the employee to the company; (2) departmental training, or training the employee for his or her specific job; and (3) on-the-job training, which enhances the performance of the employee's present job or readies him or her for another position. Regardless of the type of training, development of the employee for future growth is the aim.

The staff of the human resources department is expected to inspire confidence and respect of coworkers, executives, and applicants. The door should always be open to serve any who seek assistance. In administering company policies, fringe benefit programs, or any of its other activities, the human resources staff is expected to conduct its activities in a highly professional way, holding all information concerning employees and the hotel in the strictest confidence, and keeping the door open to any employees who have questions or problems. The human resources department must also manage the hotel's **affirmative action** program, which ensures that a proportional representation of employees on the basis of race, religion, and gender is maintained and that no discrimination occurs. Control becomes a critical factor in the hotel business. With the considerable volume of human resources required to provide services to the guest, the need to create consistency in the provision of such services and the potential for loss of assets used to create the services, a systemized and workable set of controls becomes critical.

Summary

The sales department is one of the first contacts that many persons have with a hotel. Staffed with a director of sales, sales managers, sales representatives, and their secretaries, this department's fundamental task is to bring food and beverage, sleeping rooms, and meeting room business into the hotel. Successful sales departments have multiple references available to their staff and actively participate in local, state, regional, and national organizations. Periodically, sales departments engage in telephone surveys and sales calls to develop leads. Convention bookings are a very important part of the activities of the sales department of larger hotels. The convention booking begins with entering entries in the hotel's booking software or manually in the function book. Convention planning at a hotel formally begins with the arrival of the association executive, who works closely with the convention services branch of the food and beverage department once the group has been booked. Each convention requires that separate instruction memos be sent to each department head that will have a role in supporting the convention.

The food and beverage department of a full-service hotel is a complex, diverse department. Its subunits can include a food production (kitchen) department, a food service department, a beverage department, a room service department, and a stewarding department. In addition, the catering department is part of the food and beverage department and provides support personnel to convention and group business. Convention services personnel must be knowledgeable about hotel policies and the law; the sales department's operations; hotel architecture; the hotel's public address system; audio-visual facilities; and all facilities booked by the convention.

A full-service hotel's engineering department is called to make minor repairs, to coordinate the building systems for conventions and banquets, and to assist in planning for remodeling of, or additions to, the hotel's structure. Its five major responsibilities are (1) preventive maintenance, (2) repair, (3) replacement, (4) improvement, and (5) modification.

The human resources department is responsible for recruitment and employment; training and placement; and compensation and employee relations.

References

1. Robert D. Reid and David C. Bojanic, "Marketing Organizational Structure and Management," *Hospitality Marketing Management*, 3rd ed. (New York: John Wiley & Sons, Inc., 2001), p. 30.
2. Joe Jeff Goldblatt, *Special Events—Best Practices in Modern Event Management* (New York: John Wiley & Sons, Inc., 1997), p. 143.

3. Frank D. Borsenik and Alan T. Stutts, *The Management of Maintenance and Engineering Systems in the Hospitality Industry*, 4th ed. (New York: John Wiley & Sons, Inc., 1997), p. 1.
4. Frank Go, Mary L. Monachello, and Tom Baum, *Human Resource Management in the Hospitality Industry* (New York: John Wiley & Sons, Inc., 1996), p. 10.

Review Questions

1. Describe the duties of the director of sales in a full-service hotel.
2. What factors would you utilize to determine whether a sales department in a full-service hotel is organized for success?
3. What information should be included in a function book entry?
4. Why is a one-stop service contact important for an association executive?
5. What is room pickup, and why is it important to a convention hotel?
6. Describe the monthly forecast and the instruction memo, and indicate their purpose.
7. If you were to explain to a newly hired convention services manager in a full-service hotel the key aspects of the job, what would you say?
8. How does the engineering department influence the success of the sales department in a full-service hotel?
9. What is the role of the human resources department in a full-service hotel?

Activities

1. Interview the chief engineer of a local hotel. Evaluate the department, using the checklist in Figure 6–5.
2. Ask to see the room setup for a large meeting in a local hotel. Make note of all equipment used, and evaluate the setup and note any improvements that might be made.
3. Accompany a sales manager from a local hotel in making a cold call. What were the key elements in the sales manager's preparation for, and conducting of, the call?

4. Observe a catering manager in a local hotel working with a client as they review the requirements of an upcoming event. What did the catering manager do to prepare for this meeting? What was the key information reviewed by the catering manager with the client? How did the catering manager handle any changes that were made at the meeting with the client?

Chapter 7

Control

CHAPTER OUTLINE

Control is the process of:

Evaluating actual performance

Comparing actual performance to goals

Taking action on a difference between performance and goals (1)

Much of the responsibility for control is delegated to the hotel's accounting department. The accounting department's traditional role is recording financial transactions, preparing and interpreting financial statements, and providing department managers with timely reports of financial results. Additional responsibilities, which fall to the assistant controller for finance, include payroll preparation, accounts receivable, and accounts payable. Another dimension of the accounting department deals with hotel operations, cost accounting, and cost control throughout the hotel, and often results in the department being called the controllers department to better describe its function.

Hotel and lodging managers have multiple methods of control available to them. The successful hotel and lodging manager is able to decide which type of control system is most appropriate for his or her establishment. The selected control system must be economical, accurate and understandable. Stephen F. Bollenbach has, throughout his career, done a masterful job of developing and implementing control systems (see Box 7–1). In general, controls can be grouped into three categories: (1) preliminary, (2) concurrent, and (3) feedback.

Preliminary Control

Preliminary control is designed to identify what factors are essential in the selection of a hotel's employees, vendors, materials, and supplies such that the hotel can deliver to its guests the quality of services they expect. For example, employees of a hotel must have the physical and intellectual characteristics necessary to perform assigned tasks; the materials and supplies provided to the hotel's workforce must be of sufficient quality to meet the standard the hotel has promised its guests; and the financial resources necessary to purchase materials, meet payrolls, and so forth, must be available in sufficient amount and at the right time. Preliminary control procedures are designed to increase the probability that actual results will compare favorably with planned results. Typically, preliminary control processes focus on human resources, materials, and financial resources (capital).

Human Resources

The preliminary control of human resources increases the probability that the hotel will match its needs to the skills, abilities, and attitudes of the staff that the hotel hires. Increasingly, hotels have realized that a significant

BOX 7–1
Stephen F. Bollenbach

Stephen F. Bollenbach. (Courtesy of the Hospitality Industry Archives and Library, University of Houston, Texas.)

Stephen F. Bollenbach (1943–) was named president and chief executive officer of Hilton Hotels Corporation in February 1996. He successfully led Hilton to spin off its gaming division into a new company, Park Place Entertainment, and to purchase Promus, the parent company of the Doubletree, Embassy Suites, and Hampton Inn brands.

Bollenbach credits business leader D. K. Ludwig for much of his business and financial knowledge. From 1968 until 1990, Bollenbach held a series of financial management positions with the Ludwig Group, including vice president of finance and assistant to the chief operating officer. During this tenure, he was closely involved with the development of the control infrastructure and with creating an environment that used a combination of preliminary control, concurrent control, and feedback controls to increase organizational profit.

Prior to his current positions with Hilton Hotels Corporation, Bollenbach was senior executive vice president and chief financial officer for the The Walt Disney Company, where he was instrumental in executing that company's $19 billion acquisition of ABC/Capital Cities, the second-largest acquisition in U.S. business history.

Prior to joining Disney, Bollenbach was president and chief executive officer of Host Marriott Corporation, an organization that he helped create in 1993 by leading an innovative restructuring of the Marriott Corporation. The result was two companies: Host Marriott and Marriott International.

From 1990 to 1992, Bollenbach was chief executive officer of the Trump Organization, where his primary responsibilities involved refinancing various assets and companies owned by Donald Trump. Earlier, Bollenbach was chief financial officer and a member of the board of directors of Holiday Corporation, where the recapitalization and major operational restructuring he spearheaded resulted in a 250 percent increase in stock value over a two-year period.

Source: "Hilton Hotels Corporation Press Release, March 12, 1996," Hospitality Industry Hall of Honor Archives, University of Houston, Houston, Texas.

competitive advantage can be gained when potential employees are effectively screened, interviewed, and trained. Preliminary control of human resources is the responsibility of the human resources department.

Materials The materials provided to a hotel's guest, whether it is the steak a guest orders in the hotel's restaurant, the wax used on the lobby floor, or the soap provided in a guest bathroom, must conform to quality standards. Preliminary control of materials is the responsibility of the departments in which the materials are used. In addition, satisfactory delivery and inventory control systems must be established and maintained to ensure that an adequate supply of materials are continuously provided.

Capital *Capital* for this discussion is defined as the funds that a hotel must secure in order to expand, renovate, or replace existing equipment or facilities. Preliminary control of capital, the monitoring of the acquisition and utilization of capital, is accomplished through the use of certain criteria to evaluate potential **profit margin**, or the ability of the proposal to generate net income by total revenue before a proposal is approved. These criteria include the payback method, rate of return on investment, and discounted rate of return.

The Payback Method. The **payback method** calculates the total number of years that are necessary for a proposed capital acquisition to repay its original cost; this must fall within a specific time frame. The total cost of the replacement, renovation, or expansion is divided by the increased cash flow per year after taxes and depreciation caused by the investment. For example, if the total cost of replacing an elevator is $40,000 and the increased cash flow after depreciation and taxes as a result of replacing the elevator were $16,400, then the payback period would be 2.44 years. If hotel policy is that all capital items must have a three-year payback, the purchase of the elevator would seem to be an appropriate investment.

Rate of Return on Investment. The **rate of return on investment** is a measure of profitability that is similar to the payback method. With this method, you would divide any additional net income after taxes and depreciation by the original cost of the investment. For example, if the additional net income from the elevator was $6,400, the rate of return would be 16 percent. The rate of return is then compared to a predetermined minimum. For example, if hotel policy is that a minimum rate of return should be 10 percent, then replacing the elevator is 6 percent above the minimum and appears to be a good choice.

Discounted Rate of Return. The discounted rate of return method takes into account the time value of money. In other words, a dollar collected today might be worth more than a dollar collected at a future date. Thus, the future value of the funds must be considered in order for the hotel to make an informed decision as to the potential value of undertaking various projects, such as the addition of guest rooms or the expansion of the hotel lobby.

Once the payback, return on investment, and discounted rate of return have been evaluated and the decision has been made to use the capital, a capital budget is developed. The **capital budget** is an intermediate- and long-range planning document that details sources and uses of funds, and ensures that adequate financial resources are available to meet financial obligations to employees, vendors, and others. The capital budget serves as the principal means of controlling the availability and cost of financial resources, and helps the hotel anticipate the level of business activity during a particular reporting period.

Concurrent Controls

Concurrent controls are personal, on-the-spot observations by the general manager, department heads, and supervisors to determine whether ongoing business objectives are being pursued by their employees. (2) The more successful hotel and lodging enterprises have delegated authority to managers and supervisors who use financial and nonfinancial incentives to impact concurrent control. For example, the director of sales might give an award to the sales manager who books the most business during a particular period.

Feedback Controls

Feedback controls are controls that give information about the progress of a business as it attempts to achieve its financial goals. Feedback controls target the end result or the position that the hotel wishes to reach by year-end and provide information that can be used to improve the acquisition of resources for expansion and acquisition of additional properties. The most widely utilized feedback controls in the hotel and lodging industry are financial statements and a standard cost analysis.

Financial Statements

Financial statements are summaries of the assets, liabilities, equity, revenues, and expenses of a hotel. Because they are so complete, financial statements are the principal tool used by hotel management to evaluate results. The general manager periodically receives a set of financial statements that usually include a balance sheet and an income statement. A **balance sheet** describes a hotel's financial condition at a specific point in time, and an **income statement** summarizes a hotel's financial performance over a given period of time. (3)

To completely understand a financial statement, the general manager must understand the standards of liquidity, inventory turnover, and solvency established for the hotel. **Liquidity** is a measure of the hotel's ability to meet current short-term obligations as they become due by maintaining sufficient cash. The most widely utilized measure of liquidity is the current ratio of assets to liabilities. However, the accounts receivable turnover and inventory turnover are equally important measures. Accounts receivable turnover is the ratio of credit sales to average accounts receivable. The higher the turnover is, the more rapidly accounts receivable can be converted to cash. A low accounts receivable turnover indicates a time lag in the collection of accounts receivable, which may limit the hotel's ability to meet its own obligations. One result of a low accounts receivable might be for a hotel to make the decision to tighten the hotel's standard for issuing credit to its convention or meeting business.

Inventory turnover is a ratio showing how quickly a hotel's inventory is moving from storage to productive use and is calculated by dividing the cost of goods sold by the average inventory. A high inventory turnover indicates a low balance of goods, which means that they are being consumed in large quantities by a hotel's guests. A low inventory turnover may reflect an overinvestment in inventory. The appropriate level of inventory turnover is based on the hotel's experience within the industry and its target market.

Solvency is the ability of a hotel to meet its long-term obligations. Such long-term obligations include debt to its creditors and the owner's claim to the hotel's assets, which might include cash invested in the project. The general manager is responsible for maintaining a balance that protects the interest of the owner yet does not ignore the advantages of long-term debt as a source of funds.

Standard Cost Analysis

Standard cost analysis permits the comparison of actual costs with estimated costs. If there is a large discrepancy in actual versus estimated costs, management can take appropriate corrective action.

FRONT OFFICE ACCOUNTING

Front office accounting is a system of vouchers, journals, ledgers, and folios that are designed to follow a guest's financial transactions and summarize outstanding balances in a running total, so that they will be ready to be settled whenever the guest checks out. To minimize errors and inconvenience to the guest, the folios and the journals from operating departments are audited daily. Figure 7–1 illustrates the front office accounting cycle.

A **Uniform System of Accounts for Hotels**, developed in 1925 by the Hotel Association of New York City, is a standardized system of terminology and procedures that describe hotel accounts, classifications, formats, contents, and the use of financial statements. Since that time, this system has been adopted by the American Hotel and Motel Association and most of the industry worldwide as a uniform system of hotel record keeping. (4)

Night Audit

The **night audit**, introduced in Chapter 3, provides up-to-the-minute statistics and financial statements so that management can make effective decisions regarding operations. The staff performing the night audit in a full-service hotel may include a night auditor, an assistant night auditor, a cashier, and a food and beverage auditor, all of whom work the night shift, which typically runs from 11:00 P.M. until 7:00 A.M. The audit of the guests' accounts is the duty of the night auditor(s). With an average room occupancy of 70–80 percent, the ballpark figure is one night auditor per 300 rooms, without late closing points of sale, such as restaurants, lounges, or other entertainment outlets.

The night auditor is responsible for the daily update of accounts receivable. Unlike other businesses, a hotel must constantly update records of amounts owed, since guests may check out at any time of day or night. Whatever the checkout time is, the hotel must be able to produce an up-to-the minute record of charges for the guest to settle. The room cannot be cleared for the next guest until the guest room account has been settled. Since the development of **property management system (PMS)**, or software that provides integrated financial record keeping and operating system, in

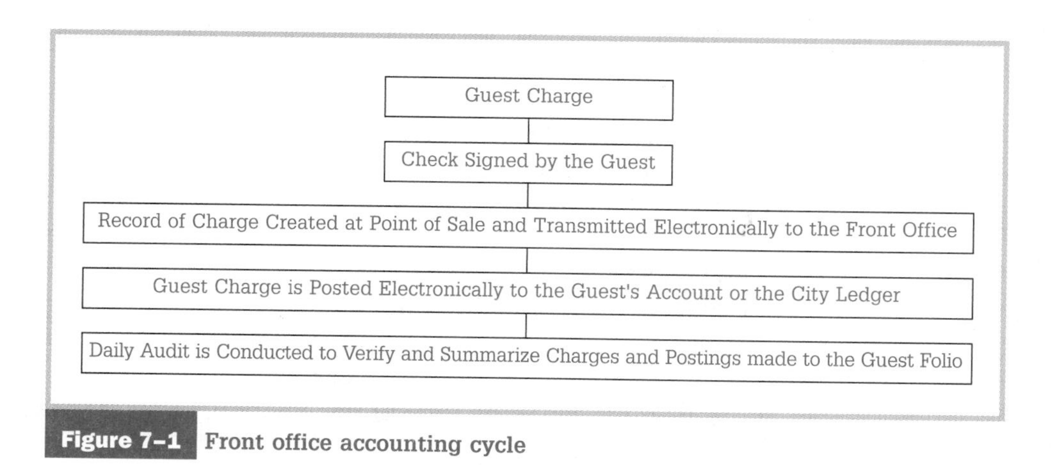

Figure 7–1 Front office accounting cycle

the 1970s, much of the work of the night auditor includes reconciling changes to guest folios.

Posting of Outstanding Charges. The first duty of the night auditor is to post (charge to the guest's account) all charge vouchers received before the close of the business day. Vouchers arriving after the **end of day**, or the time during a business day up to which the audit of all transactions are completed are not posted until the work of verifying the previous day's accounts has been completed. The closing hour of the business day may be later in hotels that have late-closing restaurants. Most of the charges are posted as they occur. The night auditor must post charges from all revenue centers of the hotel, such as the gift shop, the restaurant, and the lounge. It is not unusual for the night auditor to find some charges from previous shifts that have not yet been posted.

Verification and Posting of Room Rates and Taxes. Once all charges have been posted, the night auditor verifies the guests' account balances by comparing the accounts with the vouchers. The night auditor checks the cash receipts and allowance credits, which are a decrease in a folio balance that might be the result of compensation for unsatisfactory service or perhaps a rebate for a coupon discount.

The next step for the night auditor is to complete the accounts by charging each active account with the room rate and tax. The night auditor compares the rack rate and the rate for which the room was actually sold, and reports any discrepancies from the rates that were authorized for use to the front office manager.

Completion of Day's End Balances by Department. The night auditor reviews the day's end balance for each department to determine whether the postings to guest and nonguest accounts correspond to the amount that the departments have charged. The sales generated by the restaurant cashiers and telephone charges generated by the telephone department are usually the most detailed, and are summarized by the night auditors. The sales sheets from other, less active departments are then added in to indicate the total sales for the day.

If there is any discrepancy between the total sales recorded by the department and the total on the guest folios or city accounts, it is necessary that the night auditor check the sales record against the accounts. If there is no voucher for a charge appearing in a departmental record, the night auditor posts the charge, writing "no voucher" after the entry, and reports the missing voucher in a memorandum to the income auditor.

Once any errors have been corrected, the total of debits less the total of credits must equal the total of the balances forwarded (as when you balance your checkbook) for the night auditor's work to be finished. The night auditor then prepares a report for the controller, proving that the work has been properly completed.

Report Preparation. The night auditor prepares the following reports: a **daily operations report,** a summary of the day's business from which the general manager and different department heads can review revenues, receivables, operating statistics, and front office cash receipts and disbursements; departmental reports on revenue and expenditures; and a credit report, which lists guest accounts remaining unpaid three days after billing, and any unusually large guest charges or balances.

Preparation of Cash Deposit. If the account and departmental balancing conducted by the night auditor involves any cash transactions, he or she may be required to prepare a cash deposit. A copy of the shift report may be included in the cash deposit envelope to support any overage (i.e., if the total of cash and checks in a cash drawer is greater than the initial bank plus net cash receipts), shortage (i.e., if the total of cash and checks in a cash drawer is less than the initial bank plus net cash receipts), or due back (i.e., if the cashier pays out more in cash than is received, the difference is due back to the cashiers bank).

System Backup. As you have already learned, the hotel industry has become heavily dependent upon data compiled by computers. Thus, a complete system backup must be performed on a daily basis to ensure continued operation in the event of a computer failure. Because computer activity is lighter at night, this duty naturally falls to the night auditor.

As a part of the system backup, the night auditor typically prints out a list of guests, a room status report (i.e., occupied versus empty rooms), a guest ledger with ending account balances of all registered guests, and an activity report, which lists expected arrival and departure information for the next seven days.

Resolution of Room Status Problems. If a room charge appears on the room rack and not on the room count sheet, the night auditor must determine immediately whether the room is occupied. If the room is found to be occupied but the record is missing from the room rack (i.e., there is an open guest account), the room rack is corrected to avoid overbooking. If the rack indicates that the room is occupied but there is no open guest account, a search for the missing account information is initiated. If no unassigned account folio is found, the night auditor prepares a new one as best as he or she can from the transcript of the preceding day and by posting the charges and credits for the current day with an advisory to the front office manager.

If the re-creation of the account shows that the guest has indeed checked out, this means that the front desk agent failed to check out the guest correctly. The cashier's sheets will reveal whether the guest settled his or her bill by payment (provided the cashier recorded the payment!). The absence of a cashier's sheet entry closing out the account must be reported to the front office manager and the controller for further investigation on the following day.

Front Office Cashier

You were introduced to the responsibilities of the front office cashier in Chapter 2. The cashiering procedure involves opening the station; posting guest charges; accepting payment on guest accounts; posting city ledger charges; making corrections; processing transfers; conducting a bucket check; and closing the shift. Because the cashiering function is automated and is included in the property management system of most hotels, basically all that is necessary to start a day's work is to place working funds in the cash drawer. However, the cashier must verify the amount of cash at the beginning of the shift and again at the end.

Posting charges to a guest folio involves verifying the room number and the name on the guest account folio against the voucher before entering the charge in the guest ledger. The **guest ledger**, which is maintained at the front desk, consists of all of the charges made by guests registered in the hotel. The front office cashier also must ensure that every charge or credit has a supporting voucher and a room number.

Procedures for accepting payment on accounts fall into seven categories, based on the type of payment and the ledger into which the payment has been entered:

1. Cash
2. Check
3. Traveler's check
4. Charge
5. Foreign currency
6. Check payable in other than U.S. funds
7. Bill to be paid by a party other than the guest

Figure 7–2 illustrates the procedures that might be required of a cashier in handling each of the methods of payment.

The **city ledger** includes all nonguest accounts, or those local businesses that have been given charge privileges, including house accounts and unsettled departed guest accounts. During the cashier's shift, folios charged to the city ledger are filed by order of room number. Other charges are filed by origin, such as coffee shop, gift shop, or banquet. For example, at the end of a banquet function, the head waiter presents the bill to the guest for signature.

Cash

1. The guest is asked whether there have been any recent charges, and the folio is checked for posting.
2. Additional charges are posted.
3. The bill is presented to the guest.
4. For cash payments in excess of the bill, currency is not placed in the drawer until the guest has received change.
5. The bill is stamped "paid," and the guest is given his or her copy.

Credit Card

The cashier might accept a credit card for the amount of bill. (Currently, the hotel and lodging industry in the United States accepts various credit cards, including American Express, Visa, Master Card, and Diners Club.)

Traveler's Checks

1. The cashier requests identification (i.e., passport, driver's license, etc.) and compares it against the traveler's check.
2. The check is countersigned in the cashier's presence. Should the check have been countersigned and not witnessed by the cashier, the credit manager or assistant manager typically approves payment.
3. If the two signatures do not match, the assistant manager or credit manager typically handles approval.

Payments in Foreign Currency

1. Convert foreign currency to U.S. dollars using the foreign exchange discount list.
2. The head cashier, general cashier, or credit manager usually assists the cashier in completing the foreign currency transactions.

Payment by Party Other Than Guest

1. The cashier does not present a copy of the bill to the guest when instructions on the folio indicate the bill is being paid by another party or the charges are being waived.
2. The guest is told that the bill has been taken care of, is thanked for staying at the hotel, and is invited to return.

Figure 7–2 Accepting payment

After the bill has been accepted and signed, it is carried to the front desk. Before the check is charged to the city ledger, the cashier should verify the calculations and tip computation, and be certain that it has been signed. In the event the bill is paid at the same time that it is signed for, the check will be verified in the register and a receipt given to the head waiter, who then presents it to the guest.

Corrections are necessary when postings have been made in error or when they have been posted to the wrong account. If the incorrect charge is less than the correct amount, a posting of the additional amount will bring the account into balance, and a correction is not necessary.

There are occasions when the cashier is requested to transfer an amount from one guest account to another. Transfers also may occur between the guest ledger and the city ledger. In such cases, the cashier must fill out a charge credit slip with the amount, the name of the person being charged, and the name of the person being credited. This voucher must be validated for both transactions. Transfer of balances from one folio to another requires a credit to the old folio and a debit for the same amount to the new folio. The same room number must be indicated in both transactions.

Once during each shift, the cashier must verify each guest account folio against the room status board to see that the total of occupied rooms is in agreement with the number of folios. If a cashier finds that the room status board indicates an occupied room and there is no folio, the cashier should check with the front office manager to see if the guest may have been put in a room without the front office cashiers being notified. If this is not the case, housekeeping conducts a room check. If the room is found vacant, room status is cleared; if it is found occupied, the front office manager is notified. The front office manager will report the final disposition of the incident to the controller.

During the cashier's shift, all posted vouchers typically are separated by department. Prior to leaving the shift, the cashier takes a subtotal reading. The group totals must agree with the department totals. At this time, the "paid" (amounts received) and "paid out" (amounts paid out) totals are compared so that the cashier's "turn in," or drawer balance, can be determined.

After the paid and paid out reading has been taken, the cashier is ready to leave the station and prepare a cash turn-in. The cashier counts out the money or checks the amount of the turn-in; fills out the turn-in envelope, placing the currency in the turn-in envelope and cash in the drop spot; and counts the cash in the drawer to ensure that the amount assigned at the start of the shift is present. Any shortages must be reported to the general cashier immediately, and any overages must be turned in.

Accounts Receivable

Accounts receivable is a subdepartment of the accounting department. **Accounts receivable** are funds owed to the hotel. For example, the food and beverage provided at a wedding reception that was to be billed to the guest. If a guest checks out and does not settle the account immediately with cash or is permitted to be **direct** billed, or a guest pays charges incurred upon receipt of a bill sent at a later date, a receivable is created. Should the guest be authorized not to settle a bill upon checkout, charges are transferred by the accounts receivable clerk to the city ledger. All city ledger transactions are balanced by the night auditor and forwarded to the accounting department for further processing. At the end of the month, the accounting department creates a bill that is mailed to each guest who has an outstanding account.

The city ledger can include many subcategories, including employees, guests, and house expense. The documents that represent city ledger charges include folios, food and beverage checks, and after-departure charges. The first task of the accounts receivable clerk is to code each charge. If the name is recognized as one from the permanent accounts, the accounts receivable clerk can refer to a list of permanent codes and assign the proper number to the charge. If the name is not among the permanent accounts, the accounts receivable clerk enters the name and address next to an assigned number. If the charge is being made by a person who previously has made several charges but is not among the permanent accounts, a note is made to assign this individual a permanent number for the following month.

After charges to an account have been coded, the accounts receivable clerk runs a total on all of the charges for billing control purposes. A payment card and statement are mailed to the guest, who is requested to return the payment card with a remittance.

As payments come in, the accounts receivable clerk runs an itemized total for all checks received and records the total remittances. The checks, with totals, are then submitted to the general cashier for deposit. On occasion, the clerk will receive a check without a payment card and will be unable to relate it to any specific charge. When this occurs, the clerk will write a form letter to the sender and request the name of the person to whom the credit should be applied and the circumstances of the charge.

The accounts receivable department establishes a billing cutoff date near the end of the month. All charges incurred after the cutoff date, also known as month-end, appear on the following month's statement. For example, if the billing cutoff date is March 25 and a guest makes a charge on March 26, the March 26 charge will appear on the guest's April bill. This cutoff date gives the accounting department adequate time to prepare the statements for mailing prior to the first of the month.

After they are completed by the accounting department and before they are sent to the customer, the statements are returned to the accounts receivable clerk. These statements are reviewed for credit balances and obvious errors. Each credit balance should be checked to see that there are no duplicate payments or overpayments. After the statement balances have been verified, they are matched with the source documents and mailed to the customers.

Accounts Payable

Accounts payable are monies owed by the hotel to its suppliers of goods and services, including food and other supplies, telephone service, advertising, etc. Typically, an accounts payable clerk is responsible for assigning vendor numbers to and maintaining up-to-date addresses on all suppliers. In addition, the accounts payable clerk makes a checklist of expenses accrued on a regular (usually monthly) basis, such as telephone, utilities, and so forth, to make sure they are not overlooked.

Invoices must be compared to vendor statements for errors, such as omissions or discrepancies in amounts. When errors are found, the accounts payable clerk corrects the errors with the vendor by telephone or in writing. Figure 7–3 provides a checklist of the procedures that should be considered in processing a vendor payment.

One important vendor payment is to travel agencies that serve the hotel. A travel agency receives a commission for each room that it books for the hotel. Typically, a travel agency will not deal with a hotel that is slow to pay this commission, especially when a competing hotel makes a more prompt and timely commission payment.

One of the most essential functions of the accounts payable department is ensuring that all payments go out before the cutoff date, or month-end. If the accounts payable department is slow in preparing invoices for payment, the current month's expenses cannot be totaled and the monthly financial statement will be delayed.

- Prepare a voucher with vendor name and address.
- Assign a voucher number.
- Verify that invoices have proper approval, purchase order, and receiving slip.
- Arrange invoices by number and date.
- Code invoices to a hotel account.
- Record and code all credit memos separately.
- Submit to controller for review and signature.
- Submit to general manager for review and signature.
- Prepare check for distribution.
- File vouchers in numerical sequence by month.

Figure 7–3 Vendor payment process

INVENTORY CONTROL

We introduced the topics of inventory and control in Chapter 4, because they related to the housekeeping department. **Inventory** is a physical count of all operating equipment of the hotel. A complete inventory, including both in-use and stored inventories, should be taken at least twice a year. (This is in addition to the perpetual inventory that should be kept by housekeeping—see Chapter 4.) Operating equipment included in a hotel inventory count includes linen, china, glass, and silver.

Orientation Meeting Prior to the inventory, an orientation meeting should be scheduled by the controller, in order to assign specific duties and to discuss procedures. The topics for this meeting should include the inventory to be counted and methods to be followed. The personnel conducting the physical count are selected on the basis of their familiarity with the type of operating equipment being counted.

Counting Procedure Personnel taking inventory work in pairs and are called counting teams. One person counts; the other fills out the inventory card, providing item descriptions and quantities (see Figure 7–5). Then the inventory card is left with the counted items. A representative from the controller's office, called an auditor, who is accompanied by someone capable of identifying the items, verifies the count and item description. For example, the auditor may need someone from the housekeeping department to help distinguish among a wet vacuum, wet extractor, and rotary floor machine. The auditor and companion are called the auditing team.

Variables:

Unit	Quantity	Price	Extension (Quantity × Price)
Opening inventory (closing inventory for previous period)	+ Purchases	− Requisitions	= Total operating inventory
Cognac Glasses	500	100	600

Total operating inventory	−	Actual physical inventory	=	Loss for previous period
600		300		300

Cost per item	×	Items	=	Total dollars lost
$10.00		300		$3,000

Figure 7–4 Inventory loss calculation

Inventory cards are issued in numerical sequence, and a record is kept of the numbers issued. In the event that an inventory card is lost, the auditor checks the other cards in the sequence. The auditor should be able to identify the location of the missing card from the locations of the preceding and following cards. Such tight controls are necessary to achieve an accurate inventory count.

Linen Count

The count of linen is taken in three areas: linen room; linen closet on each floor; and laundry. Inventory in the rooms is taken from the established par stock, which is furnished by the executive housekeeper (see Chapter 4).

Because of the constant movement of linens throughout the hotel, in order to ensure an accurate linen count, a cutoff time must be established. After the cutoff time, the linen room must not issue linens, the floor storage closets must be sealed, no linens must be issued for room make up, the laundry chute must be cleared of soiled linen, and the laundry must cease processing incoming linens. This process allows the count to be undertaken without any danger of having linen moved from one area to another and counted more than once or missed.

Food and beverage linens cannot be counted until all dining and lounge facilities have closed. Once all outlets are closed, soiled linens are placed in a tagged cart and sent to the laundry area. The tag indicates that the linen has not been counted and can be processed by the laundry. These items then will be included in the laundry count. The count proceeds through the food and beverage storage areas and finally to the table setups.

It is essential that the food and beverage area stock heavily on the day of the inventory count to avoid running out after the established cutoff time in the linen room. There's nothing worse than being unable to reset a table with fresh linen when an unexpected guest arrives to dine.

Once the cutoff time has been reached and there are supposedly no linens circulating in the hotel, the actual linen count can begin. The linen count begins in the linen room and ends in the laundry. All linen should be counted, even those that appear damaged. It is the responsibility of the housekeeper to document and remove permanently all damaged linens before they are placed into storage.

China and Glassware Count

The china and glassware count should not begin until all dishes and glassware have been washed and moved to the counting area. The chief steward must be allowed sufficient time to wash and move glassware after the restaurants or clubs have closed, and all items must be ready for breakfast, so this count usually occurs during the graveyard shift. If possible, an assigned area should be used for counting in the location where the items to be counted are found. This not only facilitates the count but also insures against many inaccuracies that might arise if items to be counted are transported out of their normal location. Like dishware should be stacked and like glassware should be placed in the proper racks. Once the proper setup has been accomplished, the china and glassware count proceeds as previously outlined for the linens.

Silver Count Like the china and glassware count, the silver count must proceed after the close of business in the food and beverage outlets, and after all items have been cleaned. The most difficult items to identify in the silver count will be trays and items used on buffet lines, such as pans, trays, silver spoons, meat forks, and silver chafing dishes. To alleviate this problem, all such items should have a code number stamped on the bottom or should be otherwise easily identifiable. The counting teams must record the code numbers on the inventory card along with the item descriptions and quantities.

Accounting for Losses The beginning inventory is the initial stock issued when the hotel opened or when the previous count was taken. All items issued are added to the beginning inventory, and the results of the inventory count are subtracted. If the result of this calculation is a positive number, there is an overage (where did those purple linens come from?). More commonly, the difference is a negative number, or loss. See Figure 7–4 for a typical inventory loss calculation.

Date: 3/14/2000
Time: 10:00 AM.
Taken by Storeroom Manager (and) F/B Director
Approved by Controller

Page 1 of 12
Department F/B Storeroom
Location Shelves (Canned Goods)
Priced by Storeroom Manager
Extended by Clerical Staff

Item Description	Unit	Quantity	Price	Extension
		(Quantity × Price)		
Juices:				
Apple	46 oz	8	1.49	11.92
Grape	64 oz	9	3.18	28.62
Grapefruit	46 oz	14	1.17	16.38
Pineapple	46 oz	12	1.17	14.04
Tomato	46 oz	15	.96	14.40
V-8	5.5 oz	19	.27	5.13
Fruits:				
Peaches, halves	No. 10	7	3.98	27.86
Peaches, sliced	No. 10	15	3.86	57.90
Vegetables:				
Beets, sliced	No. 10	9	2.62	23.58

Figure 7–5 Report of inventories in service inventory card

Since each item in the inventory has a value assigned upon purchase, loss is easily transferred from a quantity missing to a dollar amount.

As we discussed in Chapter 4, loss can occur because of theft or damage. All department heads should maintain records disclosing quantities, codes, and written identification of all items taken out of service due to damage. During the inventory, any broken or cracked piece of glassware, china, or silver spotted by the counter is set aside for the stewards' inspection and disposition. At no time is damaged inventory included in the count.

The data provided by these reports and the results of a semiannual count is used to establish any discrepancy between the number of items acquired at a specific point in time and the number of that same item remaining at a later date.

Reporting After each count has been completed and audited, the inventory cards are entered into an inventory control module of the property management system. The code number and count of each item is entered, and the system is updated, resulting in a report such as the one shown in Figure 7–5.

Quality Control

In a traditional hotel operation, **quality control** is assigning the checking of quality to the last person involved in the preparation of a product or a service before delivery to the guest. For example, a food checker is responsible for checking each food item before it leaves the kitchen for the table, and an inspector is responsible for checking each room after housekeeping has finished and before a guest checks in. The principle behind quality control is that customers seek products and services of consistently high quality. Each employee provides a product or a service for an individual, and that product or service can be evaluated using the tools of total quality control.

Total quality control (TQC) is a system for integrating the quality development, quality maintenance, and quality improvement efforts of the various departments in a hotel or lodging enterprise to provide service at the most economical levels that ensure full customer satisfaction. To practice TQC is to develop, design, produce, and service a quality product that is economical, useful, and always satisfactory to the customer. (5) Employees also must be **empowered** to make decisions or to take action without a manager's prior approval.

The emphasis of TQC is on customer satisfaction. Principles behind TQC include:

1. Quality is what the customer says it is.
2. Quality is a way of managing.

3. Quality and innovation are mutually dependent.
4. Quality requires continuous improvement.
5. Quality involves a complete system connecting customers and suppliers.

In addition, there's no such thing as a permanent quality level; expectations are constantly changing. A sign of good management is the ability to mobilize the knowledge, skill, and positive attitudes of all employees in the organization, and to help them recognize that what they do to make quality better affects the entire organization.

TQC begins with planning aimed at preventing quality problems. The concerns addressed by quality planning include:

Establishing quality guidelines
Building quality into all policies and procedures
Procuring only quality products
Ensuring in-process and finished product quality
Following inspection guidelines
Handling and following up on customer complaints
Educating and training for quality (6)

SUMMARY

Controls are designed to evaluate actual performance, to compare actual performance to goals, and to take action on differences between performance and goals. Controls can be divided into three categories: preliminary, concurrent, and feedback.

Preliminary controls focus on developing procedures for human resources, materials, capital, and financial resources. Concurrent controls ensure that ongoing business objectives are being pursued. Feedback controls include financial statements and standard cost analysis.

Front office accounting is a system of vouchers, journals, ledgers, and folios that are derived from uniform accounting systems. The night audit and cashiering functions are key components of front office accounting.

In the hotel industry, the two main types of receivables handled by the accounts receivable department are guest ledger and city ledger. The accounts payable department is responsible for the prompt payment of vendors and verification that the payments are for goods or services received.

Inventory control is important to a successful hotel operation. A physical count of all operating equipment should be made at least twice a year.

Inventory involves a counting team and an audit team; an inventory includes linens, china, glassware, and silver.

Total quality control (TQC) is an effective system for integrating the quality development, quality maintenance, and quality improvement efforts of the various groups in an organization to provide service at the most economical levels that allow for full customer satisfaction.

REFERENCES

1. Joseph M. Juran, *Juran on Leadership for Quality: An Executive Handbook* (New York: The Free Press, 1989), p. 145.
2. Lawrence L. Senmetz and H. Ralph Todd, Jr., *First-Line Management*, 3rd ed. (Homewood, Ill.: Richard D. Irwin, 1986), p. 30.
3. Michael M. Coltman, *Hospitality Management Accounting*, 6th ed. (New York: John Wiley & Sons, Inc., 1997), p. 508.
4. *A Uniform System of Accounts for Hotels*, 9th rev. ed. (New York: Hotel Association of New York, 1996), p. xi.
5. V. Feigenbaum, *Total Quality Control* (New York: McGraw-Hill, 1991), p. 50.
6. Thomas Pyzdek, *What Every Manager Should Know About Quality* (New York: Marcel Dekker, 1991), p. 40.

REVIEW QUESTIONS

1. Can effective preliminary controls improve the services provided to guests and the efficient operation of a hotel? Explain your answer.
2. As a general manager, how would you utilize an income statement?
3. Does a high inventory loss signify a successful hotel operation? Why or why not?
4. How would you instruct a new trainee in conducting a night audit?
5. Summarize the key responsibilities of a front office cashier.
6. If you found a high balance of accounts receivable that were over 30 days past due, should you be concerned? What might be done to reduce the accounts receivable?
7. Explain the importance of inventory control.

ACTIVITIES

1. Interview a local hotel controller and, from the interview, prepare a summary of duties and qualifications that would be essential to successfully perform this job.
2. Interview a local hotel general manager and determine what information is collected and how the information is utilized when the hotel conducts a property inventory.
3. Interview a local hotel general manager and determine what precautions and procedures the property has in place to minimize accounts receivables.
4. Gain permission from a local hotel general manager to participate in the properties night audit. Summarize the key aspects of the job of the night auditor at this property.

Chapter 8

Developing and Opening a New Hotel

CHAPTER OUTLINE

- **Defining the Product Concept**
- **Preparing an Economic Market Study and Appraisal**
  - Selecting a Consultant
  - The Market Study and Appraisal Process
  - The Written Report
- **Financing the Project**
- **Developing the Site**
  - Acquisition
  - Design
  - Construction
- **Planning Opening Day**
  - Staffing
  - Implementation and Control
  - Organizational Structure
  - Final Month

The development of a hotel or lodging property involves all work from concept to opening. Regardless of the size or type of property, the development process is a major undertaking. A myriad of interrelated processes must be considered and acted upon. While there are no guarantees in this business, strict attention to detail will greatly enhance the project's potential success.

Generally, there are five steps in the development of a hotel or lodging business:

1. Defining the product concept
2. Preparing an economic market study and appraisal
3. Financing the project
4. Developing the site
5. Planning the opening day

While the order of these steps may change, the methods and processes used will be the same from one project to another.

The companies that are most successful in this process have given careful attention to each of these five steps. Throughout the development process, an awareness of the effects of economic cycles and social trends on demand is crucial. (1)

Defining the Product Concept

In Chapter 1, you learned about a variety of product concepts, ranging from full service to limited service. The first step in developing a hotel or lodging property is to identify market areas that show long-term potential for hotel investment. The next step is to choose a lodging product that will take best advantage of the local supply and demand characteristics.

One option in developing a hotel or lodging business is to consider a franchise product concept or an agreement with a national or internationally recognized hotel company to manage a new property, called a management contract. In Chapter 9, the concepts of franchise operations and management contracts will be discussed in detail. A variety of product concepts is already available, established by operators such as Hilton (see Box 8–1) and Marriott (see Box 11–1). Considerable time and resources already have been spent in developing market and demand data for these concepts. For some, having the research already done is worth the investment (franchising and management contracts involve some pretty substantial fees). Others may wish to develop their own hotel or lodging product concept.

Choosing a product concept is a chicken versus egg proposition: selecting is easier once a feasibility study has been completed, but, in order to

The 622-room Hotel Conrad in Queensland is a model of good hotel development. The largest hotel in Australia, it features four restaurants, a full array of recreational activities, a marina, meeting facilities for 2,300 persons, an international showroom, a nightclub, sweeping views of Australia's famous Gold Coast, and the 60,000-square-foot Jupiters Casino. (Courtesy of the Hospitality Industry Archives and Library, University of Houston, Texas.)

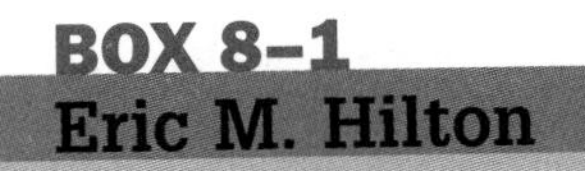

BOX 8–1
Eric M. Hilton

Eric M. Hilton. (Courtesy of the Hospitality Industry Archives and Library, University of Houston, Texas.)

Eric Hilton (1933–) began his career in 1949 with the Hilton Hotels Corporation, retiring in 1997 as the vice chairman of Hilton Hotels Corporation's board of directors.

Hilton began his career while he was still in high school as an engineer at the El Paso Hilton. He also apprenticed as a bellman, doorman, steward, cook, elevator operator, front desk clerk, and telephone operator. During his management career with Hilton Hotels Corporation, he held positions of resident manager, general manager, regional sales manager, senior vice president of the franchise division, and president and director of Conrad Hotels, Hilton Hotels Corporation's international subsidiary.

His brother Barron Hilton observed that Eric's contributions to their father's company, particularly in the areas of domestic and international strategic planning and property development, have been a key factor in the company's success.

Eric Hilton was particularly instrumental in the development of Conrad Hotels, the international subsidiary of Hilton Hotels Corporation. Conrad Hotels was founded in 1982 with a goal of acquiring and operating a network of deluxe and first-class hotels, resorts, and casinos situated in the world's major business and tourism capitals and resort destinations.

Hilton led Conrad Hotels to the news in 1983 with the development of the Hotel Conrad and Jupiters Casino in Queensland, Australia (see page 197). Developments followed in Barcelona, Brussels, Dublin, Hong Kong, Istanbul, Hurghada Resort Egypt, London, and Punta Del Este Uruguay.

Eric Hilton observed that the Conrad Hotels are first-class or deluxe facilities that are designed to be service oriented and customer driven, but that each property is unique and different architecturally from the others. In major metropolitan cities, Conrad properties are often part of mixed-use development (i.e., shopping center, office complex), coexisting within a complex of retailers, offices, and residential units. In more remote locations, they operate as freestanding resort hotels. This diversity provides the owners with a wide revenue base and the community residents and travelers with a wider range of services.

Source: "Eric Hilton," Cathleen Baird, Hospitality Industry Hall of Honor Archives, Conrad N. Hilton College, University of Houston, Houston, Texas, 1993.

undertake a feasibility study, you need a concept! It may seem a simple task to look around and see that a need exists right now for a new hotel in your community. However, you need to focus on the *long-term* economic trends and the potential for *future* supply and demand. The median economic life of a lodging facility is 35 to 40 years. So, in assessing your market, you must decide whether the need that you see today will continue to exist and whether current economic characteristics in that market are likely to continue.

To help you make your decision, you must examine the following factors: the characteristics of the existing lodging demand; the features of the existing lodging supply; and the features of successful lodging enterprises in the target market. See Table 8–1 for the data associated with each of these areas that must be collected to assist with the product concept decision.

Like any new product, a lodging product concept is more likely to be successful if one of the following market conditions exist:

1. The product does not currently exist, but the potential demand is strong.
2. The product exists, but there is a high level of demand and low levels of competition.
3. The product exists, but increasing levels of future demand are foreseen.
4. The product exists, but the existing product suffers from poor location, poor quality of facilities, and/or poor management.

Table 8–1 Information That Must Be Collected to Make a Lodging Product Concept Decision

Transient lodging demand	Price
	Facility requirements
	Seasonality
	Size, by market segment
	Future growth potential
Existing lodging supply	Number of competitive hotels
	Current levels of occupancy and average rates
	Orientation to particular market segments
	Analysis of facilities, amenities, and services
	Relative competitiveness, by market segment
	Probability of new additions to lodging supply
Reasons for existing successful lodging products in the target market	Location
	Management
	Affiliation
	Facilities and amenities
	Lack of competition

Preparing an Economic Market Study and Appraisal

If your assessment of the potential market area(s) for your product concept shows that the product concept is promising, then a more detailed analysis should be undertaken, in the form of an economic market study and appraisal, to determine whether or not the project should continue as originally conceived. Unless you have money to burn, you cannot skip this step; you cannot jump directly from product concept to construction. Obtaining financing for your lodging project more than likely depends on an independent assessment of the market conditions, the proposed site, and the product concept. Two of the three reasons many projects fail are related to the study phase:

1. The studies were incorrectly performed or incorrect recommendations were made.
2. The studies were performed correctly and the right recommendations were made, but the client was so enamored with the original concept that he ignored them.
3. The studies were performed correctly, the client adjusted the project to the recommendations, but the project was unsuccessful because of one of a myriad of variables. (2)

In other words, if you perform an economic market study and appraisal correctly and you follow the recommendations given, your chances are two out of three that your project will be a success.

If you, as a hotel developer, approached a potential lender with just a proposal, more than likely the potential lender will tell you that a feasibility study would have to be prepared by one of the major accounting firms with an active hotel accounting practice. Several months and thousands of dollars later, you would return to the potential lender, only to be told that an appraisal by a member of the American Institute of Real Estate Appraisers would be required to justify the amount of the loan. After additional time and dollars spent, you *might* obtain financing.

To avoid this costly and time-consuming process, a consultant should be hired to provide an economic market study and appraisal, which combines an all-encompassing report of the market evaluation, financial projections, and *valuation findings* and figures that show whether the economic value of the proposed project exceeds its total cost. The developer of a hotel project can expect to spend upwards of $50,000 on an economic market study and appraisal, depending on the scope of the assignment.

Selecting a Consultant

Because the market study and appraisal are so important to the progress of the project, it is important to hire a qualified individual to perform these analyses. The consultant should specialize in hotel-related studies and should have a background of exposure to multiple types of markets and products. Credibility is very important, as the consultant's recommendations may be challenged by the lender. The consultant should have access to hotel-trained personnel for both the market study and the appraisal. It is best if the consultant conducts the market study and the appraisal with the same staff (coordinating multiple staffs can be difficult). The appraiser must have adequate qualifications, background, and experience to conduct an accurate assessment of the potential economic success of the project. It is essential that the consultant take into account every category of expense in making financial projections; it is not uncommon for firms to omit fixed expenses, such as property taxes, insurance, reserve for replacement, and management fees.

The Market Study and Appraisal Process

The economic market study and appraisal should evaluate the local market demand, the area's economic and demographic characteristics, the attributes of the site, and the competition in order to determine the characteristics of an optimal lodging facility. Based on this profile, the study should then furnish estimates of future occupancy levels and average room rates for the proposed facility in order to project income and expenses over a three- to ten-year period. The three steps in the economic market study and appraisal are (1) fieldwork data collection, (2) project analysis, and (3) economic valuation.

Fieldwork Data Collection. During the fieldwork data collection phase of the study, the appraiser should focus on a number of specific characteristics, including the site and surrounding land uses, accessibility to transportation systems, the economic and demographic base, and competitive lodging facilities.

Project Analysis. After the fieldwork has been completed, the appraiser performs a project analysis, which consists of organizing the fieldwork data and stating conclusions regarding the most appropriate type of facility; occupancy and use projections for guest rooms; recommended food and beverage facilities and related amenities; and a ten-year projection of income and expenses.

Market Area. The appraiser must ask three main questions to determine the ultimate viability of a project:

Who lives in the area?

Does the area attract the desired market segment?

Can this area support a new facility?

While some preliminary answers to these questions may be found by the in-house project team, the appraiser's job is to provide more detailed information in order to eliminate inaccuracies and to ensure less biased recommendations.

Transportation Systems. The present transportation system in the market area and region must be evaluated, along with any plans for future changes in transportation. The results of the analysis will reveal how access may affect the marketability of the proposed hotel development. The following elements should be included in the transportation system analysis:

A list of all air carriers and the number of flights presently servicing the market area

U.S. government projections on changes in airline traffic in the market area

A description of the network of highways, with current and proposed traffic counts

A description of anticipated improvements in the transportation network

Competition. Knowledge of the competition is essential so that you can properly position your project in the marketplace. You need to know your competition's themes or concepts, target markets, occupancy rates, average daily rates, availability and types of services, age and condition of facilities, labor issues, market shares, and corporate affiliations. A summary of this information should be provided in the written report.

Site. A key variable in the success of a hotel or lodging business is location. However, there are other factors to be considered when evaluating a site for a proposed project. In addition to geographic location and aesthetics, the following variables need to be actively researched: accessibility; its proximity to attractions, business centers, or recreational activities; the infrastructure, including required site preparation, utilities, and transportation access; zoning regulations; an ability to expand; the political climate; environmental issues; and legal issues. Proposed or anticipated changes to any of these variables also should be considered.

Demand. Obviously, the primary objective of a hotel or lodging project is to generate a profit for the owners and investors. One of the major keys to success is to establish the number of guests who would be willing to pay the rate required for the hotel or lodging enterprise to remain profitable and then to attract at least that many guests. This section of the written report considers the demographics, target market, and current trends in the target market in the desired location. From this information, **market share**, or the number of potential guests from various segments, including individual and group markets, that may frequent the property, is predicted.

Facilities and Services. The facilities and services portion of a feasibility study is a true indication of what the prospective customers want. Successfully incorporating the recommendations of that part of the study, within reason, into the final plans for the project will help increase demand.

The identity of the target market dictates in large part the type of facility and services that the project will provide. A decision needs to be made as to whether to construct a new facility or to purchase and renovate an existing structure. Another lodging business may have the best location but may have failed because of poor management or some other variable. Other factors that might make the possibility of purchasing and renovating more attractive are local building ordinances, zoning restrictions (historical districts, environmental areas), market demand, and market share.

Projection of Income and Expense. The projection of income (revenue) and expense (cost) is the key to many projects. The cost/revenue ratio must be profitable enough to attract investors. Obviously, the lower the budget and start-up costs are, the greater potential for increased positive profit ratios if revenue projections are achieved. For example, the Paris Hotel and Casino in Las Vegas was underbudget on the projected preopening and construction costs. In contrast, Bellagio, also a hotel and casino resort in Las Vegas, exceeded preopening and construction costs. The average investor in Paris can expect a 16 percent return on their investment, but, because of these cost overruns, Bellagio investors may only achieve 11 percent.

Revenue projections must include room revenue, food and beverage sales, telecommunications revenue, and income from other departments. These projections can be compiled only after estimating annual occupancies and room rates.

After projecting all revenues and expenses, analysts prepare a statement of projected cash flow from operations before debt service and income taxes. Typically, this is presented in constant and current (inflated) dollars and covers the first five years of operation. As the rates of inflation may vary from year to year, they must be calculated separately for each revenue and expense category.

Costs include both preliminary development costs (the cost of building the facility, from groundbreaking to opening) and operating costs (the cost of operating the hotel). Preliminary development costs vary according to hotel type, size, location, amenities, and quality.

For most projects, a developer will expect to spend 10–20 percent of the total projected cost for the land, 50–53 percent for construction, 13–14 percent for furnishings, and 13–18 percent for miscellaneous expenses. Some often overlooked costs include providing an infrastructure to the site, such as utilities or site preparation; developing parking garages, retaining walls, and seawalls; and upgrading furnishings.

The calculation of projected operating costs depends on several interrelated factors: the design of the proposed facility, the prevailing local rates for salaries and wages, utilities, and other costs; the expenses incurred by comparable facilities in comparable markets; expected staffing needs; requirements of the proposed hotel operator; and predicted occupancy level. (3)

Unless the ownership or financing structure has been finally negotiated and firm commitments have been obtained from all financing partners, most analysts prepare a consolidated operating and development statement that includes an operating cash flow statement, an estimate of total development costs, financing assumptions, depreciation figures, management incentive fees, and loan origination fees.

Use of the internal rate of return (IRR) is a common method of analyzing project viability. The IRR is an approach to evaluating a capital budgeting decision based on the rate of return generated by the investment. After evaluating the project's IRR, the project analyst prepares a number of scenarios using different variables (i.e., higher or lower inflation rates, different interest rates, etc.) to reflect changes in the financing, development costs, or ownership structure that might alter the overall financial performance of a project.

Economic Valuation. The last step in the market study and appraisal process, the economic valuation or appraisal, compares the value of the project's cash flow, or the stream of receipts and disbursements resulting from the operational activities of the project, with the estimated total cost to determine the economic feasibility of the project. Professional appraisers use different approaches when appraising real estate for market value. The *cost approach* is based on the cost of replacing a property with similar square footage, construction, and amenities, with adjustments made for various forms of depreciation. The *sales comparison approach* compares the known sales prices of hotels with attributes similar to those of the hotel under consideration.

The Written Report

The written report includes the findings obtained during the fieldwork, the analysis performed on the findings, and the final conclusions and recommendations of the appraiser. In most instances, the appraiser issues the written report in draft form, so that it can be reviewed by the developer and any necessary changes can be made before it is finalized. The format of the projection of income and expenses in the written report should be in accordance with the Uniform System of Accounts for Hotels, as previously discussed in Chapter 7. Income and expense projections should be applied to cash flow before debt service, depreciation, and income taxes are noted. (4)

FINANCING THE PROJECT

A hotel can be financed through a commercial bank, a life insurance company, a credit company, a savings and loan association, a real estate investment trust, or a pension fund. Many lenders perceive hotel or lodging projects as high risk, that is, that the possible return is less than the perceived risk.

Lenders on hotel and lodging projects seek to minimize their risks by developing strong underwriting guidelines, criteria that the lender follows in evaluating the project. Underwriters focus particular attention on **cash flow risk**, the potential that revenues generated by the hotel's operation will be insufficient to cover operating expenses, debt service, or return on investment. Consideration is also given to **market value risk**, an analysis of the risk that the value of the property will decline to the extent that sale of the property would be insufficient to cover mortgage indebtedness, total equity investment, or inflationary value increases.

While assessment of the risks associated with a hotel investment are complicated, categorizing them is easy. Location, improvements, management, ownership, economy, and competitive environment are the major categories of risk.

Regardless of whether a proposed hotel is being developed or an existing hotel is being acquired and renovated, the various parties to the transaction must establish the structure of the benefits and the risks inherent in proceeding with the project. The parties to a hotel investment could include the developer, owner, lender, sellers, management company, franchiser, real estate broker, mortgage broker, and equity broker. In addition, the transaction would include accountants, appraisers, attorneys, title companies, engineers, and property tax consultants.

DEVELOPING THE SITE

Acquisition

The history of project development is littered with stories of hotels, motels, resorts, and casinos that have been aborted because of exorbitant real estate costs or other problems encountered during the development process. One example is problems with land acquisition. A single landowner, who may not even live on the property, can hold up an entire project if he or she is unwilling to accept an offer for the property.

Because of such painful and expensive experiences, many lodging companies have private individuals or holding companies make the purchases, without mentioning the developers' name. Only after all of the land and/or property has been acquired and, in some cases, only after the necessary governmental approvals have been granted, do the companies announce the extent of the project.

Once an investor has located a desirable market area, has selected a suitable type of lodging facility, and has targeted one or more appropriate properties worth pursuing, the acquisition process begins. Prospective buyers generally utilize real estate brokers who have experience in the hotel market, who continue to work with the buyer and the seller throughout the process of negotiating the numerous issues that are involved in the acquisition of property for a lodging facility.

As in any real estate purchase, the buyer and the seller must agree on general terms that are mutually satisfactory. At that point, a letter of intent is drawn up that spells out the basic terms of the agreement; it also serves as an obligation on the part of both the buyer and the seller to make an effort in good faith to complete the transaction. After the letter of intent has been accepted by both parties, the buyer must obtain financing. Negotiations regarding the final form of the purchase and the sale contract continue throughout this process. When the content, structure, and schedule of the transaction are agreed upon and the funds have been obtained, the closing takes place.

Other ways in which property may be acquired include a long-term lease, barter, and eminent domain. A long-term lease, in which the owner (lessor) retains ownership of the property but "rents" it to the developer (lessee), can benefit both the developer and the owner. The owner receives a steady income from the lease payments, and the developer is not forced to invest a large amount of capital in land acquisition. The lessee, who is permitted to build the facility to his or her own specifications, actually owns the building and whatever is contained therein for a period of up to 99 years.

In a barter arrangement, the residential landowner may trade the property for another that is to be purchased or that is already owned by the developer. The developer may assist in moving a home from the old site to the new site or may even construct a new home for the landowner. Barter is a standard practice when there are multiple acquisitions. It may also be used in negotiations with local governmental agencies, in which the developer agrees to relocate a street to city or county standards, or perhaps donate land and the design for a public facility, such as a park.

Local governments may assist in the acquisition phase through the principle of eminent domain. The local government exercises **eminent domain** when it condemns an unoccupied property and sells it to the developer, provided it can be shown that the public interest would be benefited to a greater extent than an individual would. Such matters typically find their way into the court system and may take many years to resolve.

Design

The design of a new facility is the responsibility of an architectural firm that has been hired by the developer. Although large companies usually use architectural firms that have a national reputation, they still employ local architects to review the plans in order to insure compliance with local regulations. In any such project, key considerations in the selection of the architectural team include prior experience with similar projects; familiarity with trends that may capture future demands or needs from the target market segments; a thorough understanding of the geographic and climatic conditions that

A hotel developer visiting the site of a new project.
(Courtesy of the Hospitality Industry Archives and Library, University of Houston, Texas.)

must be considered to maximize on construction and maintenance costs; and the knowledge of cultural and historic factors that are characteristic of the locale surrounding the site, which might be reflected in the construction and design.

Once the design has been completed and approved, the developer must answer some difficult questions. Is there enough money budgeted to execute the design? Will the design satisfy the target market? Can a hotel of this design be operated profitably, or is it merely what the architect thinks should be built? Have operations personnel (i.e., general managers, front office managers, directors of housekeeping, chief engineers, catering managers, food and beverage directors) been consulted to ensure that the "front of the house" (i.e., lobbies, public areas, etc.) will be pleasing to the guest and functional for the employees? Has the "back of the house" (i.e., service areas, storage, kitchens, housekeeping, etc.) been designed to ensure maximum employee efficiency? Increasingly, hotel and lodging corporations are giving considerable attention to back-of-the-house design in order to provide an efficient and pleasant working environment. For example, the Mirage Hotel and Casino in Las Vegas spent a great deal of time and money on the lighting, wall coverings, and decorations in its back-of-the-house areas in order to enhance employee productivity and satisfaction with the working environment.

The final site, architectural, and engineering plans, completed prior to final approval to begin construction, assign amounts of square footage to each use within the hotel complex. Space allocations vary considerably with the specific market area and type of hotel being built. For example, the public areas of an economy motel on an interstate highway will be much smaller than those of an urban convention hotel. Even within one chain, hotels will not be carbon copies of one another; rather, they will be designed to complement the market for which, and location in which, they have been built. Historic features of the area, cultural attractions, and ecology of the area, all might be reflected in the design. A downtown hotel in New York City will look much different than a hotel in Palm Springs, California, even though they both may cater to conventioneers.

Construction

A hotel company that is in a growth phase, that is, regularly developing new properties, may have agreements with multiple contractors to accomplish the construction phase. There are numerous regulations involved in any major construction project. Many state and local governments require "set asides"; that is, a certain percentage of contracts or local business involvement must be set aside for companies run by women and minorities. For example, the state of Louisiana stipulates that all boats used as part of a proposed hotel and casino gambling facility must be constructed in a Louisiana shipyard. Unless stipulated by law, it is not necessary to involve the local construction industry in any construction project, especially if it has been determined that requisite expertise does not exist. However, as just stated, local contractors and firms may have a better handle on local regulations. In addition, the good corporate neighbor concept dictates that there should be as much local involvement as possible without jeopardizing the on-time, underbudget mandate of the company. Pride of ownership by local construction employees will only aid in the community's acceptance of the project.

Once the design has been completed, the construction manager takes the helm of the development team ship. The services of an experienced construction manager are critical during this phase of a project. Table 8–2 outlines the key tasks of the construction manager.

Table 8–2 Tasks of the Construction Manager

Tasks of the Construction Manager
Initiate and administer contracts
Develop working drawings and specifications
Secure necessary permits and approvals
Direct the bidding selection process and conduct the negotiations with each subcontractor
Advise the project team of construction progress
Monitor change orders
Handle contract claims and disputes
Coordinate on-site facilities
Schedule construction activity
Monitor the construction activity and process
Obtain a certificate of occupancy on completion
Assist in bringing the project in on time and budget

PLANNING OPENING DAY

The most important date to all involved is opening day. This crucial date must be set with a great deal of care. There are many factors to be considered in setting a date. On the construction side, these include climate, cost and availability of materials, and accessibility to a workforce of skilled and nonskilled tradespeople. Financial factors range from budget and cost of labor and materials to inflation and meeting a debt repayment schedule. Staffing, vendors, equipment and supplies, FF&E, legal issues, and regulatory compliance and certifications are among the operational concerns. The usual length of time from setting the date to actual opening day may be as long as two years for large projects. Although projecting that far in advance is certainly difficult and there are likely to be snags along the way, changing the date, in any direction, is usually disastrous for all concerned. The reasons that adhering to the date set for opening day are so important include the scheduling of finances and promotions, and maintaining a competitive advantage. One of the reasons for a new hotel project may be a lack of competition; if competition enters the market before opening day, the financial basis for the project can shift dramatically before the first guest arrives and thus doom the hotel to financial failure.

Staffing Once the time line for opening day has been established, a staffing plan must be determined. Because there are so many different people involved, in so many different job categories, at so many different times, the staffing plan must include a hiring timetable. The electrician cannot install the electrical work until the carpenter frames the job, and the Sheetrock or drywall contractor must wait for the electrical work to be in place before putting up the walls. The first phase includes hiring the construction manager, whose responsibilities we have already discussed (see Table 8–2). Also among the first hires is the general manager, who, in addition to the duties we described briefly in Chapter 2, which will be discussed in more detail in Chapter 12, is given overall responsibility for all aspects of project construction and, during preopening planning, can be considered a project manager. Larger hotel companies usually have one or more general managers who specialize in new construction and are utilized by the company for that specific purpose. In this arrangement, as opening day nears, the company usually brings in a general manager with operations expertise to take over after opening day.

In addition, a general counsel or law firm is retained early on in the process to deal with legal issues (i.e., contracting, labor relations, etc.) and to ensure compliance with federal, state, and local government regulations. The human resources manager's role is to write a jobs compendium or the job titles and descriptions that will be required to operate the hotel successfully, to establish staffing requirements, and to produce policy and procedure manuals and employee handbooks. A controller is hired to supervise the budget, pay the bills, and monitor the equity and debt service. A construction manager is hired to work with the general contractor and all of the vendors, and to provide security for the construction site as well as the executive offices and warehouse or storage facilities.

Other temporary specialists or consultants who are part of the construction team include the designers and architects described earlier, as well as engineers. Full-time clerical support is also necessary. One of the biggest mistakes a company can make is to attempt to save money by limiting or reducing the size of the clerical force. Imagine the delays and inefficiency that would result if a human resources department in a new hotel only hired three clerical workers and then received 8,000 applications for employment! Such a mistake in the initial stage only leads to the additional expense of trying to correct the problem.

Once construction begins on interior facilities, such as rooms and restaurants, the second phase of hiring takes place. At this point, the directors of hotel operations and food and beverage should be brought on board. Both of these individuals oversee construction in their respective areas, in addition to staffing needs, policy manuals, procedure manuals, and FF&E. At this time, a staggered training schedule should be established because of variations in the length of training necessary for specific jobs. All training should end at the same time, approximately two weeks prior to opening day. This allows time for auditions for key guest contact positions and interviews for all positions, hiring, issuance of uniforms, orientation, corporate training, and dress rehearsal prior to opening day.

Employees in certain areas require licensing, which varies from jurisdiction to jurisdiction. It is the responsibility of the human resources manager to ensure that all employees have acquired the necessary licenses. Because of the shortages of manpower resulting from a strong economy, many companies are recruiting an international workforce. Failure to comply with every regulation can lead to lost workers, adverse publicity for the company, and possibly substantial fines. Thus, ensuring that international workers possess the necessary documentation is essential.

Also, during this second phase of hiring, a training coordinator is brought on board to originate, schedule, and supervise training programs for many of the departments. Exercises involving realistic scenarios are valuable to prepare employees for the diverse situations that they will encounter when the property opens. Usually there is only a short period of time available to try and mold an assortment of individuals with varying levels of training and experience into a smoothly functioning unit.

Implementation and Control

The implementation and control of the project should be the responsibility of a single person, usually the project manager, to ensure that there is a single source to bring together all consulting and permanent staff who need to give their input and analyze a particular issue. That individual should be given access to the organizational matrix and authority to achieve all tasks. For example, the president of a multimillion dollar new property, who has had no preopening or opening day experience, makes the decision to hire executives with good business credentials but no preopening or opening day experience. He informs his executives that they, in turn, are not to hire anyone with prior preopening or opening day experience, because he wants a "fresh approach," unfettered by "any preconceived notions." Although there have been indications, in the first phase, that things are not going as well as expected, he maintains this policy in the second hiring phase. As a result, it is a terrible opening day, and simple mistakes are made that could have been avoided easily by those who have had prior experience who could have anticipated such things as that not all of the guest room telephones would be connected on time and thus attendants would need to be stationed on each floor with special telephones to allow guests make local calls if the need arose, to handle reservations, to call for baggage assistance as needed, and to receive messages on a timely basis. The inexperience of the staff has cost the company millions of dollars in lost revenue and productivity; in addition, the negative publicity is devastating.

Organizational Structure

You learned about the organizational structure of a hotel or lodging business in Chapter 2. The new property needs to establish this structure prior to opening day. The basis of this structure is the job description of each employee. Job descriptions should outline the specific requirements of the job that the individual is being hired for, yet be flexible enough to allow the requirements to evolve as the job, and the project, evolves.

One Month from Opening Day

- ☐ All furniture, fixtures, and equipment (FF&E) are on site or in transit.
- ☐ All policy and procedure manuals have been written, approved, and duplicated for distribution to employees.
- ☐ Construction site clean-up is in full swing.
- ☐ Subcontractors are finishing their work.
- ☐ Letters of acceptance to all employees have been mailed.
- ☐ Training programs have been written and approved; trainers have participated in a "train the trainer" program to sharpen teaching skills. Scenarios used to train departmental employees in specific "how to" situations have been developed, approved, and tested.
- ☐ Copies of the entire properties training schedule, including room assignments, have been distributed to the trainers.
- ☐ The human resources department has employee packets ready, orientations scheduled, and employee uniforms on site.

Two Weeks from Opening Day

- ☐ Necessary employees have been brought on board.
- ☐ "Status of hiring" reports have been given to each department.
- ☐ Most employees are not yet on payroll, but they are arriving at human resources to fill out forms, get measured for uniforms, and pick up orientation and training schedules. The earlier the employees are processed, the less hectic it becomes when all employees are due to report.
- ☐ All offices have moved to the completed building.
- ☐ Landscaping is taking place.

One Week from Opening Day

- ☐ All employees report to work.
- ☐ Training and orientation begins.
- ☐ Last-minute job offers are made to fill unexpected openings left by no-shows and last minute rejections of job offers.
- ☐ Construction, landscaping, and clean-up have been completed.
- ☐ City inspectors inspect the property and issue a certificate of occupancy.
- ☐ Last-minute items and services are delivered.

Two Days from Opening Day

- ☐ At the dress rehearsal for opening day, corporate officials, as well as government, political, and religious dignitaries, are invited to attend a three-hour tour and rehearsal.
- ☐ Mystery shoppers are hired to anonymously evaluate the service and product being provided versus the standards the hotel expects to achieve for its guests.

One Day from Opening Day

- ☐ An employee family tour is conducted in the morning.
- ☐ In the afternoon, assignments are made for the following day.
- ☐ Errors that were made or observed during dress rehearsal are corrected.

Opening Day

- ☐ At last—the culmination of two years of work. Now the real work of providing hospitality and lodging begins!

Figure 8–1 Preopening planning checklist—final month

Each supervisor's job description should clearly spell out the span of control and the scope of the authority. At the preopening and opening day phases, the micromanager who tries to do everything himself or herself could doom a previously successful venture to failure.

Most large organizations opt for the departmental approach to corporate organization, which we described in Chapter 2. During this start-up period, it is important to ensure that all departments are compatible.

Final Month During the final month prior to opening day, multiple tasks must be completed in a specific order. Figure 8–1 provides a checklist for planning the major events of the final month before opening day.

SUMMARY

The development of a successful hotel or lodging property is the result of careful decision making. Critical decisions that must be made include defining the product concept, preparing an economic market study and appraisal, financing the project, developing the site, and planning opening day.

Defining a product concept depends upon the characteristics of existing transient lodging demand, existing lodging supply, and the characteristics of successful lodging enterprises in the target market.

An economic study and appraisal evaluates the local market demand, economic characteristics, demographic characteristics, location attributes, and the surrounding competitive environment. The economic valuation compares the value of the project cash flow with the estimated total projected cost to determine the project's economic feasibility.

Hotel projects are financed through commercial banks, life insurance companies, credit companies, savings and loan associations, real estate investment trusts, and pension funds. The development phase of the project typically involves land acquisition decisions, design strategies, and ultimately construction.

Preopening planning involves a series of decisions, including construction phase staffing, implementation and control, organizational structuring, and final month organization.

REFERENCES

1. Brian Bash, "The Development Process," *Hotel Development*, Urban Land Institute, 1996, Washington, D.C., p. 529.
2. Kaye Chon and Raymond T. Sparrenner, *Welcome to Hospitality: An Introduction* (Albany, New York: Delmar Publishing, 1995), p. 147.

3. Stephen Rushmore, *Hotel Investments—A Guide for Lenders and Owners* (Boston: Warren, Gorham & Lamont, 1990), p. 13-1.
4. David Arnold, Daniel Daniele, John Keeling, Nancy Landine, Christopher Lee, and James Nateware, *Hotel/Motel Development* (Washington, D.C.: Urban Land Institute, 1984), p. 79.

Review Questions

1. What are the three major elements of an economic market study and appraisal?
2. What are the five major steps in the development process? In what order do they occur?
3. I am in charge of all of the general contractors who are involved in constructing the hotel, and I am responsible for maintaining the construction schedule and for controlling costs. Who am I?
4. Why is adhering to the scheduled date of opening so important?

Activities

1. Utilizing the categories listed in Table 8–1, evaluate existing lodging supply in your local community.
2. Interview the general manager of a local hotel, using the categories in Table 8–1 to determine the factors that he or she believes will contribute to the success or lack of success of the hotel property.
3. Select a local hotel and determine what information was used in planning the project. Contrast your findings with what should be included in an economic market study and appraisal.
4. Determine from the general manager of a local hotel the primary mode of transportation of the guests. Determine from local government officials any changes in the number of flights arriving at the local airport and any improvements that may occur to local roadways and highways, and determine their effect on the local hotel.
5. Interview a general manager who has participated in a hotel opening and determine what factors were critical to its success.
6. Contact the corporate office of a national hotel company and request a summary of the information that they utilize when preparing for the opening of a new hotel property. Compare this information to the checklist in Figure 8–1.

Chapter 9

Management Contracts and Franchise Agreements

CHAPTER OUTLINE

Originally, a hotel, particularly a small hotel, was operated by the owner, who was the sole proprietor. In many instances, the owner also served as the manager, the concierge, the maitre d, and so forth. However, with the rapid growth of the U.S. hotel industry, particularly during the past 30 years, the management contract and the franchise agreement have become cornerstones of the hotel industry.

By the end of the 1980s, hotel companies discovered that they could make almost as much money with a management contract as with a property lease without assuming any of the financial risks. Consequently, they started to change their mode of operation. Today, only a few hotel property leases are still in effect; those that remain date from the 1950s and 1960s and are now nearing the end of their terms. (1) In the early 1980s, there were fewer than 65 management companies. By the early 1990s, the number had increased to over 500. However, as the lenders who had foreclosed on properties in the 1980s sold off these hotels, the need for third-party management companies dwindled. The buyers who purchased these properties were owners and/or operators who had no need for third-party services. By 1993, management companies were downsizing, consolidating, or disappearing. Some have observed that, during the early years of the 21st century, the number of management companies could drop even further. (2)

MANAGEMENT CONTRACTS

A **management contract** stipulates that the operator of the property is acting fully and completely as an agent of the owner and for the owner, and assumes full responsibility for operating and managing the property.

The operator may be an individual or a third-party management company. The employees of the hotel are employees of the owner. Any losses resulting from lawsuits or judgments against the hotel must be absorbed by the owner. Similarly, the final financial result of the operation, be it a profit or a loss, is recorded on the owner's account, not on the operator's account. For fulfilling the role of manager of the hotel on behalf of the owner, the operator receives certain fees. Hotel chains operate under the management contract concept.

American hotel companies have been eager to expand overseas using management contracts, because the foreign country assumes all of the financial risk in order to develop tourism. The management company provides the management talent, standardized training programs, and name recognition. Companies such as Hilton International, Hyatt, Sheraton, Western International (Westin), and Intercontinental are among the hotel companies that have used management contracts to expand their operations into the international market.

Advantages of the Management Contract

The management contract is a way for a hotel chain to grow with a low level of investment. Third-party management companies even have assisted the owner in some cases by providing funds such as loans to the owner to cement the deal. One advantage to the operator is that a management contract rarely requires that the operator participate in operating deficits, so the owner assumes the financial risk.

A management contract gives the owner greater control over the physical and operational quality of the hotel, thus protecting the owner's trademark and reputation.

Disadvantages of the Management Contract

Although he or she works hard to increase the value of the hotel through strong management and quality control, the operator may not reap any financial rewards upon its sale or refinancing.

The management company typically retains little control over the transfer of ownership. For example, an undercapitalized new owner can restrict the cash needed to cover the expenses that are essential to the maintenance of quality, adversely affecting operations. In the long term, this will decrease the value of the property and adversely affect the owner; in the short term, however, the task of operating the property becomes miserable for the management company.

The creditworthiness of the owner is critical to the management company. Any shortfall in the owner's cash flow, which must cover operating expenses and debt service, can result in the loss of the property to bankruptcy, loss of the management contract, and damage to the management company's reputation.

A typical management contract may contain a cancellation provision through which either party may withdraw from the contract, with penalties imposed on the party that initiates the cancellation, unless it can show that the other party has defaulted on terms that were included in the agreement. The cancellation, while requiring a fee that must be paid to the management company, although it does avoid other problems, can result in a surplus of key management personnel and a public relations problem.

Types of Management Companies

Management companies typically fall into one of two categories. Category one companies provide day-to-day management and supervision, preopening planning, staff recruitment and training, as well as a high level of name recognition. Hilton, Four Seasons, Marriott, and Hyatt are examples of category one companies. Like category one companies, category two companies provide day-to-day management and supervision and, in some cases, preopening planning, staff recruitment, and training, but they do not provide name recognition. Instead, category two companies seek to arrange a franchise affiliation that has a high level of brand recognition for the owner, which the category two company manages for the owner. Companies such as White Lodging and Thraldson Enterprises are examples of category two companies. Table 9–1 lists the top eight hotel management companies in the world today. (3)

Selection of a Management Company

The key factors in the selection of a management company include cost, market strengths, lender reputation, efficiency of operations, and flexibility in contract terms and negotiation. The management company profile describes its present status and its future plans. The number of properties and the number of years it has under contract, the locations of the properties, chain affiliations, facilities, amenities, ages, market orientations, and identities of the owners all should be considered carefully. The following are important questions that must be answered: Does the company currently manage hotels that are similar to the project under consideration? Will the selection of hotels currently under contract complement the proposed project? Have any management contracts been lost? If so, why? Has the company shown growth? Why or why not?

Cost is a key factor when you are selecting a management company, particularly when you are deciding between a category one and a category two company. Costwise, it may be difficult for a category two company to be competitive with a category one company. A category one company typically charges a basic fee of 3–4 percent of total revenue plus an incentive fee if costs are maintained at an agreed-upon level. The basic fee of a category two company is very similar to that of a category one company; in addition, a category two company must charge upwards of 5 percent of rooms revenue to pay the franchise fee. While the basic costs of either type of management

Table 9–1 Management Companies That Manage the Most Hotels

Company	Total Hotels	Hotels Managed
Marriott International	1,686	870
Societé du Louvre	601	550
Accor	2,666	368
Tharaldson Enterprises	288	288
Bass Hotels	2,738	216
Sol Melia	246	196
Starwood Hotels & Resorts	694	194
Hyatt Hotels/Hyatt International	186	183

Source: Hotels, Vol. 33, No. 7 (July 1999).

company are nearly the same, category one's incentive fee is often negotiable, reducing the cost of a management contract with a category one company to below that of a category two company.

The management company that can demonstrate greater market strength, that is, a successful track record in capturing and servicing the market segment(s) that are critical to the success of the hotel, has a distinct advantage. For example, convention and group sales require special marketing strategies, as well as significant experience in the collection and assimilation of data concerning the meeting requirements of associations, organizations, corporations, and groups. Typically, only a few hotel management companies can afford to make the investment required to secure convention and group business.

Another key factor in selecting a management company is the expectation of the lender. Lenders often are more comfortable funding projects that are operated by companies that are recognized both for their operational success in the market and for the product concept that the hotel reflects. Category one companies generally meet these expectations more easily than category two companies.

Efficiency of operation is another critical variable. Can the hotel management company make money? If a hotel provides comfortable accommodations, good service, and extensive amenities, but the operator cannot control costs and generate a reasonable profit, the owner in a management contract is the one who loses. To be considered seriously, a management company must be prepared to provide data demonstrating the financial performance of each of the properties it operates. Just as important is information about the qualifications of their key management personnel.

The methods for charging central services to the management contract should be examined thoroughly. Central services include accounting, reservations, engineering, architectural design, labor relations, insurance, and purchasing. For example, when personnel from the main office travel to a contracted hotel, is it considered a reimbursable expense or part of the management fee? Since a key variable in the selection of a management company is its ability to generate revenue through sales, the efficiency of the sales and marketing program should be given an especially critical look. Past sales and marketing experience, sample marketing plans, sales data broken down by market segment (i.e., convention, group, etc.), and public relations initiatives should all be scrutinized.

Flexibility of contract terms is another essential characteristic of a successful management company. Category one companies regularly require contract terms of at least 20 years; some require contract terms as lengthy as 50 years. Category two companies generally are more versatile with regard to contract terms. Typically, category one companies are also not as flexible regarding contract terminations.

For obvious reasons, the ability to negotiate is essential in obtaining contracts. Category two companies are less restrictive in their overall requirements than category one companies. For example, category two companies are more willing to accept shorter contract terms, performance cancellations for failure to achieve agreed-upon financial or service goals, contract buyouts that will allow the owner to change operating standards, and exclusive operating territories that might allow the owner to open a second property in proximity to the first with a different management contractor.

Management Contract Fees

Traditionally, management contract fees have been at specified rates that are set each year. More recently, this arrangement has changed to a graduated fee structure tied to the financial success of a hotel. In some cases, a maximum cap on the total management fee is negotiated by the owners.

The management fee can be calculated in different ways. If it is based solely on total revenue, the operator can spend money freely, particularly on advertising. In this case, because the revenues of the property are high, a high fee is achieved, even if the hotel might not show a profit. On the other hand, calculation of the fee on the basis of the gross operating profit places pressure on the operator to manage the hotel profitably. When results are poor, the management company may find that it is not recovering its costs. A combination fee based on a combination of total revenue and gross operating profit is the most equitable arrangement for both the operator and the owner.

Other Agreements Included in the Management Contract

In addition to stating the fee calculation method and clarifying the responsibilities of the operator to the owner, management contracts usually contain certain other clauses, as detailed in Table 9–2. These can include technical services provided by the management company, preopening services provided by the management company, and the operational duties of the management company.

During the contract negotiations stage, there are a number of issues that will be debated. For example, the owner typically wants a contract term that is as short as possible, with renewals at the owner's option, which permits the owner to change operators with minimal cost. The operator, on the other hand, wants a longer-term contract, with renewals at the operator's option. A long-term contract gives the operator an opportunity to recover costs associated with start-up (e.g., marketing, employee training, and management payroll), which might have to be paid if there is no alternative project to which a displaced management team can be assigned. For reasons indicated earlier, the owner's preference is to base fees on a percentage of net income after debt service and return on equity; the operator, on the other hand, is seeking a management fee based on some percentage of total revenue. The owner usually wants to maximize the number of financial reports,

Table 9–2 Details Included in the Management Contract

Technical Services Provided by the Management Company

A review of architectural and engineering designs prepared by the owner's architects, contractors, engineers, specialists, and consultants, including the preliminary and final plans and specifications.

Advice and technical recommendations on interior design and decorating, with the owner's decorator. A review of the owner's mechanical and electrical engineering designs, including heating, ventilating, air-conditioning, plumbing, electrical supply, elevators, escalators, and telephone.

A review of plans, specifications, and layouts for kitchen, bar, laundry, and valet equipment with the owner and the owner's consultants.

Assistance and advice in purchasing and installing furniture, fixtures, and equipment; chinaware, glassware, linens, silverware, uniforms, utensils, and the like; paper supplies, cleaning materials, and hotel consumable and expendable items, such as food and beverages.

On-site visits to assist in scheduling the installation of various facilities.

Preopening Services Provided by the Management Company

Recruitment, training, and direction of the initial staff.

Promotion and publicity to attract guests to the hotel on and after the opening date.

Negotiation of leases, licenses, and concession agreements for stores, office space, and lobby space, and employment and supply contracts.

Procurement of licenses and permits required for the operation of the hotel and its related facilities, including liquor and restaurant licenses.

Any other services that are reasonably necessary for the proper opening of the hotel, including suitable inaugural ceremonies.

Operational Duties of the Management Company

Manner of operation and maintenance of the hotel.

Hiring, promotion, discharge, and supervision of all operating and service employees.

Establishment and supervision of an accounting department to perform bookkeeping, accounting, and clerical services, including the maintenance of payroll records.

Handling of the complaints of tenants, guests, or users of the hotel's services or facilities.

Procurement and maintenance of contracts for services to the hotel.

Purchase of all materials and supplies required for proper operation.

Maintenance and repair of the premises.

Services in collection of receivables due the hotel.

Inclusion of the name of the hotel in the operator's group hotel advertising.

Designation of an agreed-upon reserve fund for the purpose of making replacements, substitutions, and additions to furniture, fixtures, and equipment.

budget data, and financial meetings in order to better control how his or her money is being spent, while the operator seeks to minimize such dealings. For similar reasons, a typical owner wants the power to approve or reject all transactions, while increased autonomy is the goal of the operator. Contract termination is another issue that is open to negotiation. The owner wants the freedom to terminate a contract upon immediate written notice; however, under no circumstances does the operator want the owner to be able to terminate before the expiration date.

FRANCHISE AGREEMENTS

Franchising has been one of the fastest-growing ways of doing business in the hotel and lodging business, both domestically and internationally. Franchises are not limited to the hotel industry; they also include restaurant businesses, such as McDonald's; income tax preparation services, such as H&R Block; and ice cream stores, such as Baskin Robbins. It is very likely that, during your career in the hotel and lodging industry, you will work for, or stay in, a franchise hotel.

A **franchise agreement** is an agreement between the holder of a named brand or product (*franchisor*) and another entity (*franchisee*), giving the franchisee the rights to use and market the franchisor's name. The franchisor provides services and conveys certain rights to the franchisee; the franchisee, in turn, has certain obligations to the franchisor, which will be discussed in detail later in this chapter. If you have a hotel concept that you wish to franchise, you must first establish the quality of your product and your expertise in the field by operating company-owned properties. Only after demonstrating the success of these properties can you make your franchise a marketable package. The franchise arrangement has provided a means for small investors to get into the hotel and lodging business with a reasonable assurance of success. Banks and lending institutions view favorably the better-known franchises and, indeed, are often reluctant to make loans to potential investors in the lodging industry unless a franchise has been acquired. In the past, the most aggressive franchisor in the hotel and lodging business has been Kemmons Wilson's Holiday Inn. However, as shown in Table 9–3, currently Cendant Corporation is the leading franchisor globally, with 500,000 rooms in 5,978 hotels. Cendant Corporation owns such names as Ramada and Howard Johnson. Following Cendant Corporation is Choice Hotels International (Quality Inn, Comfort Inn, Clarion, Sleep Inn, Rodeway Inn, EconoLodge, MainStay, etc.). The owner of the Holiday Inn name, Bass Hotels & Resorts, has fallen to third place.

The services offered by a franchisor can be broken down into three general categories: (1) operating procedures, (2) technical assistance, and (3) marketing. (4)

Franchise Operating Procedures

A reputable franchisor has established operating procedures that the franchisee can use to run the business successfully. These procedures usually are provided in the form of a series of operating manuals. The manuals should be continually updated as the franchisor amends and improves its procedures.

Table 9-3 Leaders in Hotel Franchises

Company Hotels	Total Number of Hotels	Number of Franchises
Cendant Corporation	5,978	5,978
Choice Hotels International	3,670	3,670
Bass Hotels & Resorts	2,738	2,438
Marriott International	1,686	753
Carlson Hospitality Worldwide	548	532
Accor	2,666	458
Hotels & Compagnie	326	326
Starwood Hotels & Resorts Worldwide	694	280
U.S. Franchise Systems	227	227

Source: Hotels (July 1999).

In opening any new business, the greatest challenge is obtaining qualified personnel. For this reason, many franchisors provide training programs. Such programs require some or all of the staff to attend training sessions at a franchisor-owned facility.

Regional managers or inspectors employed by the franchisor typically visit each franchise operation periodically. Although their primary responsibility is to ensure compliance with the franchisor's standards, they also provide advice and assistance covering all facets of the operation. For example, the regional manager reviews staffing and makes suggestions for payroll savings. The quality of food and beverage preparation and service might also be discussed. The inspector also may have valuable recommendations for reducing operating costs in areas such as food and beverage, purchasing, operating supplies, and equipment, as well as advice about marketing techniques, such as menu presentation and layout.

Franchise Technical Assistance

For an additional fee, franchisors also can make available various optional forms of technical assistance. Certain franchisors will aid in the study of potential sites and eventual site selection. Franchisors also may provide advice and assistance concerning financing—from help in preparing budgets and feasibility studies to actually introducing the franchisee to sources of capital or helping to negotiate a mortgage from the lender. Architectural services also may be provided. A franchisor may have its own firm of architects, whose services can be obtained for the complete architectural design of the hotel. Interior design, project management, and construction supervision are other services that are available from certain franchisors.

BOX 9–1
Howard Johnson

Howard Johnson. (Courtesy of the Hospitality Industry Archives and Library, University of Houston, Texas.)

Howard Dearing Johnson (1896–1972) is widely regarded as one of the first to introduce franchising. Johnson also developed the concept of a uniform system of operations and procedures that ensured consistency among the many facilities bearing his name.

Johnson began his hospitality empire in 1925 in Wollaston, Massachusetts, in a small patent medicine store and soda fountain that he inherited from his father. Soon after taking over the store, he revived its sales by purchasing a recipe for ice cream that contained twice the common amount of butterfat. This new ice cream caused sales to skyrocket. An admitted ice cream fanatic, Johnson spent a great deal of time developing new ice cream flavors to feature at his soda fountain, and before long he had begun to make and sell other easily prepared food items such as sandwiches, hot dogs, and fried clams. Three years later, the first Howard Johnson restaurant was born.

A family friend, Reginald Sprague, wanted to use the Howard Johnson name to promote sales at a new restaurant that he was opening. Sprague agreed to pay a cash fee, to buy all of his ice cream and many other food products from Johnson, and to allow Johnson to set the standards for all foods served at the restaurant. Johnson believed new inventions such as the automobile would change the face of America, and he wanted to be the one to provide future American travelers with a chain of restaurants

Purchasing services is extremely valuable to the new franchisee in acquiring FF&E, but their continuing availability is equally important. Purchasing services are more commonly used in the areas of operating equipment (linen, china, glass, and silver) and consumables such as paper supplies and guest supplies rather than for purchasing food and beverages. Some franchisors actually stock or even manufacture certain items, particularly identity items that embody the name of the chain, such as soap or room service menu covers. In such circumstances, the chain will invoice the franchisee at a price that includes a profit factor. In other cases, the franchisor does the purchasing for the franchisee, taking advantage of its available volume discounts.

It is also common practice for the franchisor to have strict guidelines on that would offer "good food at sensible prices." Howard Johnson signed similar agreements with other hopeful entrepreneurs, and by 1940 there were 135 company-owned and franchised restaurants along the East Coast. Most of the restaurants were located on major highways, and their now famous bright orange roofs made them highly visible to passing motorists. To support the needs of his restaurants, Johnson developed a central commissary concept, enabling customers at all of the properties to be served the same quality food.

By 1954, Howard Johnson had 400 restaurants. It was at this time that Johnson realized that the logical compliment to his nationwide food service operations was the development of lodging properties that shared the same consistent quality and service. Thus, in 1954, he franchised his first motor lodge in Savannah, Georgia. The franchise agreements enabled Johnson to quickly expand his lodging property holdings to tourist markets as well as to business travelers who needed meeting and banquet facilities.

When he ceded everyday control of the company to his son, Howard Brennan Johnson, his advice was to "make it grow," and that is exactly what his son did. Under the younger Johnson's watchful direction, the company's restaurant and lodging properties spread across the country and beyond. He took the company public in 1961, and it was eventually acquired and globally marketed by The Blackstone Group's subsidiary HFS, Inc. HFS, Inc. evolved into the Cendant Corporation, which, in turn, accelerated the globalization of the brand. By 1995, Howard Johnson's properties were in Mexico and Canada. The brand name now has been changed to Howard Johnson International, Inc. to reflect the increasing globalization of its product, and its properties can be found around the world.

Source: "Howard D. Johnson," Cathleen Baird, Hospitality Industry Archives, Conrad N. Hilton College, University of Houston, Houston, Texas, 1999.

how the franchise name can be displayed and to specify which design companies can be used. While the sign is owned by the franchisee, the right to display the sign is part of the franchise agreement. If the agreement is terminated, all signage containing the franchisor's name must be removed.

Marketing a Franchise

The most important ingredient in any franchise agreement, and indeed the reason in many cases for entering into a franchise agreement, is marketing.The franchisor's marketing techniques already have been tested and proven successful. The company name is a key element in the marketing. It appears on signs, menus, glassware, napkins, and many other places. But the nucleus of any hotel/motel franchise marketing program is the reservation system. A properly functioning reservation system should provide a steady flow of reservations to the individual franchisees. Through the "referral" process, franchisees accept reservations for other member properties and pass them along through the reservation network. Since many of these reservations are derived from guests who are currently staying at another property, the more franchises there are in operation, the more potential sources of business there are.

An extensive integrated advertising program is almost as important as an effective reservation system. An advertising campaign that keeps the name of the franchise in the public eye is called "joint advertising," since it is intended to promote the chain as a whole rather than any single property. The media targeted by joint advertising campaigns include newspapers, magazines, radio, and television. Most joint advertising campaigns, regardless of the medium, emphasize the consistent quality of all properties bearing the company name.

In another approach, a number of specifically identified properties are grouped in a franchisor-sponsored advertisement. For example, all of the franchises in a targeted geographical region might be included in the same advertisement. Properties also can be grouped by the type of facility; in a winter advertisement aimed specifically at the resort market might be included all of a resort's properties that are located in the Caribbean.

Another element of an effective franchise marketing package is a sales network. The franchisor places regional sales offices at strategic locations throughout the country, with staff who sell not only the properties in their regions but also the properties of all franchisees. This type of selling is primarily aimed at the group and convention market, but limited selling can also be done in the corporate and travel agent markets.

Advantages of a Franchise

Acquiring a franchise may be the least expensive alternative to gain access to a central reservation system and national advertising. In addition, the franchise brings customer recognition and brand loyalty.

Disadvantages of a Franchise

One of the disadvantages of a franchise is a loss of autonomy. The franchisee is obliged to meet the franchisor's standards, which have been established so that the reputation of the franchisor will be upheld. Such standards can be divided into two broad categories: brand standards and operational-quality standards. Observance of these standards is policed by the visits and reports of the regional managers or inspectors.

Brand standards outline the physical characteristics that are required of a franchised property. Some of the more common definitive standards include the size of the rooms; the amount of furniture; the size of the beds; the existence of food and beverage outlets; the hours of operation of outlets; the number of parking spaces; guest room entertainment systems (i.e., type of television, number of television channels, premium channels, etc.); and type of recreational facilities (i.e., pool, spa, exercise facility). Because they are so concrete, whether or not the property meets the definitive standards is seldom an area for disagreement between franchisor and franchisee.

Operational-quality standards are less easily defined. These standards, which relate to the operation of the franchise, include the following: housekeeping and sanitation; customer service; quality of service; rates charged; checkout times; and changing of linens.

Failure to meet either type of standard may be excused once or twice, but continued violations usually are not permitted.

Franchise Fees

Initial Fee. Most franchisors require up-front payment of an initial fee that is not refundable should the franchise agreement be terminated as a result of noncompliance with definitive or operational-quality standards. This fee, which may take the form of a dollar amount plus a per room add-on, covers franchisor costs associated with processing, site review, market study analysis, plan review, construction inspections, and preopening technical support. The initial fee is lower if the application is for a conversion of an existing property rather than for new construction, since the franchisor's costs are lower. If an application for a franchise is turned down, all or most of the fee is returned to the prospective franchisee, minus the cost of processing. (5)

Monthly Fee. In addition to the initial fee, which can run as high as $50,000 for a popular franchise, such as Hilton, there is also a monthly franchise fee. Various methods are used for computing this fee. It can take the form of a fixed monthly fee, a fixed monthly fee plus an amount per reservation made through the reservation system, a percentage of room sales, or a percentage of total sales. Still other options include a fixed dollar amount per available room and a fixed dollar amount per occupied room. A combination of two or more of these options is also possible, depending on the franchise.

A fixed monthly fee plus an amount per reservation made through the reservation system is most desirable from the point of view of the franchisee, since it obliges the chain to provide reservations in order to generate fees. However, a monthly fee is more often based on a percentage of room sales, which can range from as little as 3 percent to as much as 6½ percent.

Fixed reservation fees are desirable if they are based on the actual number of arrivals at the franchisee's facility. A per transaction fee is not as desirable from the franchisee's point of view. For example, if the fixed reservation fee is $4 and a guest makes a reservation but does not show, the franchisee would still be charged $4. If a reservation is made, cancelled, and made again with different information, the franchisee is charged for each of these transactions, so the reservation of a single room costs the franchisee $12. Reservation fees also can be based on a percentage of room sales, ranging from 1–2½ percent.

Advertising Fees. In addition, the franchisee can expect to pay for national and regional advertising, as well as the development and distribution of a franchise directory. Typically, the advertising fees gathered from the franchisees are placed into a fund that can only be expended for promotion and normally does not represent a profit center for the franchisor.

Training Fees. Since many franchisors have built their products around strong quality and guest relations, they have developed extensive training programs. Thus, training fees are often part of the cost to a franchisee for utilizing such quality and service concepts.

Franchise Financing

As you have learned already, the franchisor frequently will work with the franchisee in the search for financing. However, it is the responsibility of the franchisee to obtain a mortgage, that is, the funds to purchase the land and to construct or renovate the facility. Mortgages can be obtained from several sources—banks, insurance companies, investment trusts, and private sources. It is important to acquire information about the costs involved and the probable return on investment, so an economic market feasibility study (see Chapter 8) most likely is necessary. Many franchisors assist in the preparation of the study, and some will pay part or all of the cost.

In another arrangement, the franchisor acquires the land and constructs the facility. Once the facility is ready, a joint venture is created, giving the franchisee 50 percent of the operation. The degree to which franchisors invest in the individual operation varies. Some make no investment and derive their income solely from franchise fees and from profits on purchasing services and other forms of technical assistance. Others take active equity positions in the franchise operation.

Other Stipulations of the Franchise Agreement

See Appendix 9–1 for a sample draft of a franchise agreement. As you can see, this agreement contains all of the information we have discussed, and more. The term of the franchise agreement varies. Many will remain in effect for as long as 20 years. Many lenders want the franchise term to extend over the life of the debt. The longer the term, the better it is for the franchisee, who needs to protect his or her investment in marketing and operations. Naturally, the franchisee also will want to be able to terminate the agreement should the product concept not succeed. Most franchise agreements require that some type of financial settlement be paid to the franchisor if the franchisee terminates the agreement prior to the end of the term. (6) It is not an arrangement to be entered into lightly.

Protection against competition is another important stipulation of the franchise agreement. The details included in the agreement include a minimum distance that must exist between the new franchise and any future franchise. Sometimes franchisors will grant exclusive territories to franchisees who promise to develop a certain number of properties in the area within a specified period of time.

Another way for the franchisee to protect his or her property is to include a clause specifying a protected area or exclusive territory. In this type of agreement, the franchisor cannot own, manage, or franchise another property within a specified geographic area until the current agreement has been in place for a certain period of time or until a certain level of operating performance has been achieved (e.g., occupancy over 70 percent for two consecutive years). Frequently, the franchisee receives substantial remuneration for giving up part of a territory if a previously quiet area suddenly develops a tremendous potential for business.

The details of any technical assistance must be properly defined in the agreement. If a training program is provided, the agreement should include the number of employees to be trained and the period of time for which they will be trained. Clauses applicable to purchasing services should define the maximum markup or commission that the franchisor can receive. In particular, franchisees should protect themselves against the cost of so-called identity items that must be used under the terms of the franchise agreement.

The purchase of a computer system is often necessary for providing reservation services. In the event that procedures change and the system purchased by the franchisee is not compatible with the changes, the franchise agreement should stipulate that replacement costs are the responsibility of the franchisor. The franchise agreement will also go into specifics regarding reservation system services and fees; advertising services and fees; franchisee reporting requirements; timing and method of inspections and audits; transfer of the franchise agreement; and termination procedures. Because a franchisor in the United States is generally required by the Federal Trade Commission to amend its Uniform Franchise Offering Circular (UFOC) whenever any important terms of a franchise agreement are changed, most franchisors are reluctant to negotiate any variations from the standard agreement.

Franchise Selection

The selection of a franchise is an important decision that has a tremendous impact on the long-term profitability of the property. Guest perception, market segment, reservation system bookings, and referral opportunities all affect franchise selection. Selecting a franchise that is inappropriate for the target market or deciding to remain independent in a very competitive market can have devastating effects on a hotel's competitiveness, profitability, and financial success. (7)

The hotel's owner or management personnel must first identify from among the many franchises that are available the one that would be the best match. The economic market study and appraisal (see Chapter 8) provides an evaluation of the potential support in the market of a variety of product concepts. Location and other competitive factors identified in the study can indicate the market orientation, types of amenities, and desired quality of facility and level of services that must be provided for the property to be successful.

Another key factor is competition. Unless there is sufficient unmet room demand to allow both new and existing hotels to be successful, it is wise to avoid a franchise that is already established in the market area. If the franchisor already has a franchise in the market area, a second franchise may not be possible, for the reasons stated above in the section on franchise agreements. In this case, the franchisee's best bet is to consider another franchise with a similar product and name recognition.

Referral business is another important consideration. If the franchise company is new or has few products in operation, the opportunity for referral business is negligible. This franchise would not be a good choice if there are other franchise operations in the target market that draw heavily from referrals. A newer franchise may not have the brand identity and recognition that is so important when a traveler books a room.

- Has the franchisor's business grown over the last ten years?
- How many product concepts does the chain franchise? How are they differentiated in the marketplace?
- Has the franchisor terminated any franchises in the last five years? If so, for what reasons?
- How does the franchisor keep up with the latest technology? How is this passed on to the franchisees?
- How many reservations per month does the central reservation system produce for a franchise in similar market conditions?
- Does the central reservation system cooperate with airline reservation systems in booking accommodations?
- What percentage of reservations are no-shows?
- Does the franchisor offer training support services?
- What type of guest relations reports are available about guest perception of the franchise?
- How does a chain qualify a franchisee? Do I meet those qualifications?

Figure 9–1 Questions that a franchisee should ask before taking the plunge

After the homework has been done and several possible franchises have been identified, the next step is to make contact with a representative of the franchise. Copies of the uniform franchise offering circular (UFOC) and the most recent annual report should be requested from each of the contenders. In addition to the valuable information contained in these documents, the franchisee should obtain answers to the questions shown in Figure 9–1 to make sure that the evaluation of each franchise is as complete as possible before making the final decision.

Most management contracts or franchise agreements pertain to those hotels whose principal market is business travelers or leisure travelers in transit on their way to some far off, exotic destination. In the next chapter, we take a look at some of those destinations, including resorts, themed lodging, and unique hotel experiences.

SUMMARY

The management contract, a form of hotel operation that grew rapidly during the late 1980s and the early 1990s, specifies that the hotel or lodging facility operator (often a third-party hotel management company) is acting fully and completely as an agent of the owner and for the account of the owner. The final financial results of the operation, whether a profit or loss, is a result for the owner's account and not the operator. An operator under a hotel management contract receives fees for managerial services. The management contract enables an operator to enter the hotel and lodging industry without any significant investment or risk. However, the operator reaps no financial rewards from his or her hard work should the owner decide to sell. Management companies can be classified as category one or category two. Both categories bring operating expertise to the contract, but category one companies bring stronger brand recognition. Typically, an owner bases the selection of a management company on cost, market strengths, lender reputation, efficiency of operations, flexibility in contract terms, and flexibility in negotiation.

Management contract fees are either fixed fees based on some percentage of gross revenue or incentive fees tied to operating performance (profit). The latter is more preferable to the owner, because it provides the strongest incentive for the operator to manage the property profitably.

The terms of a management contract typically include a specified term, fee calculation provision, technical service provisions, preopening budget provisions, and operator duties.

Franchising has been one of the fastest growing ways of doing business both domestically and internationally. The services offered by a franchisor can be broken down into three general categories: operating procedures, technical assistance, and marketing.

Franchisees must adhere to a very strict set of quality and service standards with regard to housekeeping, sanitation, customer service, rates, checkout times, changes of linens, and use of the logo in order to preserve the franchisor's reputation. Failure to meet these standards can result in a loss of the franchise name.

Most franchise companies charge an initial fee, monthly fee, reservation fee, advertising fee, and training fee. The fees are negotiated as part of a franchise agreement, which the franchisor may be unwilling to modify because of the regulatory oversight by the Federal Trade Commission.

The franchise agreement includes the term of the franchise and specifies the timing and amount of fees. The franchisee must be very careful to negotiate a secure market area for the hotel and a length of agreement that will protect the investment and satisfy the requirements of the lender.

A careful evaluation of the recommendations of the economic market study is critical in selecting a franchise company. The franchisee must also take into consideration the competition and the availability of referral business.

REFERENCES

1. James J. Eyster, "Hotel Management Contracts in the U.S.: The Revolution Continues," *Cornell Quarterly* 38, no. 3 (June 1997): 14–20.
2. Karen Johnson, "Management Contracts," in *Hotel Development*, ed. by PKF Consulting (Washington, D.C.: Urban Land Institute, 1996), p. 61.
3. Stephen Rushmore, *Hotel Investments—A Guide for Lenders and Owners* (Boston: Warren, Gorham & Lamont, 1990), section 15, p. 12.
4. Bruce Batlin, James Butler, and Peter Benudiz, "Acquisition as a Development Tactic," in *Hotel Development*, ed. by PKF Consulting (Washington, D.C.: Urban Land Institute, 1996), p. 45.
5. Jerome J. Vallen and Gary K. Vallen "The Modern Hotel Industry," *Check-In Check Out*, 4th ed., (Dubuque, IA: Wm. C. Brown Publishers, 1991), p. 25.
6. Stephen Rushmore, "Hotel Franchises," in *Hotel Investments—A Guide for Lenders and Owners* (Boston: Warren, Gorham & Lamont, 1990), p. 17–3.
7. Michael L. Kasavana and Richard M. Brooks, "The Lodging Industry," in *Managing Front Office Operations*, 5th ed. (East Lansing, MI: Educational Institute AHMA, 1998), p. 3.

Review Questions

1. Explain the advantages of a management contract from the owner's perspective.
2. Prepare a presentation for a hotel owner on the benefits of selecting your company to manage. What would you include?
3. If you were preparing for the negotiation of a management contract, what would you need to research and have ready for the negotiation?
4. What are the major advantages and disadvantages of hotel franchising? Based on what you have learned, if you were to open a hotel, would you use a franchise arrangement, a management contract, or go solo?
5. What types of fees should a hotel franchisee expect to pay?
6. In preparing for the negotiation of a hotel franchise agreement, what terms should you prepare to discuss? For each of these terms, describe the position that you as a franchisee should take.
7. Before recommending a hotel franchise company, what information would you obtain?

Activities

1. Interview a local general manager and determine whether the hotel is franchised or operates under some other status. If the property is franchised, review the franchise agreement with the general manager and identify the most workable components and those that present operational problems.
2. Request a uniform franchise offering circular from two hotel franchise companies. Compare the two UFOCs and report on the differences and similarities.
3. Interview a local general manager of a franchise hotel and determine the timing and method of inspections and audits by the franchise company.
4. Survey the local hotel industry and determine how many hotels are under management contract. Select a single hotel under management contract within this group and interview the general manager about the terms of the contract.

Appendix 9–1

Sample Draft of a Franchise Agreement

__________ Corporation (hereinafter called "Franchisor") hereby grants, and __________ (hereinafter called "Franchisee") hereby accepts a non-assignable license and franchise to operate a hotel or Corporation under the name as herein provided on the premises located at __________ (hereinafter called "Hotel"), on the following terms and conditions:

1. Franchisor is a subsidiary of __________ Corporation. __________ Hotels Corporation and its subsidiaries and affiliates (hereinafter collectively called "__________") own, lease, operate, and manage a system of __________ hotels and Corporation (hereinafter called "_______ hotels"). Under an agreement with __________ Hotels Corporation, the Franchisor has developed a system for the operation of hotels and Corporation (hereinafter called "System"). The System and its distinguishing characteristics are described in this Agreement and in the Operating Manual (as hereinafter defined) as the same may be revised from time to time. __________ Hotels Corporation has authorized the Franchisor to grant licenses to selected, first-class, independently owned or leased hotel and Corporation properties for operation under the System, and to use the name "__________" as herein provided.

Franchisee hereby acknowledges Franchisor's and __________'s exclusive rights to and interest in the System and its present and future distinguishing characteristics, and Franchisor's and __________'s exclusive rights to such characteristics. These characteristics include the names "__________ Hotels," "__________", and "__________ Corporation," the stylized "Trademark" used in any form and in any design, alone or in any combination, and all other present and future names, service marks, trademarks, trade names, insignia, slogans, emblems, symbols, designs, or other characteristics used in connection with the System. Franchisee hereby acknowledges that these distinguishing characteristics have acquired a secondary meaning which indicates that the hotel, Corporation, restaurant, or similar business is operated by or with the approval of __________.

2. Grant of License. Franchisor grants Franchisee, and Franchisee hereby accepts, a nonassignable license commencing and terminating, to operate the Hotel at the above described location under the System, to use the name "__________" in the name of the Hotel, to use the name "__________" and __________'s stylized "Trademark" service mark as service marks to identify the services rendered by Franchisee at the Hotel, and to promote and advertise the Hotel under the name "__________," but in each case only in the form and manner as contained and set forth in the Operating Manual and in combination with such other color scheme, design, characteristics, and words as may from time to time be approved by Franchisor.

3. Franchisor's Duties. Franchisor shall:

a. Review the Hotel's operations periodically during each operating year and consult with Franchisee from time to time on operating problems concerning the Hotel.

b. Inspect and have the right, from time to time, to inspect the Hotel so as to maintain the high standards and reputation of the System, the goodwill of the public, and compliance with the provisions of this Agreement and the Operating Manual, but Franchisor may permit variation from the general practice of the System of the provisions of the Operating Manual wherein its opinion variation is justified by local or special conditions and will not lower the System's standards.

c. Cause __________ Service Corporation or its successor, if any, to furnish the __________ Reservation Service to Franchisee on the same basis as from time to time is furnished to other System Franchisees.

d. Cause __________ Service Corporation or its successor, if any, to include the Hotel in its directory and in its other promotional material in accordance with the standard policy of __________ Service Corporation or its successor, if any, with respect to System hotels.

e. Include the Hotel, without charge, in any national or regional directory of __________ hotels hereafter published by Franchisor or __________, and in national or regional group advertising and promotion of __________ hotels, and Corporation, in accordance with general practices with respect to System hotels.

f. Issue and revise from time to time an operating manual (the manual and its revisions are herein referred to as the "Operating Manual"), which will set out Franchisor's services and the policies, practices, and standards of the System for the hotel and motel operation, identification, advertising, and accounting. Franchisee hereby acknowledges receipt of the Operating Manual.

g. Defend the name "__________" against imitations or infringements by unauthorized hotels or Corporation.

h. Make available to Franchisee, on the same basis as to other System Franchisees for use in the Hotel, any purchase, lease or other arrangements which Franchisor or __________ may have with respect to exterior signs, operating equipment, operating supplies, and furniture and furnishings. Franchisee acknowledges that __________ or one of its subsidiaries may perform services as a representative or distributor of the manufacturer of any such items in order to secure the benefits of lower costs in connection with purchasing arrangements for Franchisee.

At Franchisee's request, use its best efforts to obtain insurance for the Hotel on a favorable basis.

i. At Franchisee's request, furnish, or cause _______ to furnish, on the same basis and at the same rate as to other System Franchisees, any one or more of the following group benefits, services and facilities:

1. technical assistance on a consulting basis in regard to: (i) front office, food and beverage, housekeeping, personnel, and other operational department supervisory and control services; (ii) maintenance and engineering services.

a. Subject to provisions of subparagraph (d) below, to consent to such sale or lease and to the assignment of this Agreement to such purchaser or tenant, if such sale or lease is, in fact, consummated. Franchisee may, at its sole option, subject its consent to satisfaction of certain conditions, including without limitation, the following: (1) the cure of any existing defaults or events that would become defaults with the giving of notice and passage of time, including without limitation, the payment in full by certified or cashier's check at the Closing of all unpaid obligations owed Franchisee and its affiliates by Franchisee; (2) receipt of evidence from the purchaser that insurance coverage, as required by the Operating Manual, is in full force and effect on the date of Closing; (3) payment by certified or cashier's check of the amount of any estimated fees and charges that will accrue to Franchisee and its affiliates through the date of Closing, which amounts cannot be calculated in full prior to or at the Closing. To the fullest practical extent, Franchisee shall give to Franchisee sufficient written notice of the date on and place at which such sale or lease is to be consummated in order to give Franchisee an opportunity to prepare appropriate transfer documents and to be present at such time.

b. To terminate this Agreement (if, and only if, Franchisee shall not have exercised its rights under clause (1) or (2) above), which notice of termination shall fix a date of termination ninety (90) days after the date of receipt by Franchisee of the Franchisee's original sixty (60) day notice. If, within ninety (90) days after the date of receipt by Franchisee of the Franchisee's original sixty (60) day notice, the Franchisee shall not consummate said sale or lease of the Hotel to the prospective purchaser or lessee named in said original notice to Franchisee, at the price or rental and on terms no less favorable to the Franchisee than those at which such property was offered for sale or lease to Franchisee, then the termination notice theretofore served by Franchisee upon the Franchisee shall be null and void, and this Agreement shall continue in full force and effect, and the Hotel shall again be subject to the restrictions of this subparagraph (b) of this paragraph 9.

c. Franchisee agrees that upon the terms and conditions set forth in subparagraph (b) of this paragraph 9, it shall elect one of the alternatives set forth in clauses (1), (2), and (3) of said subparagraph (b). If Franchisee shall fail, neglect, or refuse to so exercise any of said alternatives within said sixty (60) day period, the same shall be conclusively deemed to constitute an election and consent under subparagraph (b) (2) above, and the provisions thereof shall prevail as if Franchisee had in writing consented thereto.

d. It is the intent of the parties hereto that the Hotel shall at all times during the term of this Agreement be operated as a System hotel pursuant to the terms hereof. Accordingly, notwithstanding the provisions of subparagraphs (b) and (c) above, the Hotel shall not be sold or leased (except for leases permitted under subparagraph (b) above) unless (i) the purchaser or tenant, as the case may be, shall have first delivered to Franchisee an executed written instrument, reasonably satisfactory in form and substance to Franchisee and its counsel, expressly assuming and agreeing to perform all of the terms and provisions of this Agreement, and (ii) such purchaser or tenant shall in all respects be acceptable to, and approved by, Franchisee, which approval shall not be unreasonably withheld. Upon any such sale or lease of the Hotel in accordance with the provisions of this paragraph 9, all of the rights and obligations of Franchisee hereunder shall vest solely in the purchaser or tenant, as the case may be, and all rights of the seller or lessor shall thereupon terminate (with the exception of any liabilities or obligations incurred prior to the date of such sale or lease, as to which the seller or lessor shall remain fully liable).

e. Transfer of Controlling Interest in Franchisee. The voluntary or involuntary sale, assignment, transfer or other disposition, or transfer by operation of law (other than by will or the laws of intestate succession) of a controlling interest in the Franchisee (i.e., the possession, directly or indirectly, of the power to direct or cause the direction of the management and policies of Franchisee, whether through the ownership of voting securities or by contract or otherwise) shall be deemed a sale or lease of the Hotel within the foregoing provisions of subparagraph (b), and shall be subject to the same rights of Franchisee as set forth in said subparagraphs (b) and (d) with respect to the sale or lease of the Hotel. Franchisee from time to time, upon the written request of Franchisee, shall furnish Franchisee with a list of the names and addresses of the owners of the capital stock, partnership interests, or other proprietary interests in the Franchisee; and in the event of a contemplated sale or other disposition of a controlling interest in the Franchisee, Franchisee shall forthwith notify Franchisee in writing of such sale or other disposition and of the names and addresses of the transferee or transferees of such controlling interest.

f. Sale of Securities. In the event Franchisee shall, at any time or from time to time, "sell" or "offer to sell" any "securities" issued by it through the medium of any "prospectus" or otherwise, it shall do so only in compliance with all applicable federal or state securities laws, and shall clearly disclose to all purchasers and offerees that (i) neither Franchisee nor __________ nor any of their respective officers, directors, agents, or employees "shall in any way be deemed an 'issuer' or 'underwriter' of said securities," and that (ii) Franchisee, __________ and said officers, directors, agents, and employees have not assumed and shall not have any liability or responsibility for any financial statements, prospectuses, or other financial information contained in any "prospectus" or similar written or oral communication. Franchisee shall have the right to approve any description of this License Agreement or of Franchisee's relationship with Franchisee hereunder, contained in any "prospectus" or similar communication delivered in connection with the sale or offer by Franchisee of any "securities," and Franchisee hereby agrees to furnish copies of all such materials to Franchisee for such purpose not less than 20 days prior to the filing thereof with any government authority or the delivery thereof to any prospective purchaser. Franchisee agrees to indemnify, defend, and hold Franchisee, __________, and their officers, directors, agents, and employees free and harmless of and from any and all liabilities, costs, damages, claims, or expenses arising out of or related to the "sale" or "offer" of any "securities" of Franchisee. All terms used in this subparagraph (f) shall have the same meaning as in the Securities Act of 1933, as amended.

g. Binding Effect, etc. Subject to the foregoing subparagraphs of this Agreement shall inure to the benefit of and be binding upon the parties hereto, their respective heirs, legal representatives, successors, and assigns.

4. Direct Covenant with __________. Franchisee agrees, as a direct covenant with __________ Hotels Corporation, that it will comply with all of the provisions of this Agreement with respect to the manner, terms, and conditions of the use of any trademarks, trade names, service marks, or similar matters, and with respect to the termination of any right on the part of Franchisee to use any of the foregoing. This covenant may be enforced by any appropriate legal proceedings at law or in equity by __________ Hotels Corporation, its successors and assigns, separately or in conjunction with Franchisee, and Franchisee agrees to pay all costs and expenses, including, without limitation, reasonable attorney's fees, thereby incurred by __________ Hotels Corporation, Franchisee, or their successors or assigns.

5. Notices. Any notice by either party to the other shall be in writing and shall be deemed to have been duly given if delivered personally or mailed in a registered or certified postpaid envelope, return receipt requested, addressed as follows:

To Franchisor: To Franchisee:

__________ Corporation, Inc.
Address

or to such other address for notice of which the parties have advised each other in accordance with the provisions of this paragraph.

6. Relationship between Parties. Franchisor and __________, on the one part, and Franchisee, on the other, are not and shall not be considered as joint venturers, partners, or agents of each other, and neither shall have the power to bind or obligate the other. There shall be no liability on the part of Franchisor or __________ to any person for any debts incurred on behalf of the Hotel and the business conducted therein or for any losses, costs, liabilities, damages, claims, or expenses, including reasonable attorney's fees, arising out of or resulting from the construction or operation, or the policies, procedures, practices or alleged practices of the Franchisee in the operation, of the Hotel or any other business conducted therein or thereabout.

7. Entire Agreement. In the event for any reason any of the requirements set forth in the Franchisor's commitment letter for a __________ license have not as of the date of execution of this Agreement been met and have not otherwise been waived in writing duly signed by Franchisor, then all such requirements shall survive the execution of this Agreement

and shall be the obligation of Franchisee hereunder. This instrument, together with both franchisee's application for a __________ license and Franchisor's commitment letter, contain the entire agreement of the parties and cannot be changed or modified except in writing signed by the party against whom the change or modification is asserted. Franchisee represents to Franchisor that there has been no material change in the state of facts represented to Franchisor in the above-referred to application. To the extent reference is made herein to the Operating Manual, the provisions of the Operating Manual are hereby incorporated herein by reference. In the event any provision of this Agreement is inconsistent with the Operating Manual, the provisions of this Agreement shall prevail. No failure of Franchisor or __________ to exercise any power given it hereunder, or to insist upon strict compliance by Franchisee with any obligation hereunder, and no custom or practice at variance with the terms hereof, shall constitute a waiver of Franchisor's or __________'s right to demand exact compliance with the terms hereof.

8. Third Parties. None of the obligations hereunder of either party shall run to, or be enforceable by, any party other than the other party to this Agreement except for covenants in favor of __________, including without limitation, __________ Service Corporation and Hotel Equipment Corporation, which covenants shall run to and be enforceable by any such corporation, its successors and assigns.

9. Remedies Cumulative. The remedies granted to Franchisor or hereunder are cumulative and are not intended to be exclusive of any other remedies to which each may be lawfully entitled in case of any breach or threatened breach of the terms and provisions hereof.

10. Continuing Covenants. All continuing covenants, duties and obligations and all indemnities herein contained shall survive the expiration or earlier termination of this Agreement.

11. Partial Invalidity. Any provision of this Agreement prohibited by law or by court decree in any locality or state shall be ineffective to the extent of such prohibition without in any way invalidating or affecting the remaining provisions of this Agreement, or without invalidating or affecting the provisions of this Agreement within the states or localities where not prohibited or otherwise invalidated by law or by court decree.

12. Governing Law. This Agreement shall be governed by and construed in accordance with the laws of the State of __________.

THE FOLLOWING PARAGRAPH 13 IS APPLICABLE ONLY IF A LICENSE AGREEMENT FOR A SITE AT WHICH NEW CONSTRUCTION IS CONTEMPLATED. DELETE IF INAPPLICABLE.

13. Franchisee agrees that the plans, layouts, specifications, drawings, and designs for the Hotel, together with any substantial changes therein or departures therefrom, shall be submitted to Franchisor for its prior written approval and that the Hotel shall be constructed, outfitted, and completed in accordance with such approved plans, layouts, specifications, drawings, and designs.

The decor, design, and physical appearance of the Hotel shall be compatible with Franchisor's standards and shall also be subject to Franchisor's prior approval. Franchisor's standards referred to in this paragraph shall mean those standards established for System hotels generally. However, it is understood that it is not the policy of Franchisor to require uniformity in the decor, design, or physical appearance of all System hotels, and variations from general practices or any of such standards may be permitted by Franchisor in individual cases where, in its opinion, the same are justified or required by local or other special conditions, without the lowering of required standards.

1. Accounting and claim services; and personnel and labor relation services.

2. Central purchasing services, including without limitation, the location, testing, and selection of items of equipment in common use by hotels, and securing to Franchisee the advantages of volume purchasing and wider markets in the procurement of items of common use, such as linens, chinaware, soaps, and furniture.

3. Interior design and decoration services and architectural services on a consulting basis.

4. Convention and group sales, advertising, and business promotion and public relation services.

Any policies, procedures, or practices established at the Hotel by or through the furnishing of any such group benefits, facilities, or services shall be subject to Owner's approval, and _______ in furnishing the same shall not have the right, nor shall be deemed, to exercise control or supervision over Franchisee.

License Fees. LICENSE FEE RIDER ATTACHED HERETO IS HEREBY INCORPORATED BY REFERENCE AS A PART OF THIS AGREEMENT.

5. Franchisee's Duties. Franchisee shall, throughout the term hereof, in addition to the other provisions hereof:

a. Operate the Hotel as a System hotel, and in that connection, use, in a manner prescribed by Franchisor, the name and service mark "_______" and the "Trademark" service mark and no other name or service mark without Franchisor's approval in connection with the operation of the Hotel and related facilities as authorized in this Agreement and in the Operating Manual.

b. Operate, furnish, maintain, and equip the Hotel and related facilities in a first-class manner in accordance with the provisions of this Agreement and of the Operating Manual, in conformity to the high service, moral, and ethical standards of the System, and in compliance with all local, State, and Federal laws, customs, and regulations, including, without limiting the generality of the foregoing, maintaining and conducting its business in accordance with sound business and financial practice.

c. Refer guests and customers, wherever possible, only to other System hotels, or __________ or __________ International hotels (generally __________ hotels operated outside the United States) and Corporation, and, in general, use every reasonable means to encourage their use by the traveling public; display all material, including, but not limited to, brochures and promotional material provided with respect to __________, __________ International and System hotels, motels, and Corporation; allow advertising and promotion only of __________, __________ International and System hotels, motels, and Corporation on the Hotel premises; use the __________ Reservation Service on the terms set out in the Operating Manual; provide sufficient space at a reasonable rental in the vicinity of the front desk for a Reservation Service office; reimburse __________ Service Corporation, or its successor, if any, within ten (10) days after billing, for the Hotel's pro-rata share of that Corporation's costs and expenses for the Reservation Service allocated on the same basis or formula as allocations to other System hotels; and honor and give first priority on available rooms to all confirmed reservations referred to the Hotel through the __________ Reservation Service. Franchisee agrees that the only reservation service or system to be used in regard to outgoing reservations referred by and from the Hotel to other hotels shall be the __________ Reservation Service.

d. Honor all nationally recognized credit cards issued for general credit purposes, which are generally honored at other System hotels and Corporation, and enter into all necessary credit card agreements with the issuers of such cards, as may be necessary in connection therewith.

e. Feature in the Hotel operation, in the guest rooms, public rooms, and other public areas of the Hotel, and on the various articles therein as specified in the Operating Manual, and in advertising and promotional material, the name "__________," together with other distinguishing service marks, signs, and words of the System, in the same size, color, combination, arrangement, and manner as determined periodically by Franchisor for use generally by System hotels and motels so that the Hotel will be readily recognized by the public as part of the System, and comply with the provisions of the Operating Manual with respect to the foregoing.

f. In accordance with the provisions of the Operating Manual and to the extent permitted by law, erect, install, and maintain in complete working order on the exterior of the Hotel, in accordance with plans and specifications prescribed by Franchisor for System hotels and motels generally, large illuminated signs using the name "__________" and other distinguishing characteristics as prescribed in said plans and specifications, and, subject to any applicable law, rule, regulation, or order, keep the exterior signs illuminated from sundown to at least 12:00 A.M.

g. Advertise the Hotel and related facilities and services in a first-class manner and, upon the written request of Franchisor, cease and desist from using or continuing to use any advertising or publicity that Franchisor believes is not in the best interests of the Hotel or System.

h. Identify itself as the owner and operator of the Hotel under license from Franchisor in the use of the name and service mark "__________" and the stylized "Trademark" service mark, and in Franchisee's signs and advertising and promotional material; disclose in all dealings with suppliers and persons, other than guests, that it is an independent entity and that Franchisor has no liability for its debts and refrain from using the name "__________" or any name similar thereto in or as part of its corporate or firm name. At its option and to the extent lawful, purchase from Franchisor or whomever Franchisor designates, furniture and furnishings, operating equipment, operating supplies, consumable inventories and merchandise for resale to be used in or sold from the Hotel, on the same basis as System hotels generally, and to pay for any such items purchased within ten (10) days after billing. All such items purchased from a source other than Franchisor or Franchisor's designee shall conform to the designs and standards prevailing in System hotels generally and, at Franchisor's request, a sample thereof shall be submitted to Franchisor for its approval prior to use thereof in the Hotel.

i. Operate the Hotel directly by Franchisee.

j. Obtain the prior written approval of the Franchisor (which shall not be unreasonably withheld) as to the appointment of the manager of the Hotel. In addition, the manager and such other key employees of the Hotel as deemed necessary by Franchisor shall complete a training program with respect to operation of the Hotel under the System at such place designated by Franchisor, except that in the sole opinion of Franchisor, if it is not necessary or desirable for either the manager or such other key personnel to complete said training program, then this requirement may be waived in whole or in part by instrument in writing duly executed by Franchisor as to either the manager or such other personnel. Such training program shall be provided by Franchisor at no expense to Franchisee, except that Franchisee shall be responsible for the wages, room, board, and travel expenses of such trainees during the training period.

k. Make no major structural change or changes in design or decor without the prior written approval of Franchisor, which approval shall not be unreasonably withheld.

m. Indemnify, defend, and save Franchisor, __________, including without limitation, __________ Service Corporation, Hotel Equipment Corporation, and their respective successors and assigns, harmless from all losses, costs, liabilities, damages, claims, and expenses, including reasonable attorney's fees, arising out of or resulting from the construction or operation of the Hotel or any other business conducted in or by the Hotel or on its grounds, and at its sole expense obtain and maintain insurance of the kind, in the amounts, and with the insured (including Franchisor, Franchisee, and __________) specified in the Operating Manual.

l. Deliver to Franchisor monthly, quarterly, and annual operating statements, profit and loss statements, balance sheets, and other reports prescribed in the Operating Manual, and prepared by the persons and in accordance with the forms and methods specified therein, and permit the Franchisor to inspect the Franchisee's books and records at all reasonable times.

m. Within ten (10) days after billing, pay or reimburse Franchisor or any of its parents, subsidiaries, or affiliates for all costs and expenses actually incurred at Franchisee's request with respect to the designing, furnishing, supplying, servicing, and/or equipping of the Hotel and its facilities, and for all service and/or design fees in connection therewith.

n. Promptly deliver to Franchisor a copy of any notice of default received from any mortgagee, trustee under any deed of trust, or ground lessor with respect to the Hotel and upon the request of Franchisor provide such additional information as may be requested in respect to any such alleged default or any subsequent action or proceeding in connection therewith.

o. Upon commencement of the term of this Agreement, purchase, and thereafter replace, at its cost, computer terminal equipment as specified in the Operating Manual or otherwise specified or approved by Franchisor for utilization by Franchisee of the __________ Reservation Service. Ordinary maintenance and telephone line usage during the term of this Agreement for such equipment shall be provided by Franchisor at its cost (except as hereinafter provided) on the same basis as provided to other

System Franchisees. All or a portion of the cost of such ordinary maintenance and telephone line usage may be reimbursed by __________Service Corporation to Franchisor or otherwise paid by __________ Service Corporation and be included as a part of the cost and expense for the Reservation Service.

p. Refrain from directly or indirectly conducting, or permitting by lease, concession arrangement, or otherwise, gaming or casino operations in the Hotel or on the premises thereof.

q. Exclusively appoint __________ Hotels Corporation to provide to Franchisee without charge therefore the interior design for the guest room areas of the Hotels, and Franchisor shall cause __________ Hotels Corporation to so provide.

6. Termination by Franchisor. If Franchisee violates any provision of the Agreement or of the Operating Manual and such violation continues for a period of twenty (20) days after written notice from Franchisor, or if an order, judgment, or decree shall be entered by a court of competent jurisdiction adjudicating Franchisee a bankrupt or insolvent or approving a petition seeking reorganization of Franchisee or an arrangement of creditors, or if Franchisee makes an assignment for the benefit of creditors, or if a receiver, trustee, or liquidate is appointed to take charge of the Hotel or Franchisee's affairs generally or in respect to the Hotel, and adequate assurances of continued performance of this Agreement are not received within thirty (30) days of such order, judgment, decree, assignment, or appointment, then the Franchisor, without further demand or notice, may declare this License. Agreement and all of Franchisee's rights hereunder are terminated, but such termination shall not affect Franchisee's obligations to take or refrain from taking action after termination of the Agreement as provided elsewhere herein. Franchisee agrees, within ten (10) days after any such order, judgment, or decree, or assignment, or appointment, to give notice thereof to Franchisor.

7. Obligations of Franchisee on Termination. Upon the termination of this Agreement for any cause, Franchisee will immediately discontinue holding itself out to the public as a licensed __________ hotel, will discontinue all use of trade names, trademarks, service marks, signs, and forms of advertising and other indicia of operation as a System or __________ hotel, and will discontinue use of all distinguishing indicia of __________ hotels, including but not by way of limitation, such indicia on exterior and interior signs, stationery, operating equipment, and supplies, brochures, and other promotional material. If Franchisee fails to make such changes within thirty (30) days of termination, Franchisor may enter upon the Hotel premises without being deemed guilty of trespass or

any other tort and make or cause to be made such changes at the expense of Franchisee, to be paid by Franchisee on demand; and Franchisor and __________ shall be entitled to damages or relief by injunction, or to any other right or remedy at law or in equity.

8. Restrictions on Franchisee. Franchisee agrees that as long as this Agreement shall remain in full force and effect, it will not engage, directly or indirectly, in the hotel, motel, or related business at any place except the Hotel without the prior written consent of Franchisor, which consent Franchisor agrees not to unreasonably withhold.

9. Successors and Assigns; Sale of Securities.

a. Assignment by Franchisor. Franchisor shall have the right to assign this Agreement without the consent of Franchisee, provided that no such assignment shall release Franchisor from its obligation hereunder.

b. Sale, Lease, or Assignment by Franchisee. Franchisee shall not sell or lease the Hotel or any part thereof (except for commercial space in the Hotel customarily subject to sublease or concession arrangements), or assign this Agreement, or any interest therein, without the prior written consent of Franchisor. If Franchisee shall have received a bona fide written offer to purchase or lease the Hotel and Franchisee, pursuant to the terms of such offer, desires to sell or lease the Hotel to any person, firm, or corporation, Franchisee shall give written notice thereof to Franchisor, stating the name and full identity of the prospective purchaser or tenant, as the case may be, including the names and addresses of the owners of the capital stock, partnership interests, or other proprietary interests of such purchaser or tenant, the price or rental, and all terms and conditions of such proposed sale or lease, together with all other information with respect thereto that is requested by Franchisor and reasonably available to Franchisee. Within sixty (60) days after the date of receipt by Franchisor of such written notice from Franchisee, Franchisor shall elect, by written notice to Franchisee, one of the following alternatives:

(1) To purchase or lease the Hotel or to have its designee or designees purchase or lease the Hotel at the same price or rental and upon the same terms and conditions as those set forth in the written notice from the Franchisee to Franchisor. In the event that Franchisor shall have elected to so purchase or lease or have its designee(s) so purchase or lease the Hotel in accordance with the provisions of the preceding sentence, Franchisee and Franchisor (or its designee(s) as the case may be) shall promptly thereafter enter into an agreement for sale or lease at the price of rental and on the terms aforesaid and shall consummate such transaction in accordance with the terms thereof.

On or before ______________, 19__, Franchisee agrees, at its sole expense, to erect, install, and maintain in complete working order at the

Site, in accordance with plans and specifications prescribed by Franchisor for System hotels and motels generally, a large construction sign using the name "__________" and other distinguishing characteristics as prescribed in said plans and specifications.

The construction of the Hotel shall be commenced not later than ______________________________ and shall be completed not later than ________________________________, unless such completion shall be delayed by circumstances not within Franchisee's reasonable control. The grant of this license and the right of Franchisee to operate the Hotel under the name "____________" shall be and hereby is expressly conditioned upon Franchisee constructing, completing, and outfitting the Hotel in accordance with the foregoing provisions in compliance with Franchisor's standards as aforesaid, and, in addition, is expressly conditioned upon Franchisee meeting the requirements of Franchisor's commitment letter. If Franchisee shall fail to complete the Hotel in accordance with the foregoing or meet the requirements of such commitment letter or fail to commence operation of the Hotel on or before the date set forth above, Franchisor may, at its option, terminate this Agreement upon notice in writing thereof to Franchisee. Upon such termination, all rights of Franchisee hereunder shall cease and Franchisor shall retain all sums paid by Franchisee hereunder as liquidated damages and not as a penalty.

Franchisor agrees that it shall not unreasonably withhold its approval where required under this paragraph 19.

20. Miscellaneous.

IN WITNESS WHEREOF, the parties hereto have executed or caused this Agreement to be executed, all as of the ______ day of ______ 19____.

ATTEST:	By ___________ Corporation Inc. Franchisor
ATTEST:	By ___________ Franchisee

Source: Alan T. Stutts, ATS Hotel Management, Tucson, Arizona, 1990.

Chapter 10

Resorts, Themed Lodging, and Special Lodging Environments

CHAPTER OUTLINE

So far we have discussed hotels, motels, and bed-and-breakfasts. But there are many other forms of lodging available to the leisure, business, or convention guest. In a society dedicated to ambition, achievement, and success, leisure and escapism serve as natural relief valves for the accompanying stress. An entire segment of the lodging industry is dedicated to helping customers relieve stress and forget about the pressures of their everyday lives.

As far back as 1991, Michael Rose, an industry expert, made the following prediction about leisure travel in the new millennium: "To talk about a society in which leisure is the most important thing flies in the face of the work ethic and religious codes which have dominated our country, Japan, and many in northern Europe for generations. But it is becoming increasingly clear that the new century will see (a society) dominated by leisure." (1) Entrepreneurs are tapping into many previously unexplored leisure and recreational activities. New forms of escapist activities, including places to house the participants, spring up almost daily.

RECREATION AND LEISURE ACTIVITIES

Comprehension of the terms leisure and recreation is essential to a complete understanding of this increasingly important segment of the hospitality industry. Kaye Chon, in his book *Welcome to Hospitality: An Introduction*, defines leisure as "freedom resulting from the cessation of activities, especially time free from work or duties." Chon defines recreation as " refreshment of strength and spirits after work, a means of diversion." However, these definitions cannot be considered absolutes, as the terms mean different things to different people. No two people view leisure and recreation in exactly the same way. It is this diversity that leads to the exciting, creative thinking of the entrepreneur: How can you carve a niche and capture a segment of the leisure and recreation market, when prospective customers cannot agree on what leisure and recreation are? Is the purpose of this free time amusement, revitalization, activity, education, to be in the middle of it all, or to get away from the maddening crowds? Let's explore some of these many possibilities. (2)

Leisure and Recreation Customers

The first step in creating a leisure and recreation business is to identify your customers. This is not as easy as it sounds, especially if you are interested in developing a concept that would appeal to the entire population—from newborns to the aged, from the physically fit to the infirm, from male to female, and rich to poor. Even pets have some form of leisure or recreational activity available to them—pet shows, rodeos, state fairs, and field trials. Like the activities themselves, the customer base is limitless. The simplest

An aerial view of the Fountainbleu Hilton Resort and Spa. (Courtesy of the Hospitality Industry Archives and Library, University of Houston, Texas.)

customer model to use is yourself. What would *you* like to do on your vacation? Some research may have to be performed for target population specifics, but we already possess knowledge of most of the basics.

No longer are the more elaborate activities considered just for the young, fit, or rich. The economic success of the baby boomers has made them major consumers of leisure and recreation activities, not only as observers but also as active participants. Whitewater rafting, wilderness camping, and crewing on ships are a few examples of popular activities among this age group.

Senior citizens also are becoming more vocal about the types of activities they prefer, putting an emphasis on safety and intellectual stimulation. In other words, they want to learn while they are doing. It should be remembered that this generation has experienced a number of wars, which interrupted their lives and, in some cases, limited their educational opportunities.

The vacation as learning experience is one way to make up for lost educational opportunities.

Leisure Activities

Leisure activities can range from dropping out of a helicopter onto the top of a mountain to snowboarding down on newly fallen snow to reading a book; from experiencing virtual reality in your own home to signing on for a future space voyage. Your interests can be satisfied with thousands of people, as, for example, running in the NYC marathon or attending the millennium celebrations, or walking alone on the beach. A vacation can be well planned, like a tour. It can also be spontaneous, as many who have followed Horatio Alger's advice over a century ago found out: "Go West, young man, go West." In addition to this already overwhelming array of choices, technology is allowing for the growth of heretofore unheard-of activities. Snowboarding, X-tremesports, inexpensive air travel, and the Internet are all products of technological advances that have had effects on the leisure and recreation segment of the hotel and lodging industry.

Recreation and leisure experiences often require special lodging environments, which can be grouped by type. All types share certain characteristics: lodging (in many different forms), amenities, and a wide range of activities in addition to the primary activity. The basis for each of the three types is a central concept, activity, or theme, which remains as the focal point for the facility, regardless of the other activities or amenities offered. The four types of special lodging environments we will discuss include:

1. Activity-based lodging
2. Themed lodging
3. Unique facilities
4. Other types of nontraditional lodging

Activity-Based Lodging

The main theme of **activity-based lodging** is the type of activity, either physical or mental, in which guests participate. Examples include golf resorts, hunting lodges, music camps, and fishing camps. In addition to the primary activity, there may be a number of other activities offered. The Regent Las Vegas (formerly the Resort at Summerlin) is a 2,000-room resort with a golf course (TPC Canyons), a casino, and numerous five-star restaurants. Because of its adherence to its primary theme, no one who has been there would think it was anything other than an outstanding golf resort. Most activity-based facilities, however, offer additional forms of recreation in an attempt to keep customers (and their money) from leaving the resort for any purpose. Many go out of their way to be as self-contained as possible, while others cooperate with neighboring resorts.

Golf and tennis resorts are usually extensions of the local country club concept. These resorts may be equity clubs (not-for-profit), but most are proprietary in that they are privately owned and are operated for profit. Lodging facilities tend to be full-service hotels or condominium rentals that have banquet and meeting facilities in addition to restaurants and the obligatory pro shop. Customers at golf and tennis resorts also have come to expect a generous amount of amenities and ancillary services, for an additional charge.

Not all resorts with a golf course, either on their property or nearby, can be classified as golf resorts. Many resorts view a golf course as an amenity for their customers, with their primary focus being elsewhere. Although there is a golf course on the property, the hotels on the Disney World property hardly can be classified as golf resorts. Some examples of true golf resorts include Pebble Beach in California, Augusta National in Georgia, and the TPC at the Woodlands in Texas.

The same can be said for tennis resorts. Almost all resorts have tennis courts on their property, but few are true tennis resorts. Places like Forest Hills in New York, Wimbledon in England, and Roland Garros in France can be considered true tennis resorts.

Special activity-based or special-interest camps originated as places for people to go during the summer to get away from the city. Over the years, the concept has been enhanced to include special interests (e.g., music, scouting, the arts, specific sports activities) within the camp setting. Some of these camps gradually have developed into special-interest "camps," accommodating the different types of lodging requirements for people of varied backgrounds. Today the special-interest camp concept covers everything from sleeping on the ground at a trekking and wilderness camp to sleeping in a hammock on a tall ship to going on a celebrity cruise with sports legends. Since many of these camps are in operation throughout the year, they can no longer be called summer camps.

Many of these special-interest camps are located in areas considered off the beaten track. The fact that they are away from distractions is part of their attraction for guests, along with the opportunity to interact with people of similar interests, under the tutelage of accomplished teachers and guides, who will teach and guide them to new discoveries or to revisit past glories. Some examples of special-interest camps are the Apple Musical Camp in New Jersey, NASA Space Camps in Texas and Florida, and the sports camps available on most major college campuses.

THEMED LODGING

The variation in the topics of themed lodging is the main reason that people are attracted to them. The themes of some facilities vary, depending on the time of year. For example, South Padre Island serves as a spring-break party destination, a relaxing beach resort during the peak summer season, and an eco-tourism destination during the off-season. In most cases, the surrounding townspeople and businesses cooperate to enhance the theme's environment. The themes vary almost as much as the needs of the customers they serve. Themed lodging can be historic (Colonial Williamsburg), ecological (Yellowstone Park), gambling (Las Vegas), cultural (the Louvre), celebratory (Mardi Gras), or leisure (Club Med).

Historically Themed Lodging

As we mature, we are drawn to history in order to find out more about ourselves. We are able to read about our history, but who among us has not daydreamed of how things were in a specific period of time and wondered how we would have fared? A historically themed lodging facility, such as Colonial Williamsburg in Virginia, allows us to observe and even participate in full-dress simulations of a small 17th century settlement that became, for a short time, the capital of Virginia. People dress in authentic period reproduction clothing, use the tools and implements of the time, and cook traditional recipes in iron pots over an open hearth. You can tour and, in some instances, stay in lodging facilities that are over 250 years old. The city of Williamsburg is a willing, cooperative partner in the Colonial Williamsburg concept, with 90 percent of the city's lodging and restaurant facilities operating, specifically, to support Colonial Williamsburg tourism. Historical tours of Jamestown, Yorktown, and historic plantations are also offered, and when you get tired of history, Williamsburg boasts a large outlet mall and the Busch Gardens Theme Park.

Eco-tourism

As we have become more aware of our dwindling natural resources and the destruction of our environment, we have come to value what remains. Travel to national parks and other areas in order to admire Mother Nature's work is called **eco-tourism**. Visits to our national parks have increased to the point that the government has been forced to reduce the numbers of visitors to ensure that our children will have something to admire. Many eco-tourism packages provide guidelines to visitors on how to conduct themselves in order to best preserve the natural beauty of the site that they are visiting; for example, carry your trash out with you and do not pocket any souvenirs. It would be impossible to visit Yellowstone National Park, Bryce Canyon, the Brazilian Rainforest, or Machu Pichu in a day, or even a week. This has led to the development of lodging facilities, both within and outside the destination. In many countries, a percentage of the money that

Casino hotels are a growing segment of the lodging industry. (Courtesy of the Hospitality Industry Archives and Library, University of Houston, Texas.)

tourists spend at hotels, restaurants, and shops is dedicated to further protection of the eco-tourism area. In some cases, tourists are actually given tasks to help support the environment. During a trip to the island of Aruba, I, as well as every other tourist on the island, was requested to participate in a cleanup of the reefs and lagoons that surround the island. More than 80 percent of the citizens and tourists participated in this highly publicized, voluntary government project.

Casino Resorts

The casino industry is almost as old as time itself. The histories of all major civilizations are replete with stories or drawings of gambling as an accepted social practice. The Chinese, who have gambled for over 5,000 years, were probably not the inventors of gambling, but they have given us one of the earliest written records. The Bible chronicles gambling in the part of the world that we now call the Middle East. In their exploration of the Louisiana Purchase, Lewis and Clark found indigenous people enjoying a game that is similar to roulette, which was believed to have been invented in France.

Casinos are found all over the world—on every continent and in most countries. Even those countries, such as Russia and Venezuela, that formerly prohibited casinos for political and/or religious reasons, have allowed casinos. Presently there are more casinos on Red Square in Russia than there are in Atlantic City, the second most successful gaming venue in the world. This lucrative industry has lured many a reluctant local, state, or national government to include casinos in their economic development plans.

Casinos come in many different sizes and shapes: some float down the Mississippi River, some are on stationary barges that will never sail, some are in the middle of moats, and some are on dry land. Most casino operations either have their own hotel or are supported by a hotel complex. Generally, it is the casino in a casino/hotel complex, not the hotel, that is the economic engine that drives the operation. By the year 2001, Las Vegas will have over 120,000 hotel rooms. Because the principal target population that Las Vegas draws from is over 275 miles distant, gamblers need a place to stay. Atlantic City, on the other hand, has only 25,000 hotel rooms, because its principal target market population lives within a two-hour drive. Consequently, most of its customer base is made up of people who are staying for just one day, or "day-trippers." This has led to the growth of a previously untapped transportation format, the bussing program (see page 260).

The overnight stay has been a part of gambling in Las Vegas since the inception of legalized gaming in Nevada in 1931, but it wasn't until 1947 that an entrepreneur decided that a casino/hotel resort would appeal to gamblers. Bugsy Siegel, a well-known mobster and a member of Murder Incorporated, is credited with starting modern-day gambling in Las Vegas.

Casino hotels run the gamut as far as size, opulence, amenities, number of rooms, square footage, and food and beverage operations. Successful casino operators realize that having a place for their customers to stay is good business. These same customers are looking for a level of excellence above the norm. The casinos respond by trying to outdo one another in every aspect. Much attention is paid to details, such as large suites, air and ground transportation to and from the casino, gourmet food and beverages, and, in some cases, butler service. Ethnic chefs are hired to provide authentic ethnic cuisine for high rollers and their entourages, whether they play table games or slot machines. Lavish gifts are given on birthdays and holidays. More than one Las Vegas casino/hotel has exclusive suites that exceed 15,000 square feet—available only to a select few. The sheer volume of rooms and revenue in venues such as Las Vegas, Atlantic City, and Gulfport/Biloxi (Mississippi) is staggering.

The Park Place Entertainment Company, formerly Hilton Gaming, is the largest gambling operator in the world, due to its merger with Bally's and the purchases of Grand Casinos and Caesars' World. In September of 1999, Park Place opened Bally's/Paris Casino Resort in Las Vegas. This property is

Many casino hotels have expanded their offerings to include shows and attractions, in an attempt to increase their customer base. Families visiting Las Vegas can attend shows such as "Starlight Express." (Courtesy of the Hospitality Industry Archives and Library, University of Houston, Texas.)

a prime example of how far casino companies will go to attract customers and what a successful property can achieve. No expense was spared during the preopening phase. Planners were sent to Paris and Provence, France. The Eiffel Tower replica, an integrated part of the hotel/casino structure, was built to be exactly one-half the size of the original. The copy of the Arc de

BOX 10–1
Barron Hilton

Barron Hilton. (Courtesy of the Hospitality Industry Archives and Library, University of Houston, Texas.)

Barron Hilton was born in Dallas, Texas, in 1927. In 1935, he moved to Southern California, where he continues to make his home today. In 1954, Mr. Hilton joined Hilton Hotels as vice president, and in 1966, he assumed responsibility as president and chief executive officer of the Hilton Hotels Corporation. In February of 1979, he assumed the additional responsibility of chairman of the board. He is credited with expanding Hilton Hotels' credit card operation into the universal Carte Blanche credit card system and was also responsible for developing the Hilton Inn franchise program.

Barron Hilton expanded his company into Nevada gaming with the purchase of the Las Vegas Hilton and the Flamingo Hilton in 1970. These two hotel/casinos accounted for roughly half of the company's total operating income and made Hilton Hotels Corporation the first Fortune 500 and New York Stock Exchange company to enter the gaming business. In 1982, with his brother Eric (see Box 8–1), Hilton led the corporation into the international market by introducing the Conrad International Hotels brand name. Today, Hilton Hotels Corporation has over 250 properties with approximately 102,000 rooms worldwide. In 1999, Hilton Hotels Corporation announced its intention to purchase the Promos Hotels Corporation, which includes Doublet, Embassy Suites, Red Lion, and Hampton Inns. In the United States, the company currently concentrates its efforts in the major urban markets; its top ten properties, all located in urban areas, generate more than 60 percent of the company's gross earnings. To increase its international presence, Hilton Hotels Corporation has created a marketing alliance with Hilton International Corporation, which is owned by Ladbrooke PLC of the United Kingdom.

Source: "Barron Hilton," Cathleen Baird, Hospitality Industry Archives, Conrad N. Hilton College, University of Houston, Houston, Texas, 1998.

Triumph, which resides in the porte-cochere, is also exactly to one-half scale. The French theme is carried through in the 3,000-plus rooms. Its eight different restaurants are styled as sidewalk cafes, with staff who greet everyone in French; the streets are even authentic cobblestone. Bally's/Paris has been received with enthusiasm by both the general public and Wall Street. Its return on investment is the envy of all the other casinos in Las Vegas.

Unlike traditional lodging operations management, customer service becomes the driving force behind casino/hotel management. The usual guidelines, such as yield management, average daily rate, and occupancy rates, are no longer the standard by which the operation is judged. In fact, some casinos are attempting to drive down the average daily rate to make staying at the casino/hotel attractive to noncasino patrons. Food/cost ratios, the efficiency indicators of the food and beverage operations of a more traditional lodging facility, do not apply. The casino is able to subsidize both the lodging and the food and beverage operations in order to keep their patrons at the tables. Traditional hoteliers and food and beverage managers with traditional operations backgrounds usually have a difficult time adjusting to their secondary role as support facilities for the casinos. However, once they become involved, they realize that the sheer volume makes up for playing second fiddle to the tables. One of my students, the assistant restaurant manager for the Food Court at Caesar's Palace in Las Vegas, realized that the number of patrons the food court served in a day was equal to twice the population of her small Texas hometown!

The Complimentary Program. Although Bugsy Siegel was not terribly successful at the beginning of his casino venture, the casino industry in Las Vegas has grown tremendously since that time. There are currently 76 casinos in Las Vegas, and most large casinos have 15,000–20,000 people walk through their doors each day of the week and 40,000–50,000 on weekends. This increased competition has led to the granting of a complimentary, or comps. The **complimentary program** is a preferred customer program that is similar to those offered in other industries. Mileage rewards for airlines, preferred customer clubs for car rental companies, and point clubs for hotels and restaurants are just a few examples of such programs. Originally designed to reward wealthy table game players, comps are now offered to slot players, enhancing their appeal to the general public. It is predicted that, by the year 2005, most casinos will receive 80 percent of their casino revenue from slot machines or electronic gaming devices.

There are two types of complimentaries—hard comps and soft comps. Hard comps are those that require the casino department to pay an outside vendor for services the vendor has performed for the customer. This would include reimbursement of airfare, use of an outside limousine service, ticketing for an event at another casino, or gifts such as cars or jewelry. The term hard comp derives from the fact that the casino must pay for the service in "cold, hard cash." Some of the hard comps that have been granted include allowing a player and his wife to select his and hers matching Mercedes-Benz from a local dealership, an around-the-world cruise as a birthday present, and, in the case of one player with a $7 million line of credit, fresh raspberries in his room, regardless of the time of year. (3)

Soft comps are those handled in-house. They require only a "paper" transfer of funds from one department of the casino/hotel to another. Some examples of soft comps would be room comps, food comps, in-house limousine service, or free beverages. For obvious reasons, casinos are much more willing to grant soft comps than hard comps. You may ask yourself: "Isn't it expensive for the casino to be giving away everything free?" The answer is, yes. The saving grace, in our tax system, is that it is all tax deductible as a cost of doing business. You can be sure that the hotel is charging the casino the "rack rate" for all rooms that the casino is comping. The same holds true for restaurants, spas, retail shops, and so on. Without this tax benefit, many casinos would not comp at all, or, at the very least, comps would be much more difficult to get.

The Bussing Program. The casinos in Atlantic City have elevated bussing to an art form. With over 32 million visitors per year, Atlantic City is the number 1 destination resort in the United States, a title that it has held for the past four years. The majority of visitors live within a two-hour drive. Originally designed as a target-marketing tool to fill in the "dead" hours in the operation, the bussing program has evolved to a point at which 80 percent of all casino customers arrive by bus. Most casinos receive 50 busses per day during the week and over 100 per day on the weekend. Although it might sound like a great way to eliminate traffic and gridlock, having 650 large busses arriving in the city at all hours of the day and night has turned out to be a nightmare. However, once special "intercept" lots were set up on the outskirts of town, and all casino tour busses were assigned routes, the traffic problem was eliminated.

Riverboat Gaming. Gaming companies that rely on riverboats, such as those in the Gulfport/Biloxi area, have a similar approach to their lodging operations, but the room numbers and suite sizes are not quite as elaborate. Because most of the riverboat operations are located in towns or small cities, without the competition of Las Vegas or Atlantic City, their lodging facilities are still the most lavish and exclusive in town. Business meetings, banquets, and small conventions provide additional sources of noncasino revenue to the riverboat facilities. The casino also becomes a viable entertainment alternative for adults living in the region. In many cases, the riverboat casino becomes one of the region's largest employers.

Because of their more remote locations, most riverboat casino operations do not have access to large population bases, resulting in a smaller volume of players and a smaller profit margin. Demographic studies and market research and analysis become keys to a successful operation. A great concept, a beautiful facility, and a well-trained staff mean very little when you do not have a sufficient flow of customers to make your operation viable. Two very successful gaming venues, Lake Charles and Shreveport/

Bossier City, Louisiana, are over two hours' driving time from the two locations that comprise 80 percent of their customers, Houston and the Dallas Metroplex. Because Texas does not have casino gaming, a number of casino companies have decided to locate their facilities as close to the Texas/Louisiana border as possible. This choice has paid off for them handsomely.

Native American Gaming. Native American gaming is a relatively new phenomenon, brought into being by the National Indian Gaming Regulatory Act of 1988. Since the law was passed, over 300 Native American casinos have opened in the United States. The largest and most successful single casino operation in the world is the Foxwoods Hotel/Casino in Ledyard, Connecticut, with gross annual operating revenue of over $1 billion. The primary reason for its success is its East Coast location, approximately halfway between New York City and Boston; other tribes have not fared as well. The statute requires that the casino be built on traditional tribal land (i.e., a reservation); since many reservations are located in remote, hard to reach areas, away from population centers, many tribes have difficulty sustaining a sufficient amount of business to make their operation truly profitable. Those that also have hotels tend to be more successful, since they are able to attract new business from outside the region, instead of depending solely on the local economy.

Most of the tribes that have successful casino operations are models for reinvesting casino profits in order to improve the lives of those who need the most help. Health facilities, water treatment plants, sewage disposal facilities, and Native American schools are usually among the first projects that are paid for with revenue from these operations. Bank loans for such projects are virtually nonexistent. Start-up monies are usually provided by one or more venture capitalists, who put a management team in place before loaning the money and use a percentage of the gross revenue as collateral for the loan. Not all Native American casinos are land-based casinos. In those states that only allow commercial gaming on riverboats, the tribes have done very well. Some of the tribes have hired and partnered with successful non-Native American casino companies, usually with very lucrative results. These tribes recognize that they do not possess the expertise within the tribe to operate a multimillion dollar venture and are willing to let trusted experts do the job. In most instances, this is a very difficult decision, for most Native Americans are fiercely protective of their newly gained right to self-determination. (4)

Cultural Lodging Opportunities

The themes of lodging opportunities in and around cultural centers are usually designed to enhance the cultural experience: the hotels and restaurants in Key West and Cuba (frequented by Ernest Hemingway), the London haunts of Dickens, 221b Baker Street of Sherlock Holmes and Sir Arthur Conan Doyle fame, Giverny in France (where Monet was inspired)—the list goes on and on.

Some tourist areas are transformed into major worldwide attractions during certain times of the year. These locales become synonymous with the celebration of the event. Lodging operations are decorated in keeping with the theme of the celebration. Some examples of this phenomenon are Mardi Gras in New Orleans, Carnivale in Rio de Janeiro, Oktoberfest in Munich, New Year's Eve in New York City, and Chinese New Year in Hong Kong. These are but a few of the celebratory events that have gained worldwide reputations and huge profits for their hotel and lodging businesses.

Leisure-Only Facilities

Some resorts are devoted exclusively to the leisure of their guests. One type of leisure facility, the all-inclusive resort, includes all amenities, activities, and services in the cost of the stay. There is no need to carry cash or a credit card, since usage and/or participation is free. Sandals, which operates in Jamaica and other countries in the Caribbean, is one example of an all-inclusive resort. In some resorts, there are no telephones in the rooms, cellular phones are strictly forbidden, and the only programming available on TV are video games and movies. Messages from outside the resort may be picked up at the front desk only. By limiting distractions from the outside world, guests are better able to concentrate on those activities (or nonactivities) that will provide complete relaxation. (The first day or two is usually a difficult adjustment.)

Senior Living

This may seem a strange place to be talking about senior assisted living; however, some of the biggest names in the lodging industry have devoted their time and expertise to this oft-neglected, sometimes mismanaged segment of the lodging industry. Marriott, Hyatt, and Del Webb, to name a few, had the vision to see that many of the skills and techniques that made them successful in more traditional lodging and food service areas could be adapted to the needs of their clients in a senior-oriented atmosphere. These include paying special attention to the decor and design of the guest rooms, using colors and fabrics typically found in a hotel rather than a hospital or institutional setting; providing menus with a variety of foods, catering to the special diets of the residents but with flavors of popular restaurants; and providing recreational and leisure amenities that resemble a resort environment, including golf, tennis, spas, and aquatic sports. Overall customer satisfaction increased tremendously after these companies took over the operations. Three factors make the senior-assisted living concept an appealing and potentially lucrative area: (1) the wealthy baby boom generation is approaching retirement age; (2) with the advances in science and technology, especially medical technology, people are living longer; (3) the rising cost of health care has given birth to a new type of health insurance that is designed to cover assisted living arrangements.

Unique Facilities

There is a segment of the lodging industry that has facilities that are truly one-of-a-kind. Some are unique by reputation or location; others are unique by form and function; and still others are considered unique because of their service, decor, or amenities. Many people visit these unique facilities without ever hoping to spend the night. They are interested in the ambience, elegance, architecture, furnishings, and people watching.

Every year the Ice Palace Hotel in Sweden is carved out of a glacier, down to the tables, chairs, and beds. The Waldorf Astoria in New York City, the Palmer House in Chicago, and the Mansion at Turtle Creek in Texas all have reputations as the top hotels in their region. Where else but the Waldorf could you leave your room and run into a King, Prince, Princess, movie star, or rock star Hall of Famer in the hallway, since many make the Waldorf their home away from home.

The Greenbrier in White Sulphur Springs, West Virginia, Saratoga Springs, New York, Vichy in France, and Baden-Baden in Germany are world famous spas, some of which have been in operation for hundreds of years.

Pebble Beach Golf Resort in California, Augusta National Golf Resort in Georgia, and St. Andrews in Scotland are legendary golf resorts, famous for their accommodations as well as their spectacular, challenging courses.

The Raffles Bar in Rangoon and the Timberline Lodge in Oregon are examples of companies that have an outstanding reputation for service. Chateau de Roussan in France, Schloss Augsberg in Germany, and Parador de Trujillo in Spain are examples of castles and other historic facilities where you can sleep in rooms in which lords and princes once laid their heads. The Tunnecliffe Inn in Cooperstown, New York, allows you to sleep in one of the ten rooms that were built in 1710 and is a unique facility with the service style of a bed-and-breakfast. These facilities are but a small sampling of the truly unique lodging experiences that are available. Travel agencies and the Internet are excellent research venues for information about your next unique vacation location.

Other Types of Nontraditional Lodging

The last type of lodging that we will discuss in this chapter are those facilities that are dedicated solely to providing lodging and hospitality that do not fit into the traditional limited-service, basic full-service, and full-service framework. Included in this group are bed-and-breakfasts, rooming houses, the YM/YWCA, United Service Organizations (USO) for military personnel in transit, missions, and many others. They offer lodging with few amenities; in fact, many are simply bedrooms or sleeping rooms with shared bathrooms, dining facilities, and TV/family rooms. Although they were once very popular, these types of lodging now represent a small percentage of the lodging market. That said, they still account for billions of dollars in revenues.

The first of these are bed-and-breakfasts (B&Bs), which typically provide under 20 rooms and offer a bedroom to the guest, with bath and a breakfast after a good night's rest. Historically, B&Bs were how lodging and food and beverage hospitality was delivered prior to the advent of hotels and public houses. Travelers stayed in spare rooms provided by a host family, and meals that were eaten with the family were provided. This type of hospitality is popular today with people who want to get away from the crowds, who are looking to experience the hospitality of days gone by in a specific region, or are looking forward to coming "home" after a day spent sightseeing. The homelike feeling is enhanced by the communal dining and living areas. The clientele of B&Bs is fiercely loyal and growing. While this type of lodging is definitely not for everyone, there are a sufficient number of loyal followers for a *Guide to Bed and Breakfasts in the United States* to be compiled and published annually. Most of these facilities are individually owned and operated, with members of the family fulfilling many different functions. As in all other types of lodging, there are different prices, levels of amenities, and degrees of customer expectations and satisfaction. There are many fine examples of highly successful B&B operations throughout the United States, but do not be surprised if you do not recognize the names, unless you are a devout B&B follower. The Inn in Pacific Grove, California, is a 14-room B&B that is housed in a faithfully restored 1926 Arts & Crafts series of buildings. The Town and Country Inn near Lancaster, Pennsylvania, allows 21st century visitors to get a taste of Amish Pennsylvania Dutch life, which has not changed much since the 19th century.

In the past, the B&B's biggest problem was marketing. Mostly owned and operated by individuals, they relied on word-of-mouth advertising, repeat customers, telephone book and local newspaper advertising, and side-of-the-road signage. Today, with access to the Internet and reservation service organizations, you can find B&Bs across the country at a click of the mouse.

From the Great Depression of the 1930s through the 1950s, the Young Men's Christian Association/Young Women's Christian Association (YMCA/YWCA) and the Young Men's Hebrew Association/Young Women's Hebrew Association (YMHA/YWHA) provided clean, comfortable accommodations at a reasonable price and were a known quantity for those who were traveling to a strange city. Many had added amenities of gymnasiums and pools at no additional charge. The accommodations were very basic, but they served their purpose until better accommodations could be secured or the traveler continued on. Since the growth of budget accommodations, such as

Budgetel and Motel 6, the "Y" movement has closed many of their facilities. The few that are still in existence are found in large cities, such as New York and Houston.

At one time, every city and most towns had one or more rooming houses, also called boarding houses, the precursor of the modern extended-stay hotel (see Chapter 1). Cheaper than hotels or motels and with the added advantage that they included meals, they were the ideal accommodation for business travelers, short- or long-term workers, or those deciding whether or not to find more permanent housing in a particular city or town. Most guests contracted to stay for weeks, months, or even years. The rules of conduct were set by the owner of the rooming house, who usually owned and roomed in the house as well. While this type of lodging facility has virtually disappeared from the American scene, many people privately house newly arrived immigrants under a similar arrangement.

Throughout history, society has provided for the poor, sick, and homeless. Usually run by agencies with a religious background, missions have grown to include social service and law enforcement agencies. Even in today's positive economic climate, there are people who do not possess the means to provide shelter for themselves. Missions include communal sleeping quarters, dining facilities, and bathing facilities. Few have beds; most supply cots. Frequently, especially in inclement weather, the only space available is on the floor. Some also provide medical attention and counseling services.

The lodging industry currently is in a period of growth and change, and is meeting these challenges with renewed creativity and technological advances. The challenges of creating different forms of lodging for everyone is being met, with the full realization that these challenges will continue. It is an exciting time for everyone involved: the industry, the entrepreneur, the customers, and students like you. The future is bright for those of you who like to think outside of the norm. Those of you who are interested in the more traditional forms of lodging will be asked to "raise the bar" to compete successfully in this challenging field. The following chapter will consider a special type of lodging enterprise that, because of its meteoric rise, has opened up another opportunity for investors and managers who are seeking a bright career path—the business of vacation ownership and time-share.

SUMMARY

There are as many types of nontraditional lodging facilities as there are facilities, but they can be classified generally into four types: activity-based facilities, themed lodging, unique facilities, and other types of nontraditional lodging.

The activity-based facility evolved from children's camps to special-interest camps to the facilities of today. This is an example of the use of a classic, successful form of lodging to satisfy a totally different market need. Some examples of activity-based facilities are sports camps, celebrity cruises, space camps, hunting lodges, and fishing camps.

Themed lodging is focused on a central or specific theme. Themes include historic, eco-tourism, casino resorts, cultural, leisure-only, and senior living. Some facilities have different themes, depending on the time of year.

Unique facilities have one or more characteristics that make them stand out from all other types of lodging. At the mere mention of their names, they are recognized throughout their country, if not throughout the world. You could hardly classify staying at the Waldorf, the Mansion at Turtle Creek, or the Greenbriar as having a place to stay for the night.

Other types of facilities—nontraditional lodging—provide their customers with basic lodging: bed-and-breakfasts, YMCA/YWCAs, and YMHA/YWHAs, rooming houses, and missions. The YMCA/YWCA and local boarding houses have largely been replaced with extended-stay hotels. Bed-and-breakfasts have gained in popularity at a slow but steady rate over the past few years. Primary reasons for this are the opportunity to experience a more family/homey-type atmosphere, usually in a very desirable location, and to get away from the crowds.

References

1. Michael D. Rose, "The Advent of the 21st Century from the Chrysalis of the 1990s," speech delivered June, 1991, New York.
2. Kaye Chon and Raymond Sparrow, *Welcome to Hospitality: An Introduction* (Dubuque, IA: Delmar Publishers, 1995), p. 39.
3. Alan T. Stutts, *Gaming Marketing and Entertainment—An Overview* (University of Houston, Office of Gaming Education and Research, Conrad N. Hilton College of Hotel and Restaurant Management, University of Houston, 1997), p. 1.
4. James Wortman, "The Difference Between Hotel/Casinos and Traditional Lodging Operations," lecture given 1999.

Review Questions

1. Discuss the ways in which an individual who is interested in the various types of lodging that have been discussed in this chapter could research

business opportunities, career possibilities, growth potential, and any licensing requirements.

2. Compare and contrast the lodging requirements of activity-based facilities and themed facilities.
3. Compare and contrast lodging operations at large casino resorts with noncasino lodging business.
4. Discuss the factors that should be considered if you are developing a marketing plan for a casino resort or a themed lodging business.
5. In the past, the YMCA/YWCA organizations have provided lodging at their facilities in urban, downtown locations. Is it feasible that such organizations could create a lodging brand that would be competitive in today's urban or suburban market? Why or why not?

Activities

1. Visit a local hotel property in your community that is considered a resort or a special lodging establishment, and determine whether it could be repositioned as such a lodging establishment using any of the categories previously discussed. Explain how this repositioning might take place.
2. Contact two properties from one of the categories of lodging included in this chapter and request samples of the literature they provide to prospective guests. What is characteristic of the message that they are attempting to communicate to their guests about the experiences they provide?
3. Visit a lodging business that is included in one of the categories described in this chapter and discuss with a department head at this property those factors that are key to the success of the property. Compare this interview with what you have learned about hotel operations thus far and contrast the differences, if any.

Time-Share and Vacation Ownership

CHAPTER OUTLINE

- **History of the Time-Share Industry**
- **Resort Sales and Financing**
  - Target Market
  - Sales
  - Financing
- **Resort Amenities and Fees**
  - Amenities
  - Fees
- **Management of a Vacation Resort**
- **Rules and Regulations of Vacation Ownership**

As you learned in Chapter 1, vacation ownership or time-sharing is the right to use a vacation destination during a specific time period. Simply put, it is the prepurchase of a vacation experience. Ownership of a **time-share** is similar to ownership of a condominium, except that your rights are limited to a certain time period during the year. Ownership can be in the form of a deed, a lease, or a license. Most vacation ownership consists of a deeded interest or a long-term leased interest. A deeded interest is outright ownership. It is an absolute right , which can be sold, leased, or even willed to your heirs. Most time-shares that exist today are deeded ownership. The leased interest is much like an apartment lease; again, the right to use the property is restricted to a specific time period during the year. Upon the expiration of the lease term, your right to use the property generally terminates. The license is most commonly a membership in a club. Provided you are a member in good standing, you have the right to use the club and all its amenities during your allotted time period.

Time slots can be either fixed or floating. A fixed time slot is a specific week during the year, usually defined by number. For example, week 14 might be April 7 through April 13. Generally the week begins on a Friday, Saturday, or Sunday. By far the most popular use of time-share ownership is through a fixed-week ownership plan. With a floating time slot, the owner has the right to select any available week within a certain season of the year. If you owned a summer season week, you could pick any week that fell within the defined summer months. While this arrangement is more flexible, one disadvantage of the floating time slot is that competition between owners for prime weeks can impact availability.

It is important to decide in advance which type of arrangement best fits your anticipated travel needs. Many resorts offer special reduced rental rates for extra nights or use of other resorts owned by the same company. This can add flexibility and provide substantial cost savings. Before you buy, you must consider carefully how and where you usually vacation. If a particular time-share offers locations in Vermont and Colorado in the winter and you don't ski, this may not be the right choice for you.

As baby boomers choose more flexible and cost-effective ways to vacation, vacation ownership continues to grow in popularity. In 1980, 155,000 families owned time-shares at about 500 resorts worldwide. At the end of 1999, nearly 5 million families owned time-share vacation properties at over 5,000 resorts. This represents a growth rate of nearly 1000 percent, and makes vacation ownership the fastest growing segment of the travel and tourism industry. (1)

It is important to understand that vacation ownership is a commodity, which is purchased to be enjoyed and used over the years, and does not generally make a good investment.

HISTORY OF THE TIME-SHARE INDUSTRY

The vacation ownership (time-sharing) industry originated in Europe in the 1960s. A ski resort in the French Alps, known as "Superdevoluy," was the first known vacation ownership program in the world. The ownership of time slots brought with it the guarantee of reservations for those who wanted to ski in the area. It was an immediate success. In the 1970s, some faltering condominium projects in St. Thomas, Fort Lauderdale, and Puerto Rico were converted to vacation ownership. With the success of the conversions, time-sharing became a viable vacation alternative. Sales jumped to over $50 million by the mid-1970s and have continued to grow. The United States continues to lead the world in vacation ownership, with over 1,600 resorts and more than 2 million owners. Nearly 300,000 American families became owners of time-shares in the United States in 1999, spending over $3.5 billion. Figure 11–1 illustrates the growth in sales volume of U.S. vacation ownership. The industry worldwide displays the same healthy growth as the domestic market. In 1980, there were 155,000 owners at just over 500 resorts worldwide. Between 1985 and 1998, the number of resorts grew by 187 percent, the number of weekly intervals owned grew by more than 550 percent, and the number of owners grew by just over 500 percent. (2)

A vacation exchange, introduced in 1974 to add flexibility to the time-share arrangement, allows the owner of a vacation interest at one resort to exchange it for another one owned by someone else at another resort. The

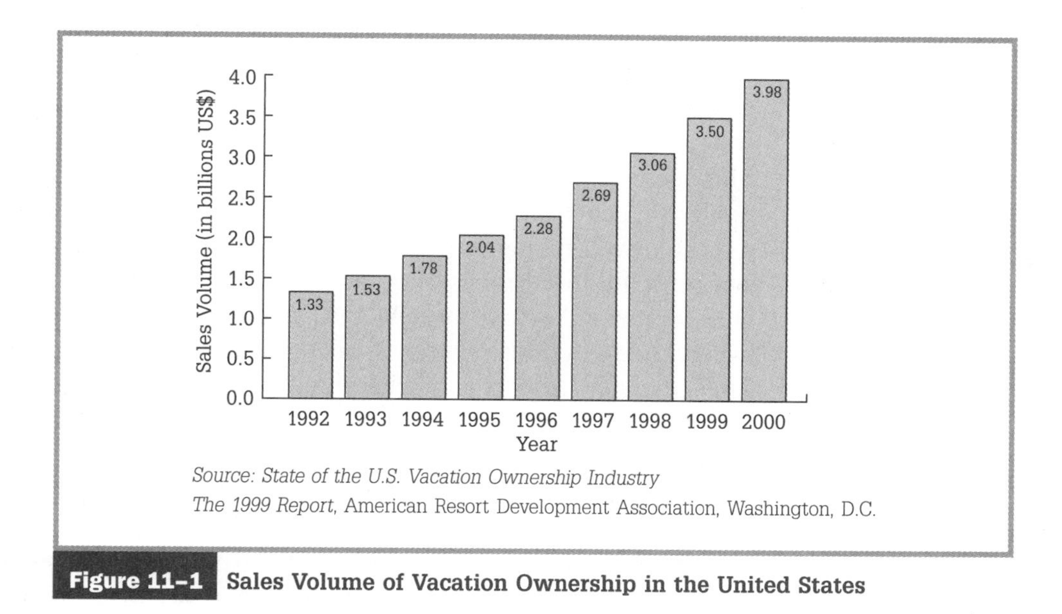

Source: State of the U.S. Vacation Ownership Industry
The 1999 Report, American Resort Development Association, Washington, D.C.

Figure 11–1 Sales Volume of Vacation Ownership in the United States

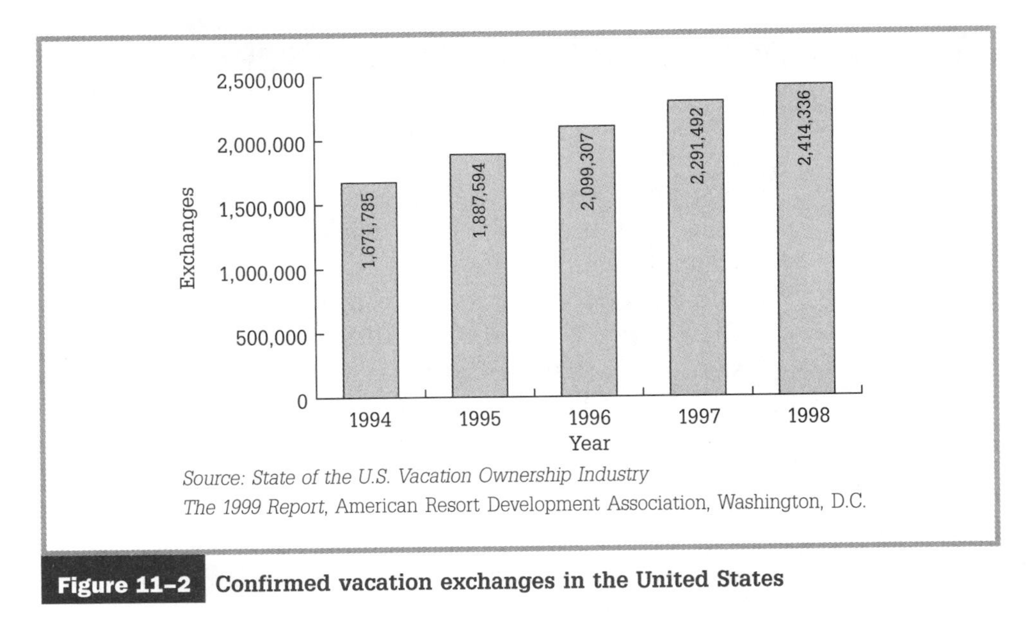

Source: State of the U.S. Vacation Ownership Industry
The 1999 Report, American Resort Development Association, Washington, D.C.

Figure 11–2 **Confirmed vacation exchanges in the United States**

exchange service is administered by an exchange company that is affiliated with the vacation ownership resort. Over 99 percent of vacation ownership resorts in the United States are affiliated with one of the two largest exchange companies, Interval International (II) with 1,200 member resorts, and Resort Condominiums International (RCI), with 2,800 member resorts. These two companies provided over 2,414,000 exchanges in 1998. (3) To date, nearly 20 million exchanges have been confirmed worldwide. Figure 11–2 illustrates the increase in exchanges from 1994 to 1998.

During its 30-year history, the industry has grown from small hotel conversions (15–20 units) to the high-quality condominium resorts of today. Management within the industry has improved noticeably, with the evolution from scattered local entrepreneurs managing failed condominium projects to well-managed professional development companies overseeing beautiful luxury resorts. For example, members of the American Resort Development Association (ARDA) are required to comply with an established code of ethics regarding management, marketing, and sales practices. The entrance into the marketplace by major hospitality chains such as Disney, Hilton, Ramada, and Marriott (see Box 11–1) has greatly enhanced the quality and image of the industry as well.

With the entry of these major players as well as more professional development and management companies, the industry is experiencing a noticeable improvement in its historically negative public image. Industry analysts have noted that the majority of time-share owners are very satisfied with their purchases; in fact, many own multiple weeks. (4)

BOX 11–1
J. W. Marriott, Jr.

J.W. "Bill" Marriott, Jr. (Courtesy of the Hospitality Industry Archives and Library, University of Houston, Texas.)

J. W. "Bill" Marriott, Jr., was born on March 25, 1932, in Washington, D.C. He learned his father's hands-on management approach by working in his parent's Hot Shoppes restaurant chain during his high school and college years. He graduated from the University of Utah with a degree in banking and finance, and joined the company full time in 1956. Just eight months later, he took over the company's Twin Bridges Motor Hotel in Washington, D.C., the company's first venture into the lodging industry.

After Marriott was elected president of the Marriott Corporation in 1964 at the age of 32, he convinced his father that to achieve growth meant taking on debt. During the next three years, Marriott became an international company by acquiring an airline catering kitchen in Venezuela and expanded its restaurant operations to include the Big Boy restaurant chain and the Roy Rogers fast-food division.

Bill succeeded his father as chief executive officer in 1972. The company continued to grow through acquisitions and by developing new lodging brands, such as Courtyard by Marriott, introduced in 1983. Marriott entered the vacation time-share business the following year. In 1985, after his father's death, he assumed the role of chairman of the Marriott Corporation.

In 1993, Marriott split into two separate companies, Marriott International, a lodging and services management company, and Host Marriott Corporation, which focuses on real estate and airport concessions. Marriott's lodging brands have continued to grow with the acquisition of the Ritz-Carlton Hotel Company. In 1996, Host Marriott Services Corporation was formed when Host Marriott Corporation divided in order to separate its real estate and airport concessions.

Marriott International employs over 130,000 people and operates in excess of 1,700 properties in the United States and 53 other countries and territories. Major brands and businesses include Marriott, Ritz-Carlton, Courtyard, Residence Inn, Fairfield, Towne Place Suites, Renaissance, and Ramada International brands; vacation club (time-share) resorts, senior living communities and services, and food service distribution.

Bill Marriott noted that his father used to say, "study well those things the company gets into"; Marriott studied the time-share business closely for a long time. The company entered the vacation ownership business in 1984. Currently, Marriott Vacation Ownership International is a part of Marriott International and operates 3,000 villas in 43 resorts, located in 21 countries worldwide, with nearly 120,000 owners.

Bill Marriott faithfully follows a set of simple business principles developed by his father: (1) take care of your employees, and they'll take good care of your customers; (2) provide customers with good service and a quality product at a fair price; and (3) stay in close touch with your business, always strive for success, and never be satisfied.

Source: "J. W. Bill Marriott," Cathleen Baird, Hospitality Industry Archives, Conrad N. Hilton College, University of Houston, Texas, 1998.

RESORT SALES AND FINANCING

Target Market The typical vacation owner is an upper-middle-income, well-educated couple, with an average age of 49 years. Over the next 20 years, more than 75 million Americans will turn 50. (A baby boomer turns 50 years old every 7.5 seconds.) With the largest concentration of vacation ownership's key demographic coming of age over the next 20 years, the time-share industry can expect sustained and significant growth. Increasingly important segments of the market include high-income households, singles, older consumers, and those with higher educational attainment.

Sales The principal factors that have been utilized to motivate the purchase of vacation ownership include the quality of the accommodations, the opportunity for exchange, and the individual amenities and features of the resort property. A company in the business of vacation ownership typically contacts potential customers using direct mail, inviting the potential customer to visit the property as a complimentary guest; the only requirement is that the potential customer attend a presentation on the benefits of ownership. Figure 11–3 illustrates the various components in the development, sale, and operation of a time-share resort.

In the 1980s, the ARDA and its members encouraged individual states to implement a standard rescission period for time-share purchases. Most states currently have a right-of-rescission period of three to ten days.

Financing The developer finances the majority of sales. Although the servicing of these funds can be extremely profitable, most resorts indicate that the primary reason developers finance their own sales is to make time-shares easier to sell. The average term of financing is six to seven years. Most consumer loans have a fixed rate of 14.5 percent, with no prepayment penalties. Credit criteria consists primarily of proof of income and credit reports. Since 1991, the minimum down payment on a vacation ownership has been 10 percent, and the average price has been $8,000 to $10,000 per week of ownership.

Because of rapid past growth and anticipated future demand, time-share developers can finance the acquisition and development of vacation ownership properties easily. Unlike a hotel or other commercial real estate properties, time-share projects are built in phases. This dramatically limits their economic exposure and avoids overbuilding. The developer waits until the previous phase nears sellout to open a new phase. Land acquisition financing, construction financing, and short-term operational loans carry the developer from one phase to the next until sales revenue is generated and is obtained primarily through conventional lenders, finance or credit compa-

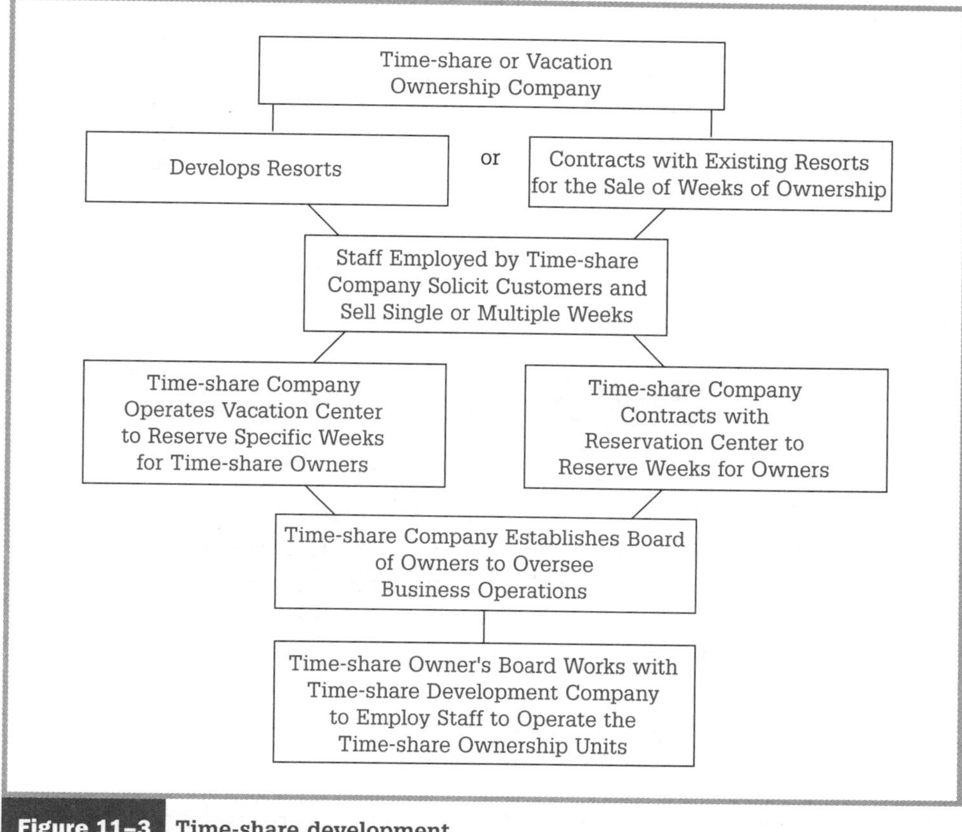

Figure 11–3 **Time-share development**

nies, and local banks. Construction loans are obtained primarily from local community banks and lenders. Based on industry financing trends, there is a demonstrated loyalty between lenders and borrowers.

Resort Amenities and Fees

What sets vacation time-share ownership apart is the combination of quality accommodations, full-service resort amenities, and unparalleled flexibility available to consumers. The typical vacation ownership unit has two bedrooms and two full baths, and can sleep up to six people. Units usually include full kitchens, outfitted with a variety of amenities, including washers and dryers.

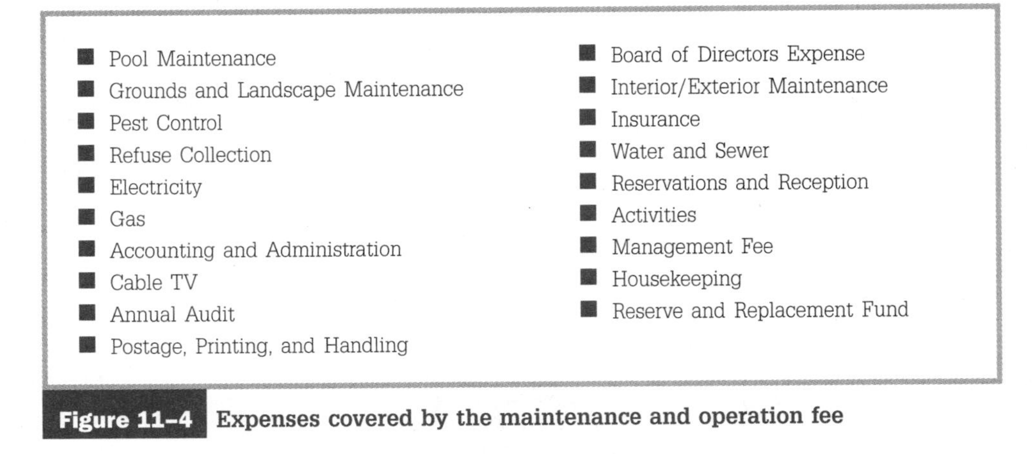

- Pool Maintenance
- Grounds and Landscape Maintenance
- Pest Control
- Refuse Collection
- Electricity
- Gas
- Accounting and Administration
- Cable TV
- Annual Audit
- Postage, Printing, and Handling
- Board of Directors Expense
- Interior/Exterior Maintenance
- Insurance
- Water and Sewer
- Reservations and Reception
- Activities
- Management Fee
- Housekeeping
- Reserve and Replacement Fund

Figure 11–4 Expenses covered by the maintenance and operation fee

Amenities The amenities offered at vacation ownership resorts rival those of many of the top-rated traditional resort properties in the world and often include fully equipped exercise facilities; tennis and racquetball courts; bicycles and paths on property; on-site shopping centers; gourmet dining; theaters and nightclubs; and children's activities. Depending upon the location and climate, a time-share property may also include indoor and outdoor swimming pools, private beach access, golf courses, ski lifts, equestrian facilities, and boats and fishing facilities.

Fees Vacation time-share ownership brings the purchaser into the membership of an association established by the developer to manage the vacation resort. The owner is required to pay an annual maintenance and operation fee to the association. In 1999, such fees averaged $600. Figure 11–4 lists the categories of expenses that a maintenance and operation fee is designed to cover.

Management of a Vacation Resort

Unlike many hotels, vacation resorts cater primarily to the vacation and pleasure traveler. The guest (the owner) is generally attracted to the vacation resort because of the reputation of the property, the area's attractions, and the resort's recreation activities. Vacation resort guests tend to participate in a variety of activities and are looking for a "total experience" during their stay. (5)

The average length of stay at a vacation resort is generally longer than at a traditional hotel. Thus, management must plan for more space for closets and for sleeping and entertainment areas in each room, as well as land for golf courses, tennis courts, Olympic-sized pools, nature walks, and other recreation, unless these activities are offered nearby. Vacation resorts in certain, more remote locations essentially must be self-contained, with a grocery store and other retailers to satisfy guests' needs.

The attitude of the staff is the indispensable ingredient that determines the quality of hospitality and service. In a commercial hotel, the guest seldom sees the manager and looks upon the hotel mainly as temporary headquarters. On the other hand, the vacation resort guest is there for a holiday and expects to be entertained around the clock.

Vacation resort management and staff are generally on hand to see to the care, comfort, and well-being of guests. Every employee in a vacation resort operation should be trained to provide total hospitality and warm interpersonal relationships. The importance of interpersonal relationships, hospitality, and service grows in inverse proportion to the size of the resort operation. The smaller the vacation resort is, the more personalized the service needs to be.

The vacation resort manager, in addition to having business knowledge, must be able to resolve nonroutine problems on a daily basis, including those involving guest relations and employee productivity as affected by a vacation environment. Facilities and equipment operation also may be a challenge, particularly if the vacation resort is located in a remote area where contract services are not easily available.

The organizational structure of a time-share resort is similar to other companies that we have considered. However, as noted in Figure 11–5, there is considerably more emphasis on sales than in a traditional hotel management structure. The actual management of the resort may be contracted out to a hotel management company or to the "parent" company of the company that developed the resort, such as Marriott International Vacation Club, whose resorts are operated by Marriott International.

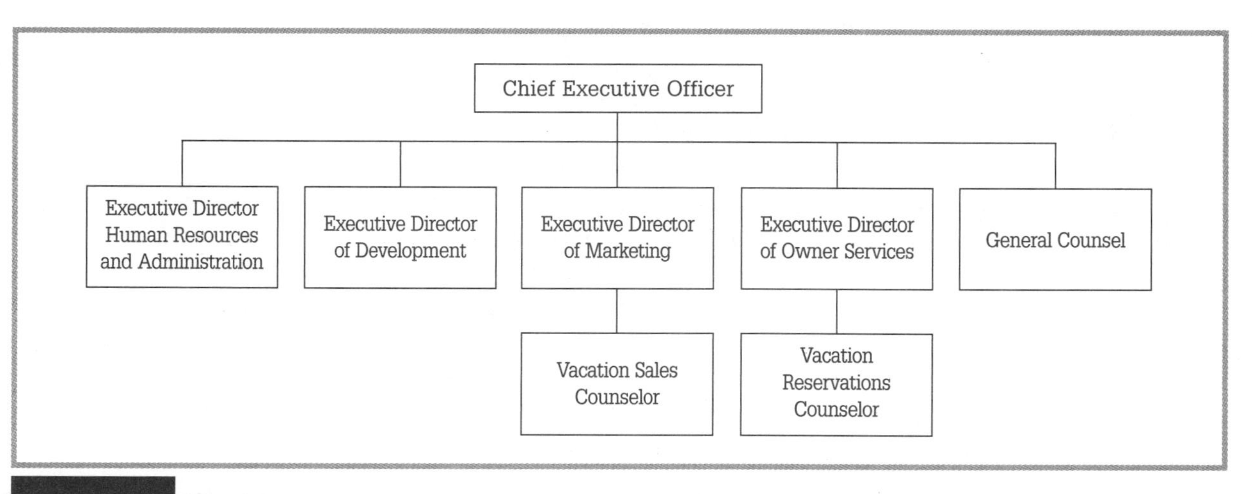

Figure 11–5 Time-share management structure

Rules and Regulations of Vacation Ownership

If ownership in a vacation resort is purchased on a floating basis, the owner will have to make a reservation with the resort or through a central reservation system in which the resort participates, such as RCI. Generally, the reserved time slot commences on a Friday, Saturday, or Sunday at 4:30 P.M. and checkout occurs seven days from check-in before 10:00 A.M. Since the guest will require a key, a front desk or a reception area is necessary. On check-in, the guest should also be provided with a packet of information that includes an inventory of items in the assigned unit, a copy of the manufacturer's instructions for operation of the appliances, and instructions for vacating the unit, such as turning off lights and electrical appliances.

Each unit is cleaned between guest stays, between 10:00 A.M. and 4:30 P.M. A vacation resort generally will provide housekeeping services at periodic intervals during the week. Most vacation resorts make available to the guest the option of additional housekeeping services for an additional fee that increases with the frequency of service desired.

Vacation ownership resorts generally are designed as studio, one-bedroom, two-bedroom, or three-bedroom units. Thus, occupancy limitations generally are applied to each unit in the resort complex. The occupancy of a studio or one-bedroom unit is typically four guests. Two-bedroom units are usually limited to eight guests, and three-bedroom units, to ten guests.

Guests should be required to report any damage or loss in a unit as soon as possible. Depending upon the source, the guest may be charged or a loss may be charged to the assigned unit. It should be clear in the rules and regulations that no structural changes, removal of furniture, wall hangings or floor coverings, or redecorating of any type are permitted.

A vacation resort should have a security team to ensure the safety of guests and to protect the assets of the resort. Since it is not necessary for the front desk of a vacation resort to be operational 24 hours per day, security may take a greater role in assisting guests regaining entry to their units, should they misplace their key.

Rules must be established to restrict storage of any extra recreational equipment (rowboats, surfboards, etc.) away from the lobbies, stairways, sidewalks, driveways, or other common areas. Because guests may arrange to leave personal articles in their assigned unit past the time of their stay, a time limit for the storage of such articles must be established.

Most vacation resorts allow an owner to have guests during their use period. Guests also may occupy the owner's assigned unit on their own during the owner's reservation period. For safety reasons, the owner must list all persons using the assigned unit.

Dangerous or unlawful substances must not be stored, introduced, or used within the resort area. Any obnoxious or offensive activities should be grounds for ejection from the property. The use of portable grills, hibachis, or other personal outdoor cooking equipment should be prohibited.

Generally, pets of any kind are not allowed on the property of a vacation resort in order to preserve the units for the other owners. However, some vacation resorts do provide separate facilities for pets. Pet lovers should raise this issue prior to their purchase of the vacation ownership.

To preserve the appearance of the resort, many vacation properties restrict the use of the balconies of the units. Sunshades, awnings, or similar devices are often prohibited. Draping of articles, such as towels and swimsuits over balcony railings, should not be permitted. Instead, management should provide adequate space inside the unit for this purpose, including a dryer and a retractable clothesline.

A vacation resort typically furnishes each unit with a private telephone with direct-line access. Any calls made during an owner's use period are charged to the owner at checkout. Vacation resorts generally impose reasonable charges for local and long-distance telephone calls.

Vacation resorts may restrict children's play to children's recreation areas, particularly if the resort caters primarily to adults. There are resorts that are adult-only—again an issue that potential buyers should discuss prior to purchase. An adult usually must accompany children under 13 years of age. Parents are held financially responsible for any disturbance or damage caused by minor children. Personal charges generally must be guaranteed by a credit card or some form of deposit.

The owner will be provided with a designated parking space, but, in many locations, extra vehicles may have to be parked at a remote site.

Failure to vacate on the designated date and at the designated time generally will result in a substantial penalty charge to the owner because of the tight scheduling of the units, the needs of housekeeping, and the arrival of the next owner.

SUMMARY

Vacation ownership, or time-sharing, is the right to use accommodations of a resort during a specific time period. The ownership can be in the form of a deed, a lease, or a license. The time of the owner's use can either be fixed or floating. Time slots are usually one-week periods. One of the most popular features of vacation ownership is the flexibility offered through the exchange opportunity.

The United States leads the world in vacation ownership. Time-shares in the United States continue to grow in popularity as baby boomers choose more flexible and cost-effective ways to vacation. The typical vacation resort owner earns a higher income and is older than the average American consumer.

Consumer loans play an integral role in the time-share sales process. The property developer usually administers the loans. The average term of contract for financing packages is six to seven years.

The basic differences between managing a vacation resort and a commercial hotel include the purpose and length of the guest's visit, requirements for additional amenities (grocery stores, etc.) due to location, and the increased needs for customer service.

In order for a vacation resort to function successfully, management must establish a reasonable set of rules and regulations. Areas for consideration include reservations, check-in/checkout, housekeeping, and restrictions on how various components of the facility can be used.

References

1. Cynthia L. Huheey, *State of the U.S. Vacation Ownership Industry—The 1999 Report* (Washington, D.C.: American Resort Development Association, 1999), p. 1.
2. Cynthia L. Huheey, "Exchanges," in *State of the U.S. Vacation Ownership Industry—The 1999 Report* (Washington, D.C.: American Resort Development Association), p. 9.
3. Richard L. Ragatz, *The Public Image of Resort Time-sharing: Major Issues and Trends, 1998 Edition* (Indianapolis: RCI Consulting, 1998), p. 60.
4. American Resort Development Association, "The Worldwide Vacation Ownership Industry," in *State of the U.S. Vacation Ownership Industry—The 1999 Report*, (Washington, D.C.: American Resort Development Association, 1999), p. 3.
5. Chuck Y. Gee, *Resort Management*, 2nd ed. (East Lansing, MI: Educational Institute, American Hotel and Motel Association, 1988), p. 16.

Review Questions

1. Should all resort hotels be converted to time-share or vacation ownership? Why or why not?

2. If you were going to organize a training program for persons engaged in vacation resort sales, what would you include about the characteristics of potential buyers?

3. Why is the management of a vacation time-share resort different from that of a full-service convention hotel?

ACTIVITIES

1. Contact two companies in the business of vacation ownership sales and request literature about their properties. Contrast experiences you had in obtaining the information and the information itself. How were you treated by the vacation ownership company? How would you compare this experience with one you had when contacting a traditional hotel property for information about the facilities?

   Contrast the information that you received from the two vacation ownership companies. What type of image did they project? What information was very clear; what information was unclear? What was your overall impression of the vacation ownership companies that you contacted?

2. Interview a local hotel general manager and determine what the general manager understands about vacation ownership and what his or her reaction would be on learning that his or her hotel was going to be converted to vacation ownership. Would this lessen his or her interest in managing the hotel? Why or why not?

Chapter 12

The General Manager

CHAPTER OUTLINE

We introduced you to the position of the general manager (GM), the person ultimately responsible for everything that goes on in the hotel, in Chapter 2. It takes about ten years of full-time hotel experience for a hotelier to become a GM. A successful GM must have a strong desire for independent action, a basic sense of fairness and honesty, and empathy for people. In addition, a GM must have a good memory, good concentration skills, the ability to analyze his or her own managerial style, and the flexibility to make adjustments in the way in which he or she handles unexpected situations. (1)

Management textbooks typically list four major functions of management:

Planning
Organizing
Directing
Controlling

Ellsworth Statler (Box 12–1) was an early implementor of these management functions in hotels. However, these four functions overlap; managers cannot divide their working days into two hours of planning, two hours of organizing, and so on. In fact, what managers actually do often bears little resemblance to any of the above! How would you classify the hours spent counseling a 20-year employee whose spouse passed away unexpectedly or babysitting one of your long-term guest's toy poodle while the guest visited a friend in a hospital where "no dogs are allowed"?

Operational Control, Organizational Development, and Business Maintenance

A better way to classify the activities of a general manager's day is by whether the demands on the GM's time have short-term, intermediate-term, or long-term results. The *short-term demands* of a GM's job revolve around the day-to-day operational issues of quality service and controlling costs and revenue. Like all operations managers, a GM is under tremendous pressure to produce positive short-term results. Therefore, the GM must devote a great deal of effort to maintain operational control and can be considered an *operational controller*.

Since the hotel's day-to-day and week-to-week operations are many and varied, the bulk of the GM's role as operational controller must be to monitor and disseminate detailed information pertaining to operational matters. For example, if there is an overbooking problem, a variety of subordinates must be involved in resolving the problem, including the reservation

The general manager organizes, manages, and relies on a team of employees to ensure that hotel operations run smoothly and that guests receive superior customer service. (Courtesy of the Hospitality Industry Archives and Library, University of Houston, Texas.)

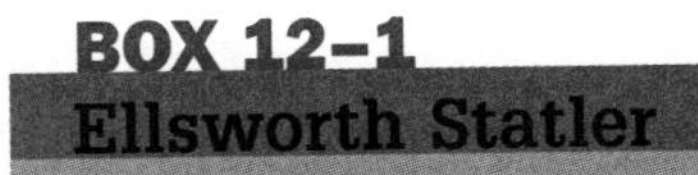

BOX 12–1
Ellsworth Statler

Ellsworth Statler. (Courtesy of the Hospitality Industry Archives and Library, University of Houston, Texas.)

Ellsworth Statler (1863–1928) was born in poverty, but his innate business sense enabled him to acquire great success in the hotel industry. From the time he became a bellman at the age of 13, he had a consuming curiosity about every aspect of the hotel business. He questioned various department heads, from the housekeeper to the engineer and bookkeeper to learn all that he could. His curiosity and enthusiasm led to greater responsibilities. From the beginning, he had innovative ideas that improved profitability. He convinced the hotel owner where he worked to add the first railroad ticket counter to ever function in an American hotel.

His own first hotel was a temporary structure that he built for the 1901 Pan American Exposition that was held in Buffalo, New York. The exposition itself was a commercial failure, but Statler earned a small profit on his venture. He used the money to build another temporary hotel for the successful 1904 St. Louis Exhibition. That profit enabled Statler in 1908 to construct his first permanent hotel in Buffalo.

Innovation and attention to guest conveniences insured Statler's success, revolutionized the hotel industry in 1908, and continued to provide standards for hospitality leadership. In the Buffalo Statler, each guest room featured a pri-

manager, the sales manager, the room's manager, and the resident manager. The skills involved include effectively communicating with personnel (in both speaking and listening), familiarity with the system and department, and the ability to analyze possible solutions. Every interaction between a GM and a subordinate is an opportunity to provide leadership. Another important leadership quality is recognition that the choice of operational issues on which to focus affects the attitudes of subordinates toward those issues. If the GM is interested, it must be important! Outstanding general managers realize that, as the final voice of authority on all hotel-related issues, they are constantly on stage whenever they are working in the hotel.

As you have already learned, a full-service hotel is a complicated, busy place. Staying on top of such a complicated business is unquestionably the most demanding element of a GM's job. The day-to-day operational devate bathroom, a closet, running ice water, telephones, and electric light switches by the door. Other guest room innovations included a lamp over each bed and a writing desk with hotel stationery. The vertical corridor for pipes and other utilities is now commonplace in most high-rise construction, but at that time, it enabled Statler to offer the rooms at competitive rates. By 1927, Statler had hotels in Cleveland, Detroit, St. Louis, and New York City, where he built the largest hotel of its day, the 2002-room Pennsylvania Hotel.

Ellsworth Statler had a unique philosophy, that "life is service"; the one who progresses is the one who gives his fellow human beings a little more, a little better service. He was the first to give hotel men and women a six-day workweek, paid vacations, and free health service. He devised a profit-sharing plan that matched a free stock share with each one purchased by employees.

Statler died unexpectedly in 1928, but his widow, Alice Statler, continued the expansion of his hotel company and avoided financial difficulties during the Depression. Statler's will created the Statler Foundation as an instrument for the perpetuation of his ideals. Those ideals not only fueled the success of Statler Hotels but also continue to fund research for the benefit of the hotel industry in the United States and to support the education of future generations of individuals who will enter the hospitality profession.

John Wiley, editor and publisher of the trade publication *Hotel Monthly*, wrote of Ellsworth Statler in 1912: "Mr. Statler's genius is both creative and adaptive and is combined with a shrewdness in selecting utilitarian features. He also combines the traits of the dreamer with those of the man in action."

Source: "Ellsworth Statler," Cathleen Baird, Hospitality Industry Archives, Conrad N. Hilton College, University of Houston, Texas, 1997.

mands of the job could easily become an all-consuming concern, leaving little time for anything else. To avoid merely being reactive to daily operating concerns, a GM must be able to adapt and fine-tune the hotel's service strategies to meet the changing conditions of the marketplace. In addition, he or she is responsible for the development and training of qualified subordinates and for implementing systems and programs to improve operational consistency and control. These initiatives constitute the bulk of the *intermediate-term demands* faced by a GM. In this role, the GM can be considered an *organizational developer*.

In the role of organizational developer, the GM steps out of the hotel into the surrounding community and in some cases up the ladder of the corporate hierarchy. Information about the changing needs of the community and the marketplace must be analyzed and disseminated to the subordinates in the hotel who can make the best use of this information. Both external and internal information must be processed so that the GM can make intelligent decisions regarding specific plans and improvements. Any new plan or program involves the expenditure of time and money; the general manager is responsible for the scheduling and funding of any new initiatives. The general manager must ensure that subordinates fully understand and accept the agenda and strategy set forth for the hotel in order for any new plans to be successful.

An important *long-term demand* of the GM's job relates to the major capital expenditure decisions required to ensure the long-term viability of the hotel. Another long-term demand is the development of a certain degree of organizational stability consistent with the hotel's strategy. In discharging long-term responsibilities, the GM can be considered a *business maintainer*.

In seeking capital, the GM's role as liaison to corporate executives and owners is critical, as is the allocation of financial resources. Depending on the corporation's structure, the GM may be required to prepare formal budget proposals and to justify any major financial expenditures. This is especially true if the GM is proposing a major shift in the hotel's service strategy. In order to maintain organizational stability, the GM must make sure that information is disseminated downward through the hotel staff as well as upward, keep his or her eyes open for new human resource development programs, and continue to develop management talent.

TOTAL QUALITY MANAGEMENT

Traditionally, managerial control is exerted by direct supervision, such as inspection of a guest room after the room attendant has finished. By its very nature, this type of supervision is negative—the manager doing the inspecting is looking for mistakes. In extreme cases, some managers use information technologies to eavesdrop on employees—an even more negative, and ethically questionable, practice. An effort must be made to make supervision a more positive aspect of managerial control. This includes the sometimes neglected area of communication. The pressure exerted on the employee because of the corporate trend toward downsizing and rightsizing can lead employees to tell supervisors what they think they want to hear, even if it leads to bending the truth. (2)

These pitfalls can be avoided by successful implementation of all of, or portions of, the **total quality management** (TQM) approach introduced in Chapter 7. TQM is a particular concern of the general manager, whose edge is the consistency and the level of service provided by the staff to the guests of the hotel. A successful TQM strategy is based on **benchmarking**, or measuring the hotel's goods, practices, and services against those of its toughest competitors and giving employees personal control over the quality of their performance. One example is a group of floor housekeepers who meet to discuss how the furnishings of a guest room might be rearranged in order to increase both housekeeping efficiency and guest satisfaction. A successful, quality-based management system is built on trust and pride in performance. The GM is responsible for creating such a working environment; the employees are responsible for using personal control wisely. (3)

In the TQM approach, the hierarchy of control of work processes is as follows: the workforce, automation, managers, and upper management. Thus, a quality-based approach locates control at the lowest levels of a hotel—the employees who provide the services.

To further employee self-management, general managers must develop policies and programs for worker participation. (4) Once they have internalized a knowledge of the company's goals and cost-control strategies, employees can perform their duties with minimal supervision. The GM must be sure that employees are armed with the knowledge, tools, and power to prevent problems from arising, and to deal effectively with those that do occur. Managers also must encourage employee input and cost consciousness by recognizing and implementing employees' suggestions for quality improvement. Employees should be given the first opportunity to solve any problems that might arise.

The transformation from traditional management practices to a TQM approach brings the role of the general manager beyond that of operational controller to one of organizational developer and, like any major change, requires a great deal of patience. Implementing the TQM approach takes time and training. Companies that fail to utilize the TQM method successfully are those that have not provided their employees with the information and training they need to be effective. (5) Most employees want responsibility and control over their work, and will understand and accept a new approach to their work if management demonstrates commitment to improving the system.

The Importance of Communication

As you have already seen, the general manager expends considerable time interacting with others. Only through successful interpersonal communication can anything be accomplished. This is true of any business but is especially important to a service-based business, such as a hotel. The general manager must understand that leadership is based on the ability to influence others and that effective communication plays a big part in that influence.

Oral communication, the use of the spoken word to transmit a message, can take the form of a face-to-face conversation, a telephone conversation, or a combination of the two, the teleconference. Oral communication enables prompt, two-way interaction between parties. Questions can be addressed, positions and issues can be debated, and a plan for action or resolution can be established. Some forms of oral communication also allow the use of gestures, facial expressions, and other emotions, such as tone of voice. The advantage of the teleconference is that people from different locations, even different parts of the world, who would otherwise be unable to communicate face-to-face, can interact personally, exchange ideas, and provide feedback. (6)

Because of its immediacy, oral communication can result in miscommunication. If one of the parties is preoccupied or upset, it interferes with the communication process. Or, a verbal message that is not clearly stated may fail to communicate the intended idea. A hurried general manager may instruct a bellman to go to Room 302 immediately and then hurry off without telling the bellman why he should go there. The immediacy of feedback also has its disadvantages. Individuals often feel the need to respond immediately in a face-to-face meeting, when, in fact, it might be better to wait and prepare a well-thought-out response.

Transmitting a message through the written word can help eliminate many of the problems associated with oral communication. Written messages can be in the form of procedure manuals, reports, memos, letters, notes, telegrams, or e-mails. Written messages allow the sender to think about the message, reread it several times, and perhaps get others to review it before transmitting it. The recipient can take time to read the message carefully and accurately. Written messages also provide a permanent record of communication, since like most business leaders, general managers often find it necessary to document their decisions for legal reasons.

Many general managers prefer the interaction and immediate feedback of oral communication. With their busy schedules, general managers need to resolve problems quickly, and written communication takes more time to prepare. It is almost always quicker to make a telephone call or attend a meeting than to put ideas on paper, distribute them to others, and receive their written responses. Because of its more permanent nature, written communication also may discourage open communication, which, as you have already learned, is essential to a smooth-running operation.

Examples of nonverbal communication, intentional or unintentional messages that are neither written nor spoken, include vocal cues, body movements, facial expressions, personal appearance, and distance or space. A certain look or glance, seating arrangements at a meeting, or a sudden change in tone of voice can communicate a strong message. Nonverbal messages can be quite powerful. The amount of silence left between a question to the general manager and his or her answer, for example, can be very telling.

The difficulty with nonverbal communication is that the recipient must know the sender's specific background to accurately decode the message. (7) Nonverbal cues such as touch, body language, and personal distance are used differently in different cultures. For instance, an early study of how often couples in coffee shops touched reported that couples in San Juan touched 180 times an hour; couples in Paris, 110 times; in Gainesville, Florida, twice per hour; and in London, once. A business deal in Japan can fall through if a foreign executive refuses a cup of green tea. It is important that hotel representatives working in foreign countries be given adequate communications training. (8)

Another potential problem with nonverbal communication is that the wrong message can be sent. An employee standing with his or her arms crossed across the chest, a stance usually interpreted as standoffishness, may simply be because the employee is standing in a cold draft. An effective communicator uses a combination of verbal and nonverbal communication to interpret what the other person is really saying.

The majority of our lives is spent communicating, whether by speaking to someone else directly, responding to e-mails, watching television, or listening to the radio. Of this time, 45 percent is spent listening. (9) Unless someone is listening, communication is not occurring. Listening is perhaps the most difficult form of communication; it needs to be learned and frequently improved. In *The 7 Habits of Highly Effective People*, Stephen Covey argued that the key to effective listening is to seek first to understand and then to be understood. Covey describes empathetic listening as listening with the intent to understand. (10) This is not easy—it requires looking at an issue from another person's point of view. It requires listening not only with your ears but also with your eyes and your heart.

Distractions such as interruptions, telephone calls, and unfinished work are a major barrier to effective listening. Selecting an environment free of such distractions will improve listening. Many listeners also take detours during a communication. For instance, if someone mentions a word that brings out certain emotions, such as a negative racial identifier or a profanity, the listener might become distracted and tune out the message. Many listeners also begin to debate a point, thinking ahead and planning a response before the speaker is even finished. A good listener shuts out distractions, assumes an attentive, nonthreatening listening posture, and maintains eye contact and a warm facial expression. Honest feedback can he used to determine if the listener understood the intended message. Effective listeners focus on the message's meaning, postpone judgment until the communication is complete, actively respond to the speaker, and avoid focusing on emotionally charged words.

Effective and empathic listening takes time and practice. It is not a passive exercise, but an active skill that must be learned and that requires full participation. Good listeners take notes, ask questions, and are totally attentive to what is being said.

Both general managers and their subordinates need to develop good communication skills. General managers must improve their ability to understand their associates, employees, and guests, and to be understood by them as well. With the trend toward more individual responsibility, inspired by the TQM concept, the development of effective communication skills should be addressed during training.

The use of simple language also can facilitate communication. Complex language and the use of confusing or misleading terms introduces noise into the communication process. Good communicators also question others, asking for ideas and suggestions, thus encouraging participation. They initiate new ideas and calls for action, and evaluate ideas of others, offering insightful summaries.

A major barrier to effective communication is resistance to change. Managers can facilitate the communication process by minimizing resistance to change. Preparation, participation, support, and negotiation are the four keys to minimizing resistance to change. Preparing employees for a major change by giving them advance warning and complete information will help smooth the transition. Also, having people who will be affected by a change participate in the process will increase their comfort level and commitment. Support can be demonstrated by understanding the difficulties faced by employees, listening to their concerns, and going to bat for them on important issues. Reducing resistance to change can also be accomplished through negotiation. For example, since change may bring the requirement that employees learn new skills, a part of the negotiation might be to give staff paid time so that they can receive the skills training necessary.

Increasingly, general managers face the challenge of communicating with a diverse workforce, of whom for many English is a second language. Managers must be aware of diversity and understand its value. We have already seen how differences in culture can influence how people communicate. A good communicator should be aware of an individual's background and experiences, and anticipate the meaning that will be attached to different messages. In addition to the skills we have already discussed, communicating with an increasingly diverse workforce requires an understanding of other cultures plus the ability to overcome one's own hidden biases and stereotypes about other people, as well as those of staff members.

A *communication audit* is a systematic method of collecting and evaluating information about an organization's communication efforts, usually conducted by a management consultant who is skilled in transforming organizational culture. Organizations use many different formats when conducting a communication audit. Information can be collected from both managers and employees via surveys, interviews, observation of operations, and reviews of formal and informal reports and procedures. The process consists of three steps:

1. Outlining communication policies
2. Identifying the communication objectives and media
3. Evaluating the overall quality of the communication system by comparing communication objectives to actual performance

Such an audit can establish a clear picture of current communication patterns, diagnose discontent or reveal problems in communication, and provide a before-and-after picture of communication in relation to major organizational changes. (11)

The Development of a Performance Culture

Performance is especially important for service businesses, such as the hotel and lodging industry. Hotels do not produce products; they perform services. And the performance of these services is often labor-intensive. If the performance of the staff is unresponsive and incompetent, so is the service. The majority of complaints that come into General Motors or Ford are about products; the majority of complaints that come into service businesses, such as Hilton or Marriott, are about people.

Management of services is often difficult, because service is an intangible product; one guest's idea of good service may differ dramatically from another's. One proven, tangible way to improve service productivity and efficiency is to invest in people and develop a performance culture. A **performance culture** is an atmosphere in which service employees have the training, knowledge, and freedom to meet customers' needs. Many hotels claim to be guest-driven, but it takes much more than rhetoric or good intentions to develop a performance culture. One foundation of a performance culture is total quality management, a style of business that is inclusive of differences of opinions and gains the support of all employees, supervisors, and managers.

The true measure of a performance culture is discretionary effort, the difference between the minimum amount of effort an employee must expend to perform his or her job (acceptable performance) and the maximum amount of effort an employee must expend to achieve the highest level of performance (peak performance). (12) It is discretionary effort that differentiates the peak performer, one who "chooses to do his or her best," from the employee who performs only what he or she has to in order to remain employed. Thus, it is discretionary effort that the general manager must focus on in order to develop a high-performance culture.

Some hotels are satisfied with acceptable performance, which their guests accept and move on. Because of today's highly competitive global economy, there is little difference between the products offered by various hotels. When the products are so similar, it is the service that makes the difference. Exceptional service will be remembered by the guest and will make the guest return. The challenge facing general managers is to unleash workers' discretionary effort, to motivate them to go that extra mile for the guest. Obviously, employees have the most control, and general managers have the least, over discretionary effort, but the general manager can provide an atmosphere in which discretionary effort is encouraged, or even rewarded. Empowering employees to make decisions and to take action without management's approval increases the likelihood that discretionary effort will be exercised. Employees who fear the consequences of making a mistake or who are not allowed to make decisions are less likely to put in extra effort. But empowerment alone does not ensure that a performance culture is created. The general manager must be committed to developing a responsive organizational structure that encourages exceptional performance, and employees must be committed to the organization's goals.

The general manager serves as a role model for the employees of the hotel. The general manager must demonstrate a commitment to customer service, if he or she expects workers to do the same. General managers must identify those activities that are most critical and focus the hotel's time, energy, and resources on being the best in the world at those activities.

Incentives are an effective means of recognizing and encouraging exceptional performance. Recognition or rewards should be given for performance that enhances job efficiency and employee effectiveness. Employees should be encouraged to participate with management in defining goals and standards against which individual performance can be judged. Every action of the general manager must demonstrate his or her commitment to the performance culture. The worst thing a general manager can do is to talk performance culture but take actions that convey the opposite message.

Most performance cultures are characterized by a high degree of training. Employees are trained not only to perform their jobs, but also to solve problems, deal with irate customers, and interact effectively with other members of the organization. Knowledge is power; an employee must know how his or her job fits into the overall scheme of the hotel, must be aware of the responsibilities of employees holding other jobs, must be conscious of the hotel's goals, and must be skilled in interacting with guests. Employee support is also essential; when an employee needs operational support or advice to help a guest, the support must be readily available. Adequate training, knowledge, and support maximizes an employee's ability to deliver discretionary effort.

As you can see, the responsibilities of a general manager are many and varied. Perhaps the most important characteristic that a general manager can possess is flexibility, since it is impossible to predict what will happen from one day to the next. For an outline of a "typical" day in the life of the general manager of a full-service hotel, see Appendix 12–1.

SUMMARY

The short-term demands on a general manager's time revolve around day-to-day operational issues of service, cost control, and revenue maximization (operational control). In the intermediate term, the general manager is concerned with responding quickly to changes in the external environment, as well as with effective staff training (organizational development). Long-term responsibilities include capital expenditures and development of organizational stability (business maintenance).

Successful general managers are those who can effectively implement total quality management (TQM). A successful TQM strategy is based on giving the employee personal control over the quality of his or her job performance.

Communication plays a key role in control of hotel operations and the development of effective internal and external working relationships. The general manager must master oral, written, and nonverbal communication, and must be an empathetic listener.

A performance culture is an atmosphere in which service employees have the training, knowledge, and freedom to meet customers' needs. The foundation of a performance culture is discretionary effort, the difference between the minimum amount of effort expended to complete a job and an employee's peak performance. Maximizing discretionary effort is the goal of a performance culture.

REFERENCES

1. Eddystone C. Nebel III, "The Day-to-Day Activities of Outstanding Hotel Managers," *Managing Hotels Effectively—Lessons from Outstanding General Managers* (New York: John Wiley & Sons, Inc., 1991), p. 397.
2. Joseph M. Juran, *Juran on Leadership for Quality: An Executive Handbook* (New York: Free Press, 1989), pp. 147–148.

3. Juran, *Juran on Leadership*, pp. 148–150.
4. A.V. Feigenbaum, *Total Quality Control* (New York: McGraw-Hill, 1991), pp. 204–209.
5. Gilbert Fuchsburg, "Total Quality Is Deemed Only Partial Success," *The Wall Street Journal*, 1 October 1992, pp. B1, B7.
6. Richard K. Allen, *Organizational Management Through Communications* (New York: Harper and Row, 1977), p. 10.
7. Cheryl Hamilton and Cordell Parker, *Communicating for Results* (Belmont, CA: Wadsworth, 1990), p. 127.
8. S. M. Jourard, *Disclosing Man to Himself* (Princeton, NJ: Van Nostrand, 1968), p. 10.
9. John R. Ward, "Now Hear This," *IABC Communication World* (July 1990): pp. 20–22.
10. Stephen R. Covey, *The 7 Habits of Highly Effective People* (New York: Fireside, 1990), p. 237.
11. Michael S. Hunn and Steven I. Meisel, "Internal Communication: Auditing For Quality," *Quality Progress* (June 1991): 56–60.
12. Scott W. Kelley, "Discretion and the Service Employee," *Journal of Retailing* (Spring 1993): 104–126.

Review Questions

1. Describe the short-term, intermediate-term, and long-term demands on a general manager's time.
2. If you were directed to prepare a briefing for your hotel's general manager about TQM, what would you say?
3. You have been assigned the task of training hotel managers in communication strategies; prepare an outline of your course.
4. What is peak performance? How does it relate to discretionary effort?

Activity

1. Interview the general manager of a local hotel, and from this interview, prepare a description of a typical day of this general manager. Contrast your results with the typical day of a general manager as outlined in Appendix 12–1. How much of each day is involved in oral and written communication? How much is involved in motivating others to achieve peak performance?

Appendix 12–1

A Day in the Life of a General Manager

Monday, 7:00 a.m. I arrived at the office, just a brief ride down the elevator from my hotel apartment, go over the weekend's operating statistics, check my e-mails, and begin going through the stack of paperwork on my desk.

8:05 a.m. A call from the company's regional vice president, my immediate superior, who is just calling to check on how things are going. I update her on weekend occupancy and revenue figures. We discuss a number of personnel issues, including a prospective marketing director for the hotel. We also swap corporate gossip, in a friendly way. It is nice to have a boss who can get the point across in a nonthreatening, yet professional manner. I request that the company's regional vice president of marketing accompany me to a neighboring city, where we will be trying to get a client to book a large convention.

8:24 a.m. The director of sales for the hotel dropped in to ask me why I was lowering next month's revenue forecast. During the conversation my secretary came in with papers to be signed, and I received a phone call from the head of security about a guest's van that was stolen from the parking garage over the weekend. I put the conversation with the director of sales on hold, because the director of sales had to attend another meeting.

8:30 a.m. Two junior executives who have been given responsibility for planning the upcoming employee picnic and golf tournament dropped by to discuss details. I made suggestions regarding the courtesy food and beverage carts that will be stationed on the golf course.

8:48 a.m. *I walked over to the resident manager's office to see how the search for a new chef is going. At the same time, I showed the resident manager the caps that will be given out during the golf tournament and mentioned some of the issues discussed earlier with the regional vice president.*

9:03 a.m. *The hotel's convention coordinator came to my office about a problem with a convention group staying at the hotel. I explained how the issue should be handled but left it to the convention coordinator to work out the details.*

9:06 a.m. *While signing papers, I got a telephone call from the hotel's chief engineer who brought up three or four operational matters.*

9:12 a.m. *I went to the eleventh floor to look over a room remodeling in progress. While there I ran into the executive in charge of the project, who updated me on the status of the project. I made several quick suggestions for the executive to follow up on.*

9:33 a.m. *The director of security caught up with me, and we talked on the way back to my office. The director of security gave me some more details on the van theft.*

9:45 a.m. *I walked to the nearby office of the food and beverage director to find out her concerns regarding the decision to hire a new chef. We also discussed how well the Friday night charity banquet went. The food and beverage director told me some corporate gossip received from the vice president of food and beverage that morning, and we laughed about corporate politics.*

9:55 a.m. *I received a call from a local businessman who wanted the address of a local celebrity. I had the information but did not give it out until I got some details on the reason for the request.*

9:58 a.m. *The hotel's attorney called and updated me on a pending lawsuit.*

10:00 a.m. *I attended the regular Monday staff meeting of all department heads. I wanted to congratulate them on the great Friday evening banquet. I joked with three or four executives and then turned the meeting over to the controller. I listened as the controller discussed some key budget projections, and I signed some equipment requisitions. Toward the end of the meeting, I told everyone what went on at last week's owners' meeting and went over the planning for this year's New Year's Eve events.*

11:00 a.m. *After the meeting formally broke, I had a short conversation with five different executives and reinforced the importance of the budget message from the controller.*

11:05 a.m. *Back in the office, I got a call from the son of the hotel's managing partner, who is looking for some comps. After checking with the reservations department, I regretfully refused the request, because the hotel is approaching 100 percent occupancy for those nights.*

11:08 a.m. *The resident manager came by to advise me that another hotel was chosen by the local tourist commission to house a group of wholesale travel agents. I called the city's director of tourism to see if we could host a luncheon for the travel agents, and I was assured that the next group will be housed at my hotel.*

11:23 a.m. *I called the chief engineer to check on an elevator problem. We also discussed the rooms rehab, the golf tournament, and the Monday night football game.*

11:45 a.m. *The hotel's managing partner called to ask a question about some expenditures on the previous month's profit and loss statement. I looked up the information and explained the details. We discussed five or six other issues, including the outlook for the local economy.*

12:02 p.m. *I reviewed an announcement about a reunion of an advanced management class I attended at the Conrad N. Hilton College at the University of Houston , which will be held next year in Europe. After deciding to attend, I made a note to inquire about some details regarding the trip.*

12:08 p.m. *While reviewing a report, I called the hotel's spa manager to determine the reason and the solutions to the excessive glass breakage that was evident in the merchandise the spa was receiving from outside vendors.*

12:15 p.m. *The director of sales stopped by to tell me that a competing hotel had offered a "ridiculously low" room rate to a large convention group for which they are competing. We both complained about this irrational competitor. No decision about how to respond was made at the time.*

12:18 p.m. *Two junior executives brought me a copy of the pairings for the upcoming employee golf tournament. I studied them carefully and suggested some changes to my team. We joked about the compatibility of certain employees and who the "ringers" were on the different teams.*

12:22 p.m. My secretary forwarded a message from the mayor's office about setting up a private dinner for about twenty people and indicated that I needed to call the mayor upon her return from Washington the next day .

12:30 p.m. I left the hotel to go down to the River View Restaurant for lunch with the owner of numerous riverboats and tour companies, who is currently president of the local tourist commission. Although our meeting had no real agenda, and no hotel business was transacted, we discussed numerous topics relating to the local tourism industry.

1:25 p.m. I arrived back in my office.

1:30 p.m. A newly hired young executive was brought around. I talked about how the hotel is trying to service small groups as well as large ones and how important it is for even the smallest meeting group to get special attention.

1:45 p.m. The controller escorted the representative of a credit card company to my office for an unscheduled meeting. There is some unusual new service being offered; before long, there were five people in an impromptu meeting that lasted forty-five minutes. The idea doesn't appear to apply to our business, and afterward I made a note to ask the controller why he brought this guy to me.

2:15 p.m. I phoned a prominent local executive who heads up the city's PGA golf tournament to drum up some tournament business. Nothing was resolved during our five-minute talk.

2:20 p.m. I asked the resident manager to come by so we could discuss five or six subjects, including recent increases in the percentage of convention no-shows, a suggested room rate policy for the next month, various plans to finish up the rooms remodeling, and others.

2:59 p.m. The catering director delivered the rough draft of a bid proposal on an Italian-American Festival the hotel is interested in hosting. I made a number of suggestions and complimented the catering director on a great effort.

3:15 p.m. I read two personnel action forms from the human resources department and called the director of human resources to discuss both. A number of other personnel issues were also discussed during this ten-minute conversation.

3:33 p.m. I got a call from a freelance writer who is doing a story about tourism and economic development. I answered questions and asked her a number of my own during our twelve-minute talk.

3:45 p.m. I received an unscheduled visit from the rooms manager about a guest who did not get a wake-up call and subsequently missed a meeting. The guest wants a free night's stay; we decided to offer him $59. The conversation went on to malfunctioning message lights on guest room phones and finally to the trophies for the golf tournament. The rooms manager got the golf trophies to show me.

4:00 p.m. The assistant laundry manager dropped by to discuss a personnel problem. I listened, asked questions, and outlined a detailed procedure for the assistant laundry manager to follow.

4:15 p.m. I checked my e-mail, did paperwork, and read mail and memos for an uninterrupted twenty minutes.

4:35 p.m. The resident manager came by with the hotel's operations analyst. We discussed a number of technical questions relating to sales forecasts and reports to corporate headquarters.

5:40 p.m. I got a call from the general manager of a company hotel in another state. We talked company gossip, including possible corporate organizational changes. Other topics included the hotel's capital budget, our families, and relations with the hotel's owners.

6:10 p.m. I called the general manager of a company hotel in another city, previously the GM's resident manager, to express sympathies over the death of her father.

6:30 p.m. I returned to my apartment for a quick dinner.

7:15 p.m. I met seven of my hotel executives at the hotel's sports bar to watch some of the Monday night football game and was introduced to a corporate engineering specialist who is in town for a few days. I asked about various aspects of the engineer's job, but no local hotel business was discussed at the table. Mostly, it was a little football and beer and a lot of joking and kidding.

8:00 p.m. I said good night and returned to my apartment. It was a full but average day.

Glossary

Accelerated depreciation A tax depreciation rule that was established by the U.S. government in the early 1980s and provided for faster recovery of capital expenditures. The rule was tightened in 1986 for real estate.

Account A document for accumulating and summarizing financial data.

Accounting department The department that identifies, evaluates, and communicates economic information about a hotel's financial well-being.

Accounts payable Monies owed by the hotel to its suppliers of goods and services.

Accounts receivable Monies owed to the hotel.

Actual market share The percentage share of the total rooms on the market that are actually captured by a particular hotel. Actual market share can be compared with fair market share to determine a hotel's capture rate or penetration.

Adjoining rooms Guest rooms that have a common wall but no connecting door.

Affirmative action A program designed to ensure proportional representation of workers on the basis of race, religion, or gender and that no discrimination occurs.

American plan A lodging plan that provides a guest with a room and three meals per day.

Availability board A system that indicates to the staff of the reservations department the periods of time that the hotel has guest rooms available.

Arrivals report The number of guests arriving on a specific date and the requirements of their reservation.

Average daily rate (ADR) A number that indicates revenue, derived by dividing net rooms revenue by the number of rooms sold.

Back of the House Operating departments of a hotel in which the employees have little or no direct guest contact.

Balance sheet Describes a hotel's financial condition at a specific point in time.

Bell Captain Supervises and directs bellpersons and baggage porter, who are responsible for carrying the guests' luggage to and from their room, familiarizing guests with the hotel upon first arriving in their room, and providing guests with information on in-house marketing efforts and local attractions.

Benchmarking The continuous process of measuring a hotel's goods, practices, and services against those of its toughest competitors.

Block An agreed-upon number of rooms set aside for members of a group that is planning to stay at a hotel.

Book The sale or reservation of hotel rooms in advance of the arrival date.

Brand standard The qualitative measure used by a franchisor of a hotel name to determine minimal standards of service and the quality of the facilities.

Call accounting The procedure that a hotel utilizes to identify a guest's telephone calls by telephone number, date, and amount of charge.

Capital budget An intermediate- and long-term planning document that details the alternative sources and uses of funds and ensures that adequate financial resources are available to meet financing obligations.

Cash flow risk The potential that revenue generated may be insufficient to cover operating expenses, debt service or return on investment.

Central reservation system An independent company or service that charges member hotels a fee for each reservation it backs for future guests to the hotel or a percentage of the revenue it generates from reservations it backs.

Centralization The process of retaining decision-making authority in the hands of high-level managers.

Checkout The procedure that a front desk agent follows when a guest is ready to settle his or her account.

Circulating par stock The number of items that are part of the operating par but are in use and will be reused.

City ledger A subsidiary ledger with an alphabetical listing of guests who have checked out of the hotel and who have an outstanding balance, along with a list of other persons or groups who owe the hotel for services or products provided.

Compensation The monetary and nonmonetary rewards that managers, supervisors, and employees receive for performing tasks essential to the successful operation of a hotel.

Complimentary program Used by casinos for their preferred customers to reward them for a certain level of gambling activity.

Connecting room Adjoining rooms with individual entrance doors from the outside and a connecting door between them.

Concierge A person who provides local and regional information on entertainment, sports, amusements, transportation, tours, churches, and babysitting to guests of a hotel.

Concurrent control The monitoring of ongoing operations to ensure that objectives are pursued by employees.

Control The process of evaluating actual performance, comparing performance to goals, and taking action on any differences.

Credit card guarantee A type of reservation by which payment is guaranteed to the hotel, should the guest not check in.

Daily operations report A report prepared by the night auditor that summarizes the financial activities of the hotel during a 24-hour period, including revenues, receivables, and operating statistics.

Decentralization The process of distributing authority throughout an organization.

Deep cleaning Intensive cleaning of a guest room or a public area that goes beyond the daily housekeeping of such areas.

Departure report Number of guests checking out on a particular date.

Direct billing Credit provided by a hotel to a guest by which the guest agrees to pay charges incurred upon receipt of the bill that is sent by the hotel at a later date.

Doorman The one who assists guests upon arrival and departure with their transportation and summons the bell staff to assist with the guests' luggage.

Eco-tourism Balancing tourism development and the preservation of natural and cultural heritages.

Emergency key A key that opens all guest room doors, even when they are double-locked.

Eminent domain The condemnation of unoccupied land by the government for use in the interest of the public or for the good of the public.

Empowered Employees who are responsible for hands-on service activities are given the authority to make decisions or take action without a manager's prior approval.

Engineering department Responsible for the maintenance and proper operation of all machinery in the hotel, including steam plants, heating, refrigeration, air-conditioning, elevators, lighting, and other systems. Includes skilled craftsmen, such as carpenters, locksmiths, painters, and plumbers; department directs the work of subcontractors who are responsible for designated building systems, such as elevators; and implements a work order system to ensure that the hotel's guests are not inconvenienced by faulty equipment.

End of day The time during a business day up to which the audit of all transactions is completed.

European plan Billing the guest for meals and room separately.

Evening shift A working schedule from 3:00 P.M. until 11:00 P.M.

Executive housekeeper The one who is responsible for the cleanliness of all public areas and guest rooms; hiring personnel; maintaining equipment inventory and personnel records; and organizing cleaning schedules.

Express checkout Providing the guest with a folio early in the morning of the day of checking out, which allows the guest to review the charges and hopefully speeds up the checkout process.

Fair market share The ratio of a hotel's available guest rooms and the total number on the market.

Family rate A special room rate for parents and children who are staying in the same room.

Feedback control A type of control by which corrective action is directed at improving either the resource acquisition process or the actual operations of a hotel.

Financial statement Summarizes the assets, liabilities, equity, revenues, and expenses of a hotel; communicates accounting information and includes balance sheets, income statements, etc.

Floor master key Will open all guest rooms on a specified floor. Used by housekeeping in the process of cleaning guest rooms.

Folio Details of all transactions affecting the balance of a single account that is assigned to an individual person or guest room.

Franchise A private contractual agreement under which a franchisee operates a business using a designated trademark and operating procedures.

Front desk agent Management's representative; the person must be a salesperson for the hotel with guests who are arriving and departing; is an information giver, record keeper, money handler, public relations agent, diplomat, problem solver, and coordinator. Also called a guest services representative.

Front of the house Operating departments of a hotel in which the employees have extensive contacts with guests.

Front office department A subdepartment of the rooms department that handles the following for the hotel's guests: information services; reservations; rooming; cash and credit; daily audits; liaison with PBX (telephone), housekeeping, and engineering; also performs daily audits.

Front office manager Supervises clerks, handles reservations, schedules staff, handles guest complaints, forecasts and provides liaison to other department managers.

Function book The listing of all group business to which a hotel has committed guest rooms or meeting space during a particular time period (i.e., day, week, month, or year).

General manager The top executive of a hotel who ultimately is responsible for the overall performance of the operation and all of the hotel's employees. The GM represents the owner's interests, directs the activities of the departments, and may get involved in the day-to-day operation of individual departments.

Guaranteed reservation A reservation that will be held until checkout time the day following the day of arrival, even if the guest fails to appear.

Guest history Data recorded after a guest visits a hotel, such as the guest's address, the guest's room preference, or special requirements that can be utilized for future advertising and upon the guest's next stay at the hotel.

Guest ledger A listing of the receivables due the hotel by all current guests.

Guest room attendants Formerly called maids and also called housekeepers. Make beds, supply each room with clean linen and prescribed amenities, and clean the guest rooms.

HAZCOMM Standard Hazard Communication Standard; regulations of the Occupational Safety and Health Administration, requiring employers to inform employees about possible hazards related to chemicals they use on the job.

Houseman In charge of wall or window washing, drapery cleaning, shampooing; vacuums for deep cleaning, chandelier cleaning, furniture moving, and carpet repairs.

Human resources department Recruits, hires, trains, and places hotel employees, manages hotel compensation and employee relations programs.

Income statement Summarizes a hotel's financial performance over a given period of time.

Inspector Also known as a housekeeping floor supervisor, this person is responsible for ensuring that each housekeeper properly cleans and prepares a guest room according to the hotel's standards.

Inventory A physical count of all operating equipment in the hotel.

Inventory turnover A ratio showing how quickly a hotel's inventory is moving from storage to productive use; it is calculated by dividing the cost of goods used by the average inventory.

Job analysis The process of gathering, analyzing, and synthesizing information about jobs.

Job description Listing of the job title, pay, tasks, reporting relationships, responsibilities, and working conditions required to perform a specific job.

Job redesign Attempts by the hotel to improve the quality of work and to give employees more autonomy.

Job specification A written explanation of skills, knowledge, abilities, and other characteristics that are needed to perform a job effectively.

Laundry supervisor The one who records laundry costs, oversees a preventive maintenance program, and supervises the work of the washers, laundry attendants, and linen distribution personnel.

Liquidity A measure of the ability of a hotel to meet current, short-term obligations by maintaining sufficient cash.

Loss prevention committee A committee that studies procedures and technology that can minimize the loss of a hotel's assets and protect the guests and their personal property from injury or loss.

Management contract A written agreement between the owner and the operator of a lodging facility in which the owner employs the operator as an agent to assume full responsibility for operating and managing the property.

Market share The number of potential guests from various segments, including individual and group markets that may frequent the property.

Market value risk An analysis of the risk that the value of the property may decline to the extent that its sale may not cover mortgage indebtedness and total equity or inflation value increases.

Marketing and sales department Includes the sales managers of the hotel, who must sell rooms, food, and beverages to potential clients by advertising, attending conferences, and client contacts.

Master key A key that provides access to all of the guest rooms that are not double-locked.

Master staffing sheet Used by the housekeeping department to provide a complete breakdown of the various hotel work stations and the staff responsible for each station.

Networking Creating contacts that might prove valuable in the future in selling a hotel's guest rooms or meeting spaces.

Night audit A daily review of guest accounts and nonguest accounts against records and transaction information.

Nonguest account A record of transactions of a local business that has been given charge privileges at a hotel.

No-show A guest who has a room reservation but who does not arrive or cancels the reservation.

Occupancy percentage A ratio indicating the proportion of rooms sold to rooms available during a designated time period.

On change A guest room from which a guest has checked out but that the housekeeping department has not made ready for the next guest.

Operator An affiliated independent operating company that is responsible for the professional management of a hotel property.

Operating par stock Number of items housekeeping must use to properly supply a guest room according to broad standards for a specific number of days.

Out-of-order A guest room that cannot be assigned to a guest because of a problem with maintenance or a mechanical difficulty.

Overbooking When a hotel accepts more reservations than it has rooms available.

Overselling The same as overbooking.

Payback method The total number of years that are necessary for a progressed capital acquisition to repay its original cost.

PBX (private branch exchange) A hotel's telephone equipment and those persons who operate and/or service such equipment.

Performance culture A work situation in which everyone can do his or her best work.

Performance evaluation A procedure used by managers or supervisors to determine which employees have achieved expected level of work during a specific period of time.

Perpetual inventory system An inventory system in which receipts and issues are recorded as they occur.

Person trip The travel from home and back of one person.

Physical plant The hotel building and related systems (i.e., heating, air-conditioning, electrical, plumbing, elevators, etc.)

Point of sale A location in the hotel where a guest has purchased goods or services and the equipment that is utilized to connect each location to a central computing system that records transactions for financial reporting and future payment by a guest.

Preliminary control A control method that focuses on preventing deviations in quality and quantity of resources used in the hotel.

Preregistration Entering selected information about a guest prior to that guest's arrival so as to speed up the check-in process.

Preventive maintenance Identifying and correcting potentially costly repairs when they occur; this consists of inspection, making minor corrections, and providing work orders.

Profit margin A measure of management's ability to generate sales and to control expenses; divide net income by total revenue to obtain this figure.

Property management system (PMS) A software system that provides an integrated financial, record-keeping, and operations system for a hotel.

Prospect A potential purchaser of room nights and/or meeting space in a hotel.

Quality circle A group of employees, usually fewer than ten, who perform similar jobs and meet once a week to discuss their work, to identify problems, and to present possible solutions to those problems.

Quality control Assigning responsibility to the last employee who handles a product or a service to ensure that the product or service is correct before it reaches the guest.

Rack rate A standard room rate with no discount.

Rate of return on investment A measure of profitability that divides any additional net income after taxes and depreciation by the original cost of the investment.

Registration A procedure that is utilized by a hotel upon the arrival of a guest to confirm the guest's stay at the hotel.

Resident manager The one who handles daily routine management tasks as directed and assigned by the general manager. In addition, he or she may be in charge of one department. A very visible position to the staff and guests because of the need for this person to be available in case of questions, emergencies, complaints, or special events.

Reservations manager The one who takes and confirms incoming requests for rooms, noting special requests for service; provides guests with information; maintains an accurate room inventory; and communicates with marketing and sales.

Reservationist Hotel employee who maintains records on guest arrivals and departures, keeps a convention history, prepares a VIP list, and may process guest confirmations.

Revenue per available room (REVPAR) Average daily rate (ADR) times occupancy.

Room attendant cart A lightweight, wheeled vehicle that is used for transporting cleaning supplies, linen, and equipment needed to fulfill a block of cleaning assignments.

Room pickup The number of guest rooms that members of a group have actually guaranteed for the group's event.

Room status report A report that identifies the availability of guest rooms.

Rooms department Includes reservations, front office, valet, and telephone.

Sales Selling of the hotel facilities and services to individual and group travelers.

Solvency The extent to which a hotel is financed by debt and is able to meet its long-term obligations. A hotel is solvent when its assets exceed its liabilities.

Span of control The number of persons who report to one manager or supervisor.

Special attention list (SPALT) Identifies guests who are VIPs and those guests who have special rooming requirements.

Time-share A resort property in which an owner does not buy a whole unit; rather, the owner buys an interval of time at a property, which may or may not be tied to a particular unit or even a particular property; also known as vacation ownership.

Total quality control (TQC) A system for integrating quality development, quality maintenance, and quality improvement efforts of various departments in a hotel or lodging enterprise so as to improve customer satisfaction.

Total quality management (TQM) Management approach to long-term success through customer satisfaction, based on the participation of all members of an organization in improving products, service, and the culture in which they work.

Turnover A measure to describe the number of new employees and the number of employees who leave.

Uniform system of accounts for hotels A standardized system of terminology and procedures describing hotel accounts, classifications, formats, contents, and use of financial statements.

VIP report A list of those guests arriving on a specific date who will receive special gifts and services.

Walk A guest who is unable to register but has a reservation and is turned away due to lack of rooms. The guest is referred to a hotel that is comparable in terms of accommodations. A walk report or turnaway report is generated so as to determine how the reservation forecast can be improved, since the cost of a walk typically becomes the expense of the hotel causing the walk.

Walk-in A guest who arrives at a hotel without a reservation.

Work team A team of nonmanagerial employees and their manager or supervisor within a department or unit, or a group of employees whose jobs are related and who self-manage their work team.

Index